COMMUNITY CARE

AND THE

MENTALLY HANDICAPPED

SERVICES FOR MOTHERS
AND THEIR
MENTALLY HANDICAPPED CHILDREN

Paperback edition,
reprinted with revised conclusions

SAM AYER
ANDY ALASZEWSKI

CROOM HELM
London • Sydney •
Dover, New Hampshire

©1984 Sam Ayer and Andy Alaszewski
Croom Helm Ltd, Provident House, Burrell Row,
Beckenham, Kent, BR3 1AT

Croom Helm Australia Pty Ltd, Suite 4, 6th Floor,
64-76 Kippax Street, Surry Hills, NSW 2010, Australia

New in paperback 1986

British Library Cataloguing in Publication Data

Ayer, Sam
    Community care and the mentally handicapped.
    1. Mentally handicapped children—Care and
    treatment—England—Humberside
    2. Community health services for children
    —England—Humberside
    I. Title II. Alaszewski, Andy
    362.3'58'088054   HV901.G72H8

    ISBN 0-7099-5104-3 Pbk

Croom Helm, 27 South Main Street,
Wolfeboro, New Hampshire 03894-2069, USA

Library of Congress Catalog Card Number: 84-45289
Cataloging in Publication Data Applied For.

Printed in Great Britain by
Biddles Ltd, Guildford, Surrey

4 Week Loan

This book is due for return on or before the last date shown below

1 7 NOV 2008		

University of Cumbria
24/7 renewals Tel:0845 602 6124

CONTENTS

TABLES

This book is dedicated to our families, especially Abena Sika, Akua Sika, Brenda, Danuta and Mieczysław, in recognition of the help, support and love they have given us.

ACKNOWLEDGEMENTS

The research on which this book is based was funded by a research studentship from the Social Science Research Council. Humberside Education Authority and the head teachers of 3 ESN(S) schools in North Humberside gave us permission to approach the parents of mentally handicapped children attending special schools.

Extracts from the Report of the Committee of Enquiry into Mental Handicap Nursing and Care and the Report of the Royal Commission on the Law relating to Mental Illness and Mental Deficiency are reproduced with the permission of the Controller of Her Majesty's Stationery Office.

Without the sympathy, patience and cooperation of 120 mothers in North Humberside this study would be impossible. To protect their privacy we have in all cases used psuedonyms and in some cases we have altered minor details to prevent identification. We hope this book repays these mothers for the time and cooperation they gave us.

PREFACE

        We began the research, on which this book is
based, in 1978. We had both worked in mental handicap hospitals and we were both convinced that there
must be a better way of caring for mentally handicapped people. However, in the literature on
services for mentally handicapped people we could
find few descriptions of how the alternatives
actually worked and we could find little discussion
of the main alternative in Britain, community care.
There was very little information on the ways in
which community care affected the lives of mentally
handicapped people and on the nature of support
received by families caring for mentally handicapped
people. Current policies and practices are determined more by the experiences and needs of the
various agencies providing services than by the
experiences and needs of mentally handicapped people
and their families.
        We felt that this was an unsatisfactory state
of affairs and it was important that policies should
be based on information about family life. We
decided to collect information about the needs and
experiences of families with severely mentally handicapped school children in North Humberside. We
wanted to examine the experience of caring for a
mentally handicapped child at home, especially the
additional problems that families encountered and
the resources they could mobilise to overcome them.
This book is one of the products of that research.
        Our research was an exploratory pilot study.
We aimed at generating insights and information that
could be used in policy-making and that other studies
could and would develop. We did not start by trying
to prove any particular theory nor were we attached

1

to any particular set of methods. We do not think
theory and methods are unimportant. It is, in our
view, impossible to do research without a theoretical framework and a waste of time trying to do
research without proper methods. Rather we wanted
to subordinate both the theory and methods to the
basic objectives of our research - a description of
the experience of caring for a severely mentally
handicapped child at home. In this book we have
attempted to maintain a balance between discussions
of the literature and theory and information from
our talks with the mothers of severely mentally
handicapped school children.

We start the book with two chapters which
discuss different aspects of services for the mentally handicapped. In Chapter 1 we discuss the
changes in official attitudes to the mentally handicapped and their families. In Chapter 2 we identify
the different interpretations of the policy of
community care. In the middle section of the book
we draw on mothers' accounts of caring for their
mentally handicapped children. In Chapter 3 we
briefly describe the methods we used in our study.
In Chapter 4 we discuss the problems of assessing
disability and the disability of the children in our
study. In Chapter 5 we examine the ways in which
mothers in our study discovered that their children
were mentally handicapped and their initial encounter with formal services. In Chapter 6 we discuss
the nature of care within the family, especially
the division of labour within the family. In
Chapter 7 we assess the role of the community in the
form of assistance and help provided by relatives,
neighbours and friends. In Chapter 8 we examine the
support available from different welfare agencies.
Chapter 9 is based on the experiences of two
mothers and draws together the themes of the middle
section of the book in two case studies. In the
conclusion we develop the implications of the
experiences of the mothers in our study for the
policy of community care.

Chapter 1

FAMILIES OF MENTALLY HANDICAPPED PEOPLE AND OFFICIAL
POLICY

INTRODUCTION

In this book we examine the experiences of a
group of mothers in caring for their mentally
handicapped children and the type and nature of
support they receive. We will be interested in
identifying the shortcomings of the support and
suggesting ways of overcoming these shortcomings.
However to understand some aspects of the situation
in which mothers find themselves it is important
to examine official policy towards families with
mentally handicapped children. In this chapter we
shall examine changing official attitudes to the
mentally handicapped and their families and in
Chapter 2 we shall concentrate on one aspect of
official attitudes and policies towards the
mentally handicapped by examining the origins and
nature of the policy of community care.
        Mentally handicapped people can broadly be
defined as individuals who have, when they are born
or in early childhood, sustained some kind of brain
damage and who subsequently experienced arrested
intellectual, social and in some cases physical
development. The official label for this group of
individuals has changed over time and in the last
50 years they have in England been referred to as
mental defectives, the mentally subnormal and
mentally handicapped people. The changes in
official labels have, as we shall show in this
chapter, been associated with different attitudes
and policies. There can be no doubt that in all
societies such damaged individuals exist. Societies
differ in the extent to which these individuals are
given a distinctive social identity and status and
the precise implication of this identity and status.
        In Great Britain the mentally handicapped were

first, unequivocably, given a clear and distinctive
status as a social group in the 1913 Mental
Deficiency Act and the equivalent Scottish
legislation. These Acts established an administrative and legal framework for the care and control
of mental defectives. Subsequent policy developments can be seen as either modifications of or
reactions against this framework.

This chapter will be divided into three
sections. In the first section we shall discuss the
origins of the 1913 Act. In the second we shall
discuss the period of consolidation and service
development between the wars and in the third
section we shall discuss the collapse of the framework based on the 1913 Act after the Second World
War and the hesitant movements towards a new policy
and pattern of services based on new assumptions
about the cause of handicap and new attitudes
towards the family.

THE ORIGIN AND NATURE OF THE 1913 MENTAL DEFICIENCY ACT

Although terms such as idiot and imbecile have
a long history and there is the odd mediaeval law
that mentions fools or idiots, at the beginning of
the 19th century the mentally handicapped did not
form a distinctive group either in law or in
provision of facilities. For example Rothman in his
study of American Asylums in the 1820s and 1830s
discusses separate institutions for paupers,
lunatics, criminals and juvenile delinquents but no
separate institutions for idiots.[1]
In the 1850s the situation changed and a
number of institutions reserved for idiots were
opened in England including: a small 'school for
idiots' in Bath (1846); an Asylum for idiots at
Park House Highgate (1847) which later moved to
Redhill and became Earlswood Asylum; Essex Hall in
Colchester (1859); Starcross Asylum in Exeter
(1846); and Northern Counties Asylum for Idiots
and Imbeciles in Lancaster (1868).[2] These institutions were very much local ventures and, despite
different central initiatives such as the Idiots
Act of 1886,[3] remained isolated. In 1881 a census
of idiots in public institutions identified 29,452
and only 3% were in special idiot's asylums.[4] In
1914 there were still only 6 special institutions
with 2,040 idiots.[5]
The identification of the mentally handicapped

4

as a distinctive group at the end of the 19th
century is associated with the development of a
system of universal and compulsory education.[6]
Within this education system the mentally defective
were identified both as a distinctive group and as
a problem. The education system was orientated
towards providing the basic skills required by
workers in an industrial society, especially
literary and numeracy. Pupils were tested in the
three R's and transferred between grades according
to the results of these tests. Any individuals
who had difficulty with these skills, as did the
mentally defective, would create a problem and
stand out as a group.
     Deaf and blind children were the first
'problem group' to attract official attention and a
Royal Commission was established to consider what
steps should be taken for their care and education.
The Commission not only dealt with deaf and dumb
children but also identified 'feeble-minded'
children as a problem and recommended that they
should be separated from other children.

> Feeble-minded children ... should be separated
> from ordinary scholars in public elementary
> schools, in order that they may receive
> special instruction, and that the attention
> of school authorities be particularly directed
> towards this object.[7]

     Following the Report of the Royal Commission
the Board of Education established a departmental
committee to:

> To enquire into the existing systems for the
> education of feeble-minded and defective
> children not under the charge of guardians,
> and not idiots or imbeciles, and to advise as
> to any changes, either with or without
> legislation, that may be desirable.[8]

The departmental committee endorsed and fleshed out
the recommendations of the Royal Commission. They
recommended the establishment of special classes
for feeble-minded children and the use of medical
certificates as a basis of allocation. The
recommendations of the committee formed the basis
of legislation.[9]
     Parallel changes were taking place in other
industrial countries. For example, in France,
Binet was given the job of devising a method for

identifying children in Parisian schools who could
not adapt themselves to the curriculum and therefore interfered with the smooth management of
classes. With Simon he devised a scale for
measuring intelligence.   The development of
systematic screening of the intelligence of school
children and other groups such as conscripts to the
army led to the identification of a large number of
mental defectives.

> The I.Q. test was accepted by medical and
> educational authorities in many countries as
> putting the diagnosis of mental retardation on
> a scientific basis and has led to the
> discovery of many more subnormals than had
> previously been thought to exist, and contri-
> buted greatly to the eugenic scare of the
> period.[10]

The mentally defective were not only identified as a problem in the education system but also
came to be seen as a threat to society through a
combination of ideas about the intrinsic degeneracy,
moral deficiency and high fertility of the mentally
deficient.   These ideas are clearly expressed in an
early and influential report by Howe, an American
social reformer, to the Legislature of the State of
Massachusetts. Howe had been commissioned to
investigate and report on the condition of idiots
in the state and conducted a thorough survey of
contemporary conditions. He not only visited the
various asylums, prisons and poor houses in
Massachusetts, but also visited European
institutions.
Howe discovered a large number of idiots and
argued that they presented a major threat to the
well-being of society:

> Idiots form one rank of that fearful host
> which is every (sic) pressing upon society
> with its suffering, its miseries, and its
> crimes, and which society is ever trying to
> hold off at arm's length, - to keep in
> quarantine; but all in vain.[11]

Furthermore Howe argued that mental defect was
hereditary and the family was therefore responsible
for the defect.

> It may be assumed as certain, that in all
> cases where children are born deformed, or

blind, or deaf, or idiotic, or so imperfectly
and feebly organised that they cannot come to
maturity under ordinary circumstances, or have
the seeds of early decay, or have original
impetuosity of passions that amount to moral
insanity, - in all such cases the fault lies
with the progenitors. Whether they sinned in
ignorance or in wilfulness, matters not as to
the effect of the sin upon the offspring.[12]

The ideas of Howe were very similar to those
that became associated with the eugenics movement
at the end of the 19th century. A number of
investigators performed "scientific studies" that
purported to show that both intelligence and mental
defect are hereditary. For example Goddard in his
study of the offspring of Martin Kallikak claimed
to show how:

a scion of a family of good English blood of
the middle class in an unguarded moment,
stepped aside from the paths of rectitude and
with the help of a feeble-minded girl, starts
a line of mental defectives that is trully
appalling. After this mistake, he returned
to the traditions of his family, married a
woman of his own quality, and through her
carried on a line of respectability equal to
that of his ancestors.[13]

Beliefs in the degeneracy of mental defectives
and fears of their high fertility led to the formation of a number of societies for their control and
to a number of experiments in care of the mentally
defectives. For example Pinsent as chairman of the
After-Care Committee of the Birmingham School Board
developed a system of community supervision for
defective school leavers to raise public
consciousness about the problem and to prevent some
mentally defective school leavers from reproducing.

A poor mother with other children cannot give
her whole time and strength to the weak-
minded member of the family. The child must
take her chance during the busy hours of the
day. These girls are often of a clinging and
affectionate disposition and will follow any
man who chooses to speak kindly to them. We,
who pay the rates and taxes, will have to
support these girls in the end. Would it not
be wiser to do so at once, instead of waiting

until they have produced others for us and our
children to support? Once more it is for the
permanent industrial and custodial homes which
we must work and the chief duty of an after-
care committee is to collect the evidence which
will demonstrate their necessity. No after-
care committee, however vigilant its members,
can watch over the feeble-minded at all hours
of the day and keep them from harm; but what
an after-care committee can do is to show the
public the result of its investigations and go
on publishing facts until rate-payers, poor-
law guardians, and city councillors are
convinced.[14]

The various committees for the care of the
feeble-minded campaigned to raise public consciousness and in 1904 succeeded in getting the government
to appoint a Royal Commission to investigate the
Care and Control of the Feeble Minded. The various
committees were represented on the Commission, for
example Pinsent was a member, and had an important
influence on the findings of the Commission. The
Commission accepted the argument, that the mental
defectives formed a separate and distinctive group
of people and this group was a social threat.

Of the gravity of the present state of things,
there is no doubt. The mass of facts that we
have collected, the statements of our
witnesses, and our own personal visits and
investigations compel the conclusion that
there are numbers of mentally defective
persons whose training is neglected, over
whom no sufficient control is exercised, and
whose wayward and irresponsible lives are
productive of crime and misery, of much injury
and mischief to themselves and to others, and
of much continuous expenditure wasteful to the
community and to individual families.[15]

The Commission also accepted the argument that
parents were responsible for and transmitted the
defect. As the family in some way created and
sustained the defect, defectives should be removed
from their families as soon as possible to prevent
further damage and harm.

In conclusion, we may fairly sum up the
general evidence as follows:

1. that both on the grounds of fact and of theory there is the highest degree of probability that 'feeble-mindedness' is usually spontaneous in origin - that is not due to influence acting on the parent - and tends strongly to be inherited.
2. that, especially in view of the evidence concerning fertility, the prevention of mentally defective persons from becoming parents would tend largely to diminish the number of such persons in the population.
3. that the evidence for these conclusions strongly supports measures ... for placing mentally defective persons, men and women, who are living at large and uncontrolled, in institutions where they will be employed and detained; and in this and in other ways, kept under effectual supervision so long as may be necessary.[16]

The main assumptions and recommendations of the Royal Commission were accepted by Commissioners in Lunacy, who were responsible for existing services.

The Royal Commission devoted much attention to the causation of mental defect, and arrived at the conclusion that feeble-mindedness is largely inherited; that prevention of mentally defective persons from becoming parents would tend to diminish the number of such persons in the population; and that, consequently, there are strong grounds for placing mental defectives of each sex in institutions where they will be detained and kept under effectual supervision as long as may be necessary. Public opinion would not, the Royal Commission think, sanction legislation directed to the prevention of hereditary transmission of mental defect by surgical or other artificial measures, and they regard restrictions on the marriage of persons of unsound mind as inadvisable, in view of the fact that this form of mental disability is often of a limited or temporary character. As respects, however, congenital and incurable forms of mental defect no such considerations apply, and the only remedy is to place persons so suffering under such restrictions as to make procreation impossible ... We concur in the advisability of ... (these proposals).[17]

The government was rather less enthusiastic. Implementing the recommendations of the Commission would involve legislation, a new central adminis-trative structure and a network of institutions. All of these would involve resources in short supply. Following the publication of the Commission's Report, the National Association for the Care of the Feeble-Minded and the Eugenics Education Society organised a joint campaign to implement its findings. For example during the 1910 general election they asked each candidate "would you undertake measures.. that tend to discourage parenthood on the part of the feeble-minded and other degenerate types?"[18] In 1912 they sponsored two private members bills. The Liberal Government introduced its own bill in 1912 and again in 1913. It became law as the Mental Deficiency Act.

The objectives of the Act were described by the Commissioners in Lunacy in the following way:

> The Act is a public recognition that congenital mental defect is practically incurable, that it is essential that persons so suffering should, both in their own interests and in that of the community, be placed under proper supervision, and that it is the duty of the state to contribute to the cost of maintenance, care and treatment, education, training and control of such persons, and to the provision of suit-able accommodation for their detention.[19]

The Act was built around the principle of life-long segregation within mental deficiency colonies. A central feature of the new system was certification. This was modelled on current Lunacy Act practices but had fewer safeguards. All individuals admitted to institutions had to be certified as mentally defective. This process could be initiated by the parents of low-grade defectives and high-grade defectives under 21 but once parents had made a request for certification they could not withdraw it. The certificates were renewed at the end of the second year or when the defective reached 21 years of age but thereafter it was every 5 years. The certified person and his parents had limited rights of representation at the re-certification and no rights of appeal. If a person certified as insane managed to escape and remain at large for 2 weeks then the certification lapsed. However there was no such 'escape' clause under the Mental Deficiency Act. Furthermore section 15 of the Act

permitted the detection of a person believed to be a
mental defective in a place of safety until such
time as a petition was presented. There was no time
limit on the clause.

The opponents of the proposed legislation in
Parliament were quick to point out the negative
assumptions underlying the proposed measure and its
hostility towards the mental defectives and their
families. One opponent argued that:

> We have come to an age in which the State is
> supposed to do everything by compulsion, an
> age in which the policeman is a God, and in
> which he has to rule the people. The Govern-
> ment now say we will put these mentally
> defective children away at seven years of age,
> and keep them in these institutions, asylums,
> where there are bolts and bars, for the rest of
> their lives. We will segregate them in order
> that the breed of the race may be improved and
> in order that the wealth producing power of the
> working classes may be increased.[20]

Opponents of the Bill did succeed in limiting some
of the more blatant attacks on the rights of the
mentally defective. For example in the original
government bill individuals could be certified if
they were defectives

> in whose case it is desirable in the interests
> of the community that they should be deprived
> of the opportunity of procreating children.[21]

In the final act this was restricted to female
defectives who were

> in receipt of poor relief at the time of
> giving birth to an illegitimate child or when
> pregnant of such a child.[22]

However negative attitudes to and views of the
mentally handicapped and their families pervaded the
legislation. In the case of low-grades, the
severely defective idiots and imbeciles, the defect
itself was sufficient grounds for certification.
For the more able 'high-grades' additional evidence
of social incompetence was needed. In the case of
moral imbeciles the whole emphasis was on social
incompetence.

> Moral imbeciles; ... persons who from an early

11

        age display some permanent mental defect
        coupled with strong vicious or criminal
        propensities on which punishment has had little
        or no deterrent effect.[23]

Discussion. The development of comprehensive and
compulsory education in industrialised countries at
the end of the 19th century highlighted the
existence of individuals who found it difficult to
cope with the contemporary school curriculum and
acquire basic skills in numeracy and litaracy. The
contemporary interest and concern with eugenics and
the quality of the population served to identify one
such group, the mental defectives as a major social
threat. Advocates of legislative control argued
that defectives as a group were highly fertile and
were a threat to the welfare of society.
     The negative attitudes were not limited to the
mentally defective but extended to their families
and the communities they lived in. The parents must
somehow themselves be defective and therefore unable
to adequately care and control for their defective
children. Therefore the solution was to create a
system of long-term segregated care in which the
mentally defective would be removed from the
damaging influence of their home environment and
placed in the controlled environment of the
institution.

THE INTERWAR YEARS: DEVELOPMENT OF A SEGREGATED
SYSTEM

     The 1913 Act created the legal framework for
the segregation of mentally defectives but its
implementation was delayed by the First World War.
Central government was preoccupied first with the
war effort and then reconstruction. In local
authorities there appears to have been little
commitment to the Act. The major pressure for the
implementation of the Act came from the central
agency established under the Act, the Board of
Control. The Board of Control established a
number of initiatives to heighten public awareness
of the problem and to generate action. These
included the establishment and financing of a
voluntary organisation, the Central Association for
the Care of the Mentally Defective, and the
establishment of an interdepartmental committee with
the Board of Education, the Wood Committee, which
reported in 1929.

The Reports of the Wood Committee were based on similar assumptions to the Royal Commission and the 1913 Mental Deficiency Act. Mental defectives were seen as a major cause of social problems, including crime.

> Let us assume that we could segregate as a separate community all the families in this country containing mental defectives of the primary amentia type. We should find that we had collected among them a most interesting social group. It would include, as everyone who has extensive experience of social service would readily admit, a much larger proportion of insane persons, epileptics, paupers, criminals (especially recidivists), unemployables, habitual slum dwellers, prostitutes, inebriates and other social inefficients than would a group of families not containing mental defectives. The overwhelming majority of the families thus collected will belong to that section of the community, which we propose to term the 'social problem' or 'subnormal' group. This group comprises approximately the lowest 10 per cent in the social scale of most communities.[24]

Again there was a concern with high fertility and the quality of the population.

> Prevention however is concerned not with end results but with antecedents and sometimes remote antecedents. If we are to prevent the racial disaster of mental deficiency we must deal not merely with mentally defective persons, but with the whole subnormal group from which the majority of them come. Primary amentia may be and often is an end result - the last stage of the inheritance of degeneracy of this subnormal group. The relative fertility of this (subnormal) group is greater than that of normal persons. In point of fact the disparity in the actual as opposed to the potential fertility of the normal and subnormal sections of the population is increasing, the families of the subnormal groups remaining as large as hitherto while those of the better social groups are steadily diminishing in size.[25]

The Committee produced different reports on children and adults and there were important

differences between the two reports. The two
departments agreed to divide responsibilities for
children. The Board of Education and local
education authorities were to maintain their
responsibilities for the education of 'educable'
defectives. For these children the committee
recommended that the existing barriers between
Special Schools and Public Elementary Schools
should be reduced. For example transfer between the
two types of school should be an administrative
rather than the quasi-legal procedure of certification. The Board of Control and local mental
deficiency authorities were to take responsibility
for the training of all ineducable children. These
children were to be trained in an occupation centre
or sent to a residential institution or colony if
they were too difficult or dangerous.[26]
     In the case of adults the committee believed
it 'to be a fundamental condition of any comprehensive scheme for the care, training and control of
defectives that every practicable step should be
taken to concentrate all existing powers in regard
to adult defectives... in the hands of a single
Authority, namely, the Local Mental Deficiency
Authority'.[27] The centre piece of the system of
care and control was to be the mental deficiency
institution or colony. The institution would be a
repository for all difficult cases and a base for an
active programme of ascertainment and community
supervision. Through ascertainment, the local
Mental Deficiency Authority would identify all
mental defectives in its area; through supervision
the Authority would keep a check on the activities
of the mental deficient in the area; and in the
institution the Authority could segregate the most
difficult and dangerous defectives and care for the
most defective. The committee described the
functions of the institutions in the following way:

> Segregation - The segregation of mentally
> defective adults in institutions or homes is
> generally acknowledged to be one of the most
> efficient methods of dealing with the mentally
> defective. But efficient methods are often
> costly, and to this segregation is no exception.
> The problem of the group of defectives
> requiring permanent segregation should be
> considered first. This group contains a good
> proportion of the lower grade defectives.
> Another section of this group of cases
> requiring permanent segregation is that

containing the older defectives, most of whom
are unemployable. Still another section of
this group consists of the temperamentally
unstable, whose behaviour is often markedly
anti-social. It is generally recognised that
large numbers of the young mentally defective
men and women who would beneift greatly by a
few years training in these institutions cannot
gain admission, not only because of the insuf-
ficiency of accommodation but largely because
the managers of institutions naturally think
more of the safety of those already within the
institution than of the danger of those outside.
The institutions owing to these conditions tend
to become stagnant pools. The new conception
which we have advocated strongly in the preceding Chapter is that while many have to remain
in the institution all their lives, the colony
of the future should be a flowing lake of the
greatest fluidity, always taking in and always
sending out. One of the chief aims of the
institution will be to fit as many as possible
of the suitable higher grade defectives for
life in the general community under proper
supervision. Our colonies and institutions
would become co-ordinating centres of all kinds
of activities and agencies for the welfare of
the mentally defective.[28]

Following the Report of the Wood Committee, the
Board of Control established a departmental committee to design a low-cost model colony. The
Board was worried that the high cost of existing
designs were preventing cost conscious authorities
from building colonies.

The grave danger that the further successful
carrying out of the provisions of the Mental
Deficiency Act, 1913, may be impeded if not
altogether prevented, by the refusal of local
authorities to face the cost unavoidably
involved, is in our view clearly shown by the
small progress made since the war in the
provision of colonies, and we have had direct
evidence bearing out this view. Throughout this
report we have endeavoured to keep in mind the
necessity of confining our suggestions to the
minimum requirements consistent with the
reasonable welfare of the inmates and the
efficient administration of the Act.[29]

The Board of Control set a target for the development of the colony system:

> The Wood Committee's Report suggests that two-thirds of the mentally defective population in England and Wales may be left to live in the community without undue risk to themselves or others if adequate provision is made for their care, training and protection. But the remainder - estimated at, approximately, 100,000 - who are in need of institutional care, only 28,000 are at present in institutions under the Mental Deficiency Act.[30]

To achieve this target the Board of Control put considerable pressure on the local mental deficiency authority through visits and through the annual report. As a result of this pressure in the 8 years up to the Second World War, the provision of places for mental defectives nearly doubled and reached nearly half of the Board's target. (See Table 1.1.)

Table 1.1   Rise of Institutional Provision during the 1930s
            (1st January each year)[31]

Date	Places in Institutions Certified under the MDA	Places in Institutions Approved under the MDA	Places in State Institutions	Other Places	Total
1931	17,200	9,219	1,043	722	28,234
1932	19,964	9,027	1,122	771	30,884
1933	22,493	8,880	1,196	790	33,359
1934	24,494	9,262	1,231	807	35,794
1935	26,782	9,128	1,268	809	37,987
1936	28,933	9,162	1,319	842	40,256
1937	30,798	9,408	1,376	859	42,441
1938	32,653	9,301	1,445	864	44,263
1939					46,054

Although the main thrust of development in the 1930s was the provision of institutional facilities, the Board of Control maintained an active role in the work of ascertainment and supervision. The

Board publically criticised in its annual reports
local authorities with poor supervision rates and
ascertainment rates below 1 defective per 1,000
population. As a result the growth of ascertained
and supervision paralleled the growth in the colony
system (see Table 1.2).

Table 1.2   Growth of Mental Deficiency System 1924 to 1954[32]

Date	Total Number Reported & Ascertained	Total under community supervision (including statutory supervision, voluntary supervision, guardianship and on licence from institutions	Total in institutions	Total in all forms of care
1924	36,413	17,964	17,104	35,067
1929	66,458	41,729	24,207	65,936
1934	106,439	59,173	35,794	94,967
1939	129,395	72,653	46,054	118,707
1944	127,411	72,321	51,214	123,535
1949	129,700	73,640	54,887	128,527
1954	137,456	81,880	55,984	137,864
Estimates of the Wood Committee	300,000	200,000	100,000	300,000

Discussion

   The 1913 Mental Deficiency Act laid down a
legal and administrative framework for the identification, supervision and control of mental
defectives and it created a central administrative
agency, the Board of Control to supervise the
system. However there was no guarantee that this
system would ever be established. It required
political will and finance both at central government and local government level.
   The report of the interdepartmental committee
on mental deficiency was an important element in
the Board of Control's incessant struggle to

implement the 1913 Act. The assumptions behind the committee's report were very similar to those on which the 1913 Act was based and therefore the attitude to the mentally deficient and their families was much the same. The mentally deficient were seen as a threat to society. They were a product of a particular environment and community. Therefore they had either to be supervised and controlled within that environment or better still segregated within an institution or colony. There was little evidence in the various reports of the view that having a mentally deficient child was a misfortune that could occur to any families and that families with deficient children needed sympathy, understanding and help.

POLICY DEVELOPMENT SINCE THE SECOND WORLD WAR

The 1913 Mental Deficiency Act gave the mentally deficient a distinctive legal identity and established the framework for their care and control. The Board of Control in the interwar years began to flesh out this framework by pressurising local mental deficiency committees into identifying defectives, supervising them and build-ing colonies. Policy after the Second World War was initially a modification of this framework and later became a reaction against the framework and a search for a new framework based on new attitudes.

Broadly there have been four policy-making cycles since the War. These four cycles roughly fit into the four decades. The first was related to the establishment of the National Health Service in the 1940s, the second was associated with the Royal Commission on the law relating to mental illness and mental deficiency and took place mainly in the 1950s and early 1960s, the third started with the inquiries and scandals in the mental handicap hospitals in the late 1960s, the fourth was the period of consolidation in the 1970s.

The 1940s were an important phase in the development of social policy for the mentally deficient but it was very much policy by default. The mentally deficient were not the main focus of government policy and initiatives but policy development in other areas had important impli-cations for the organisation and provision for the mentally deficient. The most obvious example of such an intiative was the formation of the National Health Service in 1948.

In the run up to the formation of the NHS there was very little discussion about the future of services for the mentally deficient. The main negotiations took place between the Minister of Health, Bevan and representatives of the acute hospital consultants and of the general practitioners.[33] Apart from the Board of Control the services for the mentally deficient were not represented by any body. The Board of Control had continually pressed for more uniformity of management and standards and therefore also supported the nationalisation of the institutions implicit in the formation of the NHS. Local authorities had only reluctantly taken on responsibility for the mentally deficient and were willing to allow central government and the central exchequer to take over responsibility for the colonies.

The deciding factor appears to have been Bevan's own determination that the new NHS should include services for both the mentally ill and the physically ill. He described the integration of the two in the following way:

> Mental illness is no longer regarded as belonging to a world of its own. I consider this to be one of the outstanding features of the British Health Service. The segregation of mental from physical treatment is a survival from primitive conceptions and is a source of endless cruelty and neglect.[34]

The administrative pattern of the new national health service was built around the administration of services for the physically ill. Services for the physically ill could be divided between community services administered by local health authorities, primary care services administered by executive councils and hospital services administered by hospital management committees.

This administrative division made little sense in relationship to services for the mentally deficient. The bulk of services for the mentally deficient were provided by or within the mental deficiency colonies and these institutions were totally different to acute hospitals. For example medical practitioners palyed a different role in the two settings. In acute hospitals, medical practitioners were clinicians. They took little responsibility for the administration of the hospitals but used facilities within the hospitals to treat their patients. In mental deficiency

institutions medical practitioners were administrators rather than clinicians. Similarly residents
in mental deficiency institutions generally did not
suffer from acute physical illness and they were not
seen as requiring therapeutic programmes. Most
were there for supervision. Indeed when researchers
came to examine the residents of mental subnormality hospitals in the 1960s they found that very
few needed either medical or nursing care. For
example Leck, Gordon and McKeown assessed the
medical, nursing and social needs of 1,652 residents
in 13 mental handicap hospitals. They found only 2
residents who needed active investigation for neuro-
psychiatric patients and only 5 who needed active
treatment for other conditions. 795 residents
needed some form of treatment by a general
practitioner. About half the residents needed
minimal supervision and could live in sheltered
housing.[35]

The formation of the NHS created a number of
problems for services for the mentally deficient.
At national level the mentally deficient did not
gain a high priority on the policy agenda. The
Ministry of Health remained preoccupied with the
problems of acute services and primary care. The
Board of Control remained but its administrative
responsibilities were transferred to the Ministry
and it retained an inspectorial and quasi-legal
role. At local level the mentally deficient did
not form a high priority within local health
authorities. The local health authorities took on
the statutory responsibilities of ascertainment and
supervision but little else. Hospital Management
Committees did not really know what to do with the
mental deficiency colonies. They provided little
guidance, paid little attention to these institutions and devoted few resources to them. The
colonies, renamed hospitals, were left with a
confused role. Their traditional functions were
no longer seen as appropriate but they were given
little guidance on how to develop new roles.

The second cycle of policy-making focused
more directly on the problems of the mentally
deficient or rather on the institutions that
segregated them. This phase of policy-making was
initiated by the National Council for Civil
Liberties who published a pamphlet '50,000 Outside
the Law'. The pamphlet attacked both the practice
of segregated care and the assumptions on which it
was based. The report highlighted two main
assumptions about the nature of mental defect - that

mental defect was permanent and that defectives
were dangerous. The report cited epidemiological
evidence that ascertainment rates for mental defect
reached a maximum for individuals aged 12 years,
30 per 1000 individuals, and then declined. In the
age range of 20 to 29 years 8.4 individuals were
classified as mentally defective. As there was no
evidence of a higher death rate amongst defectives
this meant that out of every 30 individuals classified as defective at the age of 12, 20 would be
normal when they reached their twenties. Similarly
the report challenged the view of defectives as
innately morally defective.

> It is, however, not generally realised that
> the great majority of certified patients have
> no criminal record and that the number of cases
> in which there is any suggestion of violence,
> constitutes only a tiny proportion of the whole.
> Moreover, the facts related in this pamphlet
> may offer some explanation of some of those
> acts of violence and of the desparation which
> may give rise to them.[36]

The report identified important shortcomings in
the law and with the operation of the institutions.
The parents and families of certified defectives
were denied rights. For example the law made
provision for parents to obtain an independent
medical report when an order for detention was due
for renewal. Parents were not generally informed
when the renewal was due. When they did exercise
their rights and obtain an independent report, it
was frequently rejected.

> the presentation ... of an independent medical
> report clearly demonstrating that the indi-
> vidual is not deficient, and produced by
> experts who may have superior qualifications to
> those of the officers of the institution, is
> still no guarantee of the release of the
> patient. The evidence may be, and sometimes is,
> rejected by the Board of Control without any
> statement of reasons and without disclosure of
> evidence to the contrary.[37]

Once admitted it was difficult to obtain
discharge from the institution. Even the more able
patients could not obtain their own release because:

Many institutions have been staffed, since

21

> their inception, on the assumption that there
> will always be a proportion of high-grade and
> borderline cases available, and without their
> services the institution could not be
> efficiently run.[38]

Patients who were released were generally neither
discharged completely nor returned to the care of
their family. More usually they were released on
license and returned to institutions for periodic
recertification.

> Defectives who are allowed out in license are
> often sent to a private employer rather than
> to relatives who are able to look after them.
> They have little protection from the whims of
> this person, and the wages paid depend on the
> arrangements made between the institution and
> the employer.[39]

The change in the climate of opinion between
the 1930s and 1950s can be judged by the fact that
the NCCL judged the very objectives of the 1913 Act
and the Interdepartmental Committee as the root
cause of the problem. Permanent segregation was no
longer acceptable.

> In a few (institutions), both the adminis-
> tration and traditions are progressive. In the
> majority, the treatment appears to be designed
> to condition the defective to a life of
> permanent segregation.[40]

In 1954 a Royal Commission was appointed to
review current legislation. The terms of reference
of the Commission specifically excluded the administration of the hospital service and indicated the
Minister's desire to dismantle the existing
comprehensive legal framework. The Commission was
appointed to

> inquire ... into the existing law and
> administrative machinery governing the certifi-
> cation, detention, care (other than hospital
> care or treatment under the National Health
> Service Acts, 1946-1952), absence on trial or
> licence, discharge and supervision of persons
> who are or are alleged to be suffering from
> mental illness or mental defect, other than
> Broadmoor patients; to consider ... the
> extent to which it is now, or should be made,

statutorily possible for such persons to be
treated, as voluntary patients, without certification; and to make recommendations.[41]

The Commission concentrated on the legal
aspects of existing procedures such as hospitali-
sation. The Commission found the legal basis of
current procedures unhelpful and recommended they
should be replaced by administrative procedures.
The law was to be used as a last resort. In some
ways the implications of the Commission's report
were relatively conservative. The existing services
and practices were to be maintained but with
changed names. For example the Commission received
evidence that the exclusion of severely defective
children from the school systems and their training
in occupation centres administered by local health
authorities both deprived these children of certain
services and was distressing to parents. The
Commission argued that there was no need to change
the existing pattern of services and that the
problems could be overcome by a cosmetic exercise
of re-labelling.

> We do not consider that the proper answer to
> these criticisms (of the present arrangement)
> is to recommend the transfer of administrative
> responsibility for these centres - which we
> recommend should be called training centres
> rather than occupation centres - from the
> local health authorities to the local education
> authorities. It is more important to revise
> the procedures and terminology so that the
> approach is more positive and less negative.
> It should not be necessary to label any child
> as 'ineducable' ... a child should ... be
> recommended for special training in a training
> centre or hospital.[42]

Some of the relabelling exercises were more
important than others. The Commission revised the
classification and terminology of the mentally
disordered. Under the Mental Deficiency Act
classification, ideas of moral defect, social
incompetence and low intelligence had inextricably
been linked together and this association helped to
promote the view that all defectives were a social
threat and that normal people were about to be
swamped by a tide of mental defect. The Royal
Commission recommended that the mental disorder
should be classified in three groups: the mentally

ill, the severely subnormal and psychopaths.
Psychopaths were the dangerous criminal element and
were clearly separated from the severely subnormal.

> We consider that in the general administration
> of hospital and community services, and in
> connection with compulsory powers, the higher-
> grade feeble minded and moral defectives and
> other psychopathic patients should be recog-
> nised as together constituting one main group
> of mentally disordered patients, the other two
> being the mentally ill and the severely sub-
> normal...
> Our second group (psychopathic patients)
> comprises those patients suffering from a
> personality disorder which does not make them
> severely subnormal ... but which is recognised
> medically as a form of mental disorder resul-
> ting in abnormally aggressive or inadequate
> social behaviour.[43]

The Commission also developed the concept of
community care. In practice this meant the expansion of services for the mentally disordered within
local health authorities. Equally important was
the ideological view. The Commission rejected the
view that the mentally disordered should have their
own segregated services, instead they recommended
that the mentally disordered should have access to
and use the same services as other citizens.

> In present-day conditions no one should be
> excluded from benefiting from any of the
> general social services simply because his
> need arises from mental disorder rather than
> from some other cause.[44]

The Commission focused mainly on the problems
of current services and associated procedures and
did not devote much space to discussing the role of
the family. When they did discuss the family the
hostility underlying the 1913 Act and the Interdepartmental Committee was replaced by a rather
lukewarm approval.

> Many persons now classified as imbeciles and
> the majority of those now classified as
> feeble minded are able to live in the general
> community with relatives or friends and are
> accustomed to mix and work with other people;

if their relatives or friends die or become
unable to give them a home any longer, they
need to be provided with a home by some
public authority.[45]

Again in discussing the position of defectives
discharged from hospital the Commission emphasised
the role of social workers as supporters of the
family rather than controllers or supervisors:

When a patient is living with his own family,
one of the most important functions of the
social worker or mental welfare officers is to
advise his family and to try to ensure that
they understand his needs and difficulties.[46]

The report of the Royal Commission resulted in
a number of ministerial policy initiatives based on
the assumption that the bulk of the services for
the mentally handicapped would continue to be
provided within the NHS. In 1959 the Mental Health
Act introduced changes in legal classification and
procedure along the lines recommended by the
Commission.[47] In 1961 the Minister of Health,
Enoch Powell, announced plans to invest in hospital
services and at the same time requested information
from local health authorities about their plans to
develop community services.[48] The early 1960s saw
investment in and expansion of services for the
mentally handicapped within the general framework of
the NHS.

The third major cycle of policy-making was
initiated by a series of scandals and inquiries in
mental subnormality hospitals at the end of the
1960s. The most important of these was probably
the report of the committee of inquiry at Ely
Hospital in Cardiff.[49] The inquiry was set up by
the Minister of Health, Kenneth Robinson, to
inquire into allegations into irregularities
reported in the News of the World. The inquiry
team found that these irregularities had indeed
taken place and found that the irregularities
exposed serious shortcomings in services and
policies for the mentally handicapped. Some of
these shortcomings related to the organisation of
the hospital, some to the administrative structure
of the NHS, some to low levels of funding and
staffing of hospitals for the mentally handicapped
and some related to the lack of clear policy
guidance and objectives.

By the time the Committee of Inquiry reported

the Ministry of Health had been replaced by the
Department of Health and Social Security and Richard
Crossman had replaced Kenneth Robinson. Richard
Crossman decided to publish the inquiry report in
full and used it as an opportunity to initiate a
wide range of policy initiatives.[50] One initiative
was the establishment of a working party to review
policies for the mentally handicapped. This working
party reported in 1971 and its report was published
by the subsequent Secretary of State for Social
Services, Sir Keith Joseph, as the White Paper,
Better Services for the Mentally Handicapped.[51]
     The report envisaged major shifts in the
responsibility for the care of the mentally handicapped. The Health Service was no longer the
dominant service. The newly created local authority
personal social services and social workers were to
provide a significant proportion of support services
for families and residential services. The NHS was
to provide services for assessment and for the long
term care of individuals requiring medical or
nursing care. At the same time responsibility for
the education of severely handicapped children was
transferred from local health authorities and the
DHSS to local education authorities and the Department of Education and Science.[52]
     Although the legal terms remained 'severe
subnormality', the White Paper introduced the term
'mental handicap' into official policy to emphasise
the similarity between the mentally handicapped and
other handicapped groups.

> 'Mental handicap' is used in preference to any
> of the alternative terms because this helps to
> emphasise that our attitude should be the
> same as to other types of handicap, i.e., to
> prevent it whenever possible, to assess it
> adequately when it occurs, and to do every-
> thing possible to alleviate its severity and
> compensate for its effects.[53]

     The authors of the various reports before the
Second World War were confident that they had
identified the main cause of mental deficiency. It
was heredity and therefore they believed the
defect was restricted to specific groups in society.
The White Paper stressed that the causes of most
mental handicap were unknown. Heredity was a
factor but one amongst many. Mental handicap was a
misfortune that could occur to anybody or within

any family.

> In most cases the causes are not known. Mental
> handicap can result from conditions arising
> before or at birth which affect the function-
> ing of the brain; some of these are becoming
> rarer owing to improvement in the maternity
> services, but more children with very severe
> handicap are now surviving birth and infancy.
> It is often the result of unpredictable and
> unavoidable factors - hereditary or environ-
> mental or both - including the lower end of the
> normal range of variation of intelligence.[54]

The White Paper emphasised the key role played
by the family in caring for the mentally handicapped
and the inadequacies of existing support for
families.

> Most parents are devoted to their handicapped
> children and wish to care for them and to
> help them to develop their full potential.
> About 80 per cent of severely handicapped
> children and 40 per cent of severely handi-
> capped adults - and a higher proportion of the
> more mildly handicapped - live at home. Their
> families need advice and many forms of help,
> most of which at present are rarely available.[55]

The policy initiatives of the 1968 to 1971
period marked a major transformation of services
for the mentally handicapped. Prior to 1969 the
Health Service and the medical profession had been
primarily responsible for the development of these
services. After 1971 the services were divided
between three main agencies: the NHS, local
authority personal social services and local
education authorities and three separate professional groups took a leading role in each of these
services: medical practitioners in the NHS, social
workers in social services and teachers in education
authorities.
  In one way the fragmentation of services for
the mentally handicapped between different agencies
was a logical development of the view that the
mentally handicapped should have access to the same
services as other individuals. However, the
emergence of a fragmented service was also a
product of inter-professional rivalry. The end of
the 1960s was a major period of restructuring in
English public administration and this restructuring

included the formation of the local authority
social service departments and the reorganisation of
the NHS and the reorganisation of local government.
The restructuring created agencies built around the
interests of a dominant professional group and the
services it was willing and able to provide. The
mentally handicapped were in the front line of the
battle. The scandals in long-stay institutions
indicated that the medical profession could not
provide the required leadership or policy direction
and laid the basis for the development of services
by social workers and teachers.[56]
     The fourth cycle of policy-making since 1971
can be characterised as a period of consolidation
both nationally and within local agencies. At
local level agencies have had the problem of
operationalising national policies and local
agencies have had to answer a number of questions
including: what their responsibilities are in
relationship to the mentally handicapped; what type
of provision they should make to discharge this
responsibility; how this provision should relate
to the services and facilities they provide for
other client groups; and how the services they
provide for the mentally handicapped should relate
to the services provided by other agencies. It has
in general been a fairly confused and muddled
process and many agencies have failed to develop
comprehensive strategies, let alone provide comprehensive services.
     To assist the process, central departments
have established a number of working groups to
review services and provide guidance for local
agencies. For example, the DHSS established the
Jay Committee to review mental handicap nursing and
care[57] and the DES established the Warnock Committee
to investigate the special education needs of handicapped children and young persons.[58]
     The Jay Committee emphasised that the family
played a key role in the life of the mentally handicapped and that the family must form the starting
point and focus of any service for the mentally
handicapped.

> It is within the family that the overriding
> need for helping the mentally handicapped
> person to live as normal a life as possible
> starts and it continues throughout the differ-
> ent phases of the individual's life. The
> contribution of families is not fully recog-
> nised by those who plan and provide residential

care. This has led us to set down ... the
guiding principles of care which should apply
wherever mentally handicapped people have to
resort to services outside their own families.[59]

The Jay Committee has argued that one of the major
rights of a mentally handicapped child should be to
live with a family.

> Mentally handicapped children should be able to
> live with a family. The first question to be
> asked must always be 'How can we provide
> support which will allow the child to continue
> to live with his own parents and his own
> brothers and sisters, in his own house, in his
> own community?' If this proves impossible, we
> must look first to a long term placement with a
> substitute family.[60]

Discussion. Since the Second World War there has
been a revolution in official attitudes to the role
of the family in caring for the mentally handicapped.
The services developed during the 1920s and 1930s
were based on the assumption that the family were
somehow responsible for the development of mental
defect and that official agencies should supervise
the family or place defectives in segregated
instutitons. Mental handicap is now seen as a misfortune that can occur within any family. The
family is seen as the best and most efficient way of
caring for the mentally handicapped and a major
objective of official agencies is to maintain and
support the family. Indeed there has been a reversal of official concern. It is now the mental
handicap hospitals that are a major source of
concern and there are serious worries about whether
they can provide an adequate quality of care. The
emphasis is on maintaining the mentally handicapped
within their families and the community and only
admitting them to long term residential care as a
last resort.

CONCLUSION

Official policy towards the mentally handicapped is based on assumptions about the cause and
nature of mental handicap. The mentally handicapped
first became the subject of official concern at the
end of the 19th century. The development of comprehensive and complusory education highlighted the

existence of individuals who found it difficult to
acquire basic skills in literacy and numeracy.
Theories about the cause and nature of mental defect
were based on eugenic concepts that intelligence
was influenced, if not determined, by heredity and
therefore parents were in some ways responsible for
their child's incompetence. Furthermore in a period
of declining middle class fertility there was a fear
that the race was degenerating. These views and
assumptions were accepted by policy-makers and
formed the basis of legislation and the framework of
service.

The period since the Second World War has been
marked by a radical change in official thinking
about the nature and cause of mental handicap.
Mental handicap is now seen as a misfortune that can
occur in any family. Heredity is seen as a factor
but only one factor amongst many. The mentally
handicapped are no longer seen as a dangerous and
threatening group but rather as a group of unfor-
tunate individuals requiring special support, help
and protection. The movement from one set of
assumptions to another has been rather slow and
hesitant. At central government level it has now
been accomplished. However these assumptions are
more difficult to change within local agencies.
Frequently local agencies have inherited services
based upon traditional assumptions and these take
the form of bricks and mortar or staff attitudes.
These have proved more difficult to alter.

NOTES

1.   D.J. Rothman, The Discovery of the Asylum,
      Social Order and Disorder in the New Republic,
      Little, Brown and Co, Boston, 1971.
2.   K. Jones, A History of the Mental Health
      Services, Routledge and Kegan Paul, 1972, p.182.
3.   Idiots Act, 1886, 49 and 50 Victoria, C. 25.
4.   Jones, A History of the Mental Health Services,
      p. 183.
5.   68th Report of the Commissioners in Lunacy,
      H.M.S.O., 1914, p. 14.
6.   Elementary Education Act, 1870, 33 and 34
      Victoria, C. 75. The provisions of the
      education act were not made compulsory until
      1880.
7.   Report of the Royal Commission on the Blind,
      Deaf and Dumb ... of the United Kingdom, C.
      5781, H.M.S.O., 1889, para. 724.

8. Departmental Committee on Defective and Epileptic Children, Report, Vol. 1, C. 8746, H.M.S.O., 1898, p. xxvi, para. 1.
9. Elementary Education (Defective and Epileptic Children) Act, 1899, 62 and 63 Victoria, C. 32.
10. J. Ryan 'The Production and Management of Stupidity, The Involvement of Medicine and Psychology', in M. Wadsworth and D. Robinson (eds.), Studies in Everyday Medical Life, Robertson, 1976, p. 164. Also J. Ryan, 'I.Q.: The illusion of objectivity' in K. Richardson, D. Spears and M. Richards (eds.), Race, Culture and Intelligence, Penguin, 1972.
11. S.G.Howe, Report of the Commission to inquire into the Conditions of Idiots in the Commonwealth of Massachusetts, 1848, reprinted in M. Rosen et al, The History of Mental Retardation, Vol. 1, University Park Press, Baltimore, 1976, p. 34.
12. ibid., p. 35.
13. H.H. Goddard, The Kallikak Family: A Study in the Heredity of Feeble-Mindedness, Macmillan, 1931 (1st edition, 1912), p. 50. See also F. Galton, Hereditary Genius, Macmillan, 1869 and R.L. Dugdale, The Jukes: A Study in Crime, Disease and Heredity, Putnam, 1877.
14. E.F. Pinsent, 'On the Permanent Care of the Feeble Minded', The Lancet, New Series 1, 513-515, 1903, p. 514.
15. Report of the Royal Commission on the Care and Control of the Feeble-Minded (Chairman, the Earl of Radnor) Cd. 4202, H.M.S.O., 1908, para. 9.
16. Ibid., para. 553.
17. 63rd Report of the Commissioners in Lunacy H.M.S.O., 1909, pp. 4-5.
18. Jones, A History of the Mental Health Services, p. 197.
19. 68th Report of the Commissioners in Lunacy, H.M.S.O., 1914, p. 3.
20. J. Wedgwood, 28.5.13, Debate on the second Reading of the Mental Deficiency Bill, Parliamentary Debates, Commons, Official Report 5th series, 1913, Vol. 53, p. 248.
21. R.A. Leach, The Mental Deficiency Act, 1913, The Local Government Press, 1913, p. iv.
22. Ibid., p. 9.
23. Mental Deficiency Act, 1913, 3 and 4 George 5, C. 28, Section 19.
24. Report of the Mental Deficiency Committee, Part III, The Adult Defective, H.M.S.O., 1929

pp. 80-1
25. ibid., p. 82.
26. Report of the Mental Deficiency Committee, Part II, The Mentally Defective Child, H.M.S.O., 1929, pp. 157-161.
27. Report of the Mental Deficiency Committee, Part III, pp. 100.
28. ibid., pp. 90-91.
29. Report of the Departmental Committee appointed by the Board of Control with the approval of the Minister of Health to consider matters relating to the Construction of Colonies for Mental Defectives, H.M.S.O., 1931, p. 4.
30. The Board of Control, Annual Report for the Year 1932, Part 1, H.M.S.O., p. 63.
31. Source, Board of Control Annual Reports 1930-1938.
32. Source: M. Rooff, Voluntary Societies and Social Policy, Routledge and Kegan Paul, 1957, p. 169.
33. H. Ecktein, The English Health Service: Its Origins, Structure and Achievements, Harvard University Press, Cambridge Mass., 1958.
34. A. Bevan, In Place of Fear, Heinmann, 1952, p. 182.
35. I. Leck, W.L. Gordon and T. McKeown, 'Medical and Social Needs of Patients in Hospitals for the Mentally Subnormal', British Journal of Preventative and Social Medicine, 21, 115-21, 1967.
36. National Council for Civil Liberties, 50,000 outside the Law: Report on the treatment of those certified as mental defectives, N.C.C.L., 1951, front page.
37. ibid., p. 15.
38. ibid., p. 19.
39. ibid., p. 24.
40. ibid., p. 19.
41. Royal Commission on the Law relating to Mental Illness and Mental Deficiency, 1954-1957, Report, Cmnd. 169, H.M.S.O., 1957, p. iii.
42. ibid., para. 640.
43. ibid., paras. 187 and 190.
44. ibid., para. 592.
45. ibid., para. 592.
46. ibid., para. 669.
47. Mental Health Act, 1959, Elizabeth II 1959, C. 72.
48. Hospital Plan for England and Wales, Cmnd. 1604, H.M.S.O., 1962. Health and Welfare: The Development of Community Care, Cmnd. 1973,

H.M.S.O., 1963.
49. Report of the Committee of Inquiry into
    Allegations of Ill-Treatment of Patients and
    other Irregularities at the Ely Hospital,
    Cardiff, Cmnd. 3975, H.M.S.O., 1969.
50. R. Crossman, The Diaries of a Cabinet Minister,
    III, 1968-1970. Hamish Hamilton and Jonathan
    Cape, 1977, pp. 409, 411, 418.
51. D.H.S.S., Better Services for the Mentally
    Handicapped, Cmnd. 4683, H.M.S.O., 1971.
52. Education (Handicapped Children) Act, 1970,
    Elizabeth II 1970, C. 52.
53. D.H.S.S., Better Services for the Mentally
    Handicapped, para. 4.
54. Ibid., para. 9.
55. Ibid., para. 20.
56. P. Hall, Reforming the Welfare, Heinemann, 1976.
57. Report of the Committee of Enquiry into Mental
    Handicap Nursing and Care, (Chairman, Peggy
    Jay), 7468-1, H.M.S.O., 1979.
58. Special Educational Needs: Report of the
    Committee of Enquiry into the Education of
    Handicapped Children and Young People, Cmnd.
    7212, H.M.S.O., 1978
59. Report of the Committee of Enquiry into Mental
    Handicap Nursing and Care, para. 17.
60. Ibid., para. 91(a).

Chapter 2

THE DEVELOPMENT OF COMMUNITY CARE

INTRODUCTION

The policy of community care for mentally handicapped people and other dependent individuals is now well established. As we showed in Chapter 1 the policy was developed by the Royal Commission on the Law relating to Mental Illness and Deficiency and has been the accepted basis of ministerial policy for over 25 years.

Like many policies, community care sounds attractive but like many policies it means different things to different people. In this chapter we shall examine some of the ambiguities of the policy by examining three separate meanings of community care: as an alternative to institutional or hospital care; as an alternative to segregated specialised services; and as care by the community. We shall argue that all three meanings tend to be inextricably confused in official policy and many of the problems of community care, which we shall identify in our study, are a result of this confusion.

COMMUNITY CARE AS AN ALTERNATIVE TO INSTITUTIONAL CARE

In the 1950s and 1960s the traditional large scale institutions for the mentally ill and the mentally handicapped came under increasing criticism. In the foregront of the criticism were academic writers. In 1961 an American sociologist, Goffman, published his seminal study of institutional care, Asylums.[1] Goffman had worked for a period as a recreational therapist in a large American institution. Drawing on his experience and on

an extensive and diverse literature of different
types of institutions ranging from concentration
camps to monasteries, Goffman created the image of a
'total institution'. Goffman's total institution
was cut off from tne rest of society. As inmates
were admitted they were ritually stripped of all
links with the outside world. Inside the institutions there were two separate and mutually
antagonist cultures, a dominant staff culture and
an alternative patient culture. The institution was
a mechanism of subordination and control and the
apparent incapacity and dependency of inmates was a
product of institutional life and an essential
feature of its operation.

Criticism of specific types of institutions was
not new. Since the Second World War a number of
English writers had identified the debilitating and
damaging effect on inmates of different types of
institutions. For example, Lady Allen of Hurtwood,
a distinguished voluntary worker, had exposed the
unimaginative and depersonalizing treatment of
children in children's homes.[2] Russell Barton, a
psychiatrist, had written a training manual for
nurses in which he argued that many of the patients
in the long-stay wards of British mental hospitals
suffered from two illnesses - one illness was
related to their admission and a second was created
by their stay in hospital.[3] However Goffman's
Asylum suggested that problems were not limited to
one specific type of institution or to one specific
client group but were shared by all institutions
and by all institutionalised populations.

There followed a number of English studies that
drew on Goffman's analysis and offered empirical
support for his findings. Townsend, working at the
Institute of Community Studies in Bethnal Green
examined residential facilities for the elderly and
the influence of Goffman's work is evident in his
theoretical discussion of 'The Effects of Institutions on Individuals'.[4] Terence and Pauline
Morris produced a sociological study of Pentonville
that described the effects of the exercise of power
over inmates in the institutions and related it to
the social and personal deterioration of inmates.[5]

The work of Goffman influenced two major
studies of hospitals for the mentally handicapped;
Pauline Morris's Put Away[6] and King, Raynes and
Tizard's Patterns of Residential Care.[7] Morris's
research was funded by the National Society for
Mentally Handicapped Children. A research team
visited a national sample of 35 mental handicap

35

hospitals and in each administered detailed and
lengthy questionnaires about facilities and care.
The report of the study was published in the same
year as the report of the Committee of Inquiry into
Ely Hospital and suggested that the specific failing
and shortcomings in patient care identified by the
Ely Inquiry could be found in many other hospitals.[8]
Morris concluded that 'There are many things wrong
with our subnormal hospitals, conditions in some
places are Dickensian and grotesque'.[9]

Morris suggested that the existing institutions
based on a medical ideology and using a clinical
model of mental handicap should be replaced by
organisations with a community orientation based on
a socio-therapeutic model. Morris envisaged three
levels of support or care for the mentally handicapped. For mentally handicapped individuals who
could no longer live at home and who needed constant
medical or nursing care, the restructured hospital
would provide care and therapy on a long-term basis.
For mentally handicapped individuals who could live
in a domestic environment but who needed additional
medical or nursing care the restructured hospital
would provide care and therapy on a daily basis.
These two groups formed a minority and Morris
envisaged the major demand for residential care
would come from mentally handicapped people who
could no longer live at home but who did not require
additional medical or nursing care. For these
individuals local authorities would provide small
community homes and training facilities. Thus the
concept of community care implicit in Put Away was
the development of small-scale residential facilities
administered by local authorities as an alternative
to large-scale isolated mental handicap hospitals
administered by the National Health Service.

In the introduction to the report, Townsend
offered a theoretical explanation for the shortcomings and inadequacies reported by Morris.
Townsend argued that the segregation of the mentally
handicapped was the result of a desire to create
clear cut boundaries between the normal and abnormal.
The hospital created the boundaries between normal
and abnormal by stunting the development of mentally
handicapped people. Patients in hospitals were
treated as subnormal. They conformed to these
expectations and appeared to the outside world to be
subnormal. Like Morris, Townsend defined community
care mainly in terms of developing small scale
residential provision in the community:

The long-term aim should be to allow the great

majority of persons with the same handicaps as
those in hospitals for the subnormal to live in
sheltered housing or small family homes in the
community - when they can no longer be cared
for by their families.[10]

King, Raynes and Tizard's study of residential
care confirmed many of the findings of Morris's
study. The research was part of a child welfare
project and the researchers were interested in
examining the effect of different types of residential care facilities on the management and care of
children. Using Goffman's work, they developed a
child management scale which differentiated between
child-oriented and institution-oriented environments.
Using their scale they compared child management
practices in the living units of children's hostels,
voluntary homes and mental handicap hospitals.
   The researchers found important differences
between child management patterns in mental handicap
hospitals and hostels. The hospitals were insti-
tutionally oriented and managed by lengthy
hierarchies. Unit heads had little contact with
residents and many of the features of Goffman's
total institutions could be identified as the
depersonalisation and block treatment of patients.
In contrast hostels tended to be child oriented with
far less emphasis on hierarchy. Unit heads tended
to be closely involved in resident care. Hostels
tended to provide a warm and homely environment.
Patients tended to be treated as individuals and
unit staff and residents shared many activities,
such as eating meals.[11]
   Both Morris's and King, Raynes and Tizard's
studies identified the large mental hospital as a
major problem and both advocated the development of
small residential units in the community. The role
of researchers was not limited to examination of
existing facilities. Tizard had been involved in an
experiment to develop a small residential unit for
mentally handicapped children run as a residential
nursery rather than a nursing home.
   Tizard reported on the Brooklands unit in his
study of <u>Community Services for the Mentally
Handicapped</u>.[12] The results of the experiment had
been very favourable. Young mentally handicapped
children, admitted to the Unit, from traditional
hospital care, made marked and significant improvement when compared to control children who remained
in the mental handicap hospital. Tizard described
the children's changes in the following way:

Thev became able to play socially and construc-
tively at a level approaching that of their
mental age. Emotionally thev became much less
maladjusted ... they developed strong attach-
ments to members of staff and to other children.
They were able to play co-operatively with
other children, to take turns with as much
grace as comparable normal children and to
share. They were thus affectionate and happy
children, usually busy and interested in what
thev were doing, confident and full of fun.
In all these respects the behaviour of the
children at Brooklands was in striking contrast
to their earlier behaviour in the parent
hospital, and to the behaviour of their peers
who remained in the hospital.[13]

Thus one of the earliest meanings associated
with communitv services and community care was the
development of small residential units in the
community as opposed to the provision of residential
facilities in large isolated institutions.

This concept of community care provides a recurrent theme within policy statements about
communitv care and can be found in the Report of the
Royal Commission in 1957. Existing residential
facilities were entirely in hospitals and the Royal
Commission recommended that local authorities
should develop a parallel system in the community.

Whatever form of accommodation is favoured in
any particular localitv, we are convinced that
the aim should be a deliberate re-orientation,
awav from institutional care in its present
form and towards residential homes in the
community.[14]

The Royal Commission stressed that these residential
homes should be small local units.

Residential homes provided by the local
authorities themselves should not be large
institutions. Twentv to thirtv residents might
be a usual size, with a maximum not much over
fifty. Thev should not be in isolated places,
but in or near enough to towns or villages for
the residents to participate in the life of the
general community as far as thev are able.[15]

The authors of the White Paper Better Services
for the Mentally Handicapped were preoccupied with

the problems of the mental handicap hospitals. This
is hardly surprising as the White Paper was published in the middle of a spate of scandals in these
hospitals. Furthermore the Director of the newly
established Hospital Advisory Service had also
published his first annual report. The Hospital
Advisory Service had been established after the Ely
Report to investigate conditions in long stay
hospitals and teams of professional officers had
visited all the hospitals for the mentally handicapped in more than half of the English RHBs and in
the whole of Wales. The first report was critical
of the general standard of services in these
hospitals.

Broadly the White Paper accepted the findings
of and built on the work of academic critics. The
White Paper acknowledged that large scale institutions could be dehumanising and depersonalising
and described the consequences of institutional
shortages in the following way.

> In the worst places this produces boredom and
> tension and even occasional violence. Patients
> become apathetic and institutionalised, and
> sink into a state of complete physical and
> social dependence. Nurses are frustrated by
> having no time to provide more than attention
> to basic physical needs, without using the
> psychiatric nursing skills in which they have
> been trained.[16]

The White Paper recommended an immediate and
rigorous bar on the construction of or expansion of
any hospital over 500 beds and rapid expansion of
parallel networks of local authority residential
homes. The local authorities had been directed by
the Minister of Health in 1959 and were obliged by
the 1959 Mental Health Act to provide a full range
of community services, including residential facilities but the White Paper found progress had been
slow. At the end of 1969 only 39 of the 157
English local authorities and 4 of the 17 Welsh
local authorities had residential homes for both
children and adults.[17]

The White Paper did acknowledge the need to
support families caring for mentally handicapped
people but the main thrust of the proposals and the
main details of its recommendations were on the rundown of the mental handicap hospitals from some
60,000 beds to just over 30,000 and the parallel
expansion of local authority residential homes from

some 6,000 places to nearly 35,000 places. Broadly
the hospitals were to provide facilities for the
more handicapped and disabled whereas local
authorities were to provide facilities for the more
able. The expansion of other community facilities
such as training centres was related to this general
restructuring of services. Mental handicap hospitals had traditionally provided a comprehensive
range of services whereas local authority homes were
only residential facilities and needed the support
of other facilities such as training centres.[18]
    The policy proposals of the Royal Commission
and the White Paper were incremental. Both started
with the current pattern of services, examined its
shortcomings and then made proposals to remedy these
shortcomings. Both identified large scale institutional facilities as the major problem and both
recommended the development of small residential
units in the community as the alternative. The Jay
Committee, in contrast, took a more radical approach.
It started with the rights and needs of mentally
handicapped people, developed the framework of a
service that would meet these rights and needs and
then examined the changes needed to create this
service.
    The Committee took for granted the criticisms
of institutional care and therefore did not repeat
them. However it did note that these problems were
not restricted to large isolated institutions but
could also develop in residential accommodation in
the community;

> Institutional approaches of the kind described
> by King, Raynes and Tizard are not confined to
> institutions. They can emerge in professional
> practice in the community ... We need to in-
> vestigate whether the style of new purpose-
> built homes for mentally handicapped people is
> in fact perpetuating the old 'institutional'
> approach to care.[19]

    The Committee, in contrast to the Royal
Commission and White Paper, did not advocate an
uncritical acceptance of local authority residential
homes as an alternative to mental handicap hospitals. In the words of the Committee 'A purpose
built unit on the outskirts of a housing development or a town is not in our view "in the community"'.[20] The Committee wanted all new residential
facilities to be in houses organised in the same
way as ordinary homes and to be as small as possible:

The needs of a small number of mentally handicapped children will, however, best be met by
small, special houses which are locally based.
Our preference is for such houses to be in
specially adapted private houses ... But whereas a 40 bed ward was regarded as small by
comparison with a 70 bed ward 15 years ago,
many people now think of 'small' as meaning a
maximum of 6 children in a house. As with the
children's homes we would envisage meals being
cooked in the house and the residents having
personal space, with individual bedrooms
(except in the case of those who expressly
wanted to share their sleeping accommodation
with someone else). The climate of experience
for adults, depending on their personal, social
and physical development, would be one in which
personal competence and personal identity were
continually strengthened; in particular in
making decisions, as much freedom as possible
would be normal.[21]

The Committee rejected the view held by the
Royal Commission and the authors of the White Paper
that facilities for the less disabled should be in
the community whereas facilities for the more
disabled should be in mental handicap hospitals.
They felt that all mentally handicapped people
should have the right to live in domestic houses in
the community.

We found no valid reason for a distinction
between 'treatment' and 'residential care',
since in our thinking an active developmental
programming is required by mentally handicapped
people with all degrees of handicap and all
kinds of problems.[22]

The Committee did accept reluctantly the need for
some more specialised accommodation but argued that
'these homes should share as many of the characteristics of normal living which we envisage in our
staffed local homes as possible'.[23]
Like the Royal Commission and the authors of
the White Paper, the Jay Committee emphasised the
view of community care as the provision of residential facilities in the community. Unlike the
previous reports the Jay Committee envisaged all
residential facilities in the community and left no
role for the traditional mental handicap hospital
and the committee was more specific about the nature

and form of the residential facilities it wanted in
the community, viz. specially adapted private
houses.

Comment
      The development of community care was
associated with criticisms and dissatisfactions of
the existing system of care within large scale
institutions and hospitals, especially criticisms
based on Goffman's concept of the total institution.
Large scale institutions came to be viewed as intrinsically bad and damaging to inmates. They were
seen as creating the very problems that they were
supposed to be solving. As a result one way of
viewing community care was as an alternative to
large scale institutional care and as care for
mentally handicapped people in small-scale residential units in the community.
      This conceptualisation has been a major if not
at times dominant one within official policy statements. For example a group of officials in the
DHSS recently reviewed the policies for the development of community care. The review was initiated
because of 'some uncertainty about the general
policy objectives underlying the concept of community care'[24] and the authors of the report acknowledged that the term '"community care" seems to mean
very different things depending on the context in
which it is used'.[25] Both in the report's discussion of departmental concerns about community
care and in the discussion of specific implemen-
tations of the policy it is clear that the committee
gave priority to the concept of community care as an
alternative to institutional care.[26]
      However there have been other competing
conceptualisations and in the remaining sections of
this chapter we shall discuss two: community care
as the integration of mentally handicapped people
within the community and community care as care by
the community.

COMMUNITY CARE AS INTEGRATION OF THE MENTALLY
HANDICAPPED WITHIN THE COMMUNITY

      Community care as small scale residential
facilities within the community and community care
as integration within the community are related
concepts. Both start with a critique of existing
services and facilities, especially large scale

institutions. However they criticise large scale institutions for different reasons and in different ways. One set of criticisms are directed at the organisation of the institutions and the damage it does to individuals, the other is directed at the role of the institutions in society. Institutions are seen as segregating normal from abnormal and in some way creating abnormality or deviance. Thus the intellectual roots of moves to reintegrate the mentally handicapped can be found within socio-logical theories about the nature and cause of deviance.

In the 1950s and 60s sociologists began to challenge the clinical view of deviance. In the clinical view of deviance the identification of deviance and deviants was seen as a straightforward business and the deviant acts were somehow a product of the innate characteristics of deviant indi-viduals. Sociologists argued that in practice it was difficult to distinguish between deviant and non-deviant acts. Similar actions could be classified in very different ways depending on the social context in which they occurred. Similarly it was difficult to find any intrinsic characteristics that differentiated deviants from the rest of the population. What identified or labelled an action or individual as deviant or different was the social context and societal reaction. These socio-logists emphasised the social processes or societal reactions involved in creating deviance.

The emphasis on societal reaction in the creation of deviance marked an important shift in the focus of sociological research. Rather than asking how much crime, deviance, disease or handicap existed, researchers asked how and in what circum-stances did an action or activity become defined as a crime, deviant or evidence of disability and the individual become defined as a criminal, deviant or mental retardate. By rephrasing the problem the centre of research interest shifted from the 'victim' and his characteristics to the agencies that defined specific problems, gave these problems names or labels and prescribed certain actions in response to these problems. Rather than mechani-cally and automatically responding to problems and individuals 'out there', policemen, magistrates, doctors and psychologists were seen as playing an active part in the way social problems were defined and therefore created. Becker defined this approach in the following way:

social groups create deviance by making the
rules whose infraction constitutes deviance,
and by applying those rules to particular
people and labeling them as outsiders. From
this point of view, deviance is not a quality
of the act the person commits, but rather a
consequence of the application by others of
rules and sanctions to an 'offender . The
deviant is one to whom that label has successfully been applied; deviant behavior is
behavior that people so label.[27]

The societal reaction approach suggested that
the process of labelling an individual as a deviant
was an important social process that could have pro-
found repercussions on the individual and literally
changed him or her into a different person. Individuals labelled as deviant could, for a variety of
reasons, conform to a specific societal stereotype
of a deviant and experience a loss of status or
social stigma. Becker described the process in the
following way:

When the deviant is caught, he is treated in
accordance with the popular diagnosis of why he
is that way, and the treatment itself may like-
wise produce increasing deviance. The drug
addict, popularly considered to be a weak-
willed individual who cannot forego the inde-
cent pleasures afforded him by opiates, is
treated repressively. He is forbidden to use
drugs. Since he cannot get drugs legally, he
must get them illegally. This forces the
market underground and pushes the price of
drugs up far beyond the current legitimate
market price into a bracket that few can
afford on an ordinary salary. Hence the treatment of the addict's deviance places him in a
position where it will probably be necessary to
resort to deceit and crime in order to support
his habit. The behavior is a consequence of
the public reaction to the deviance rather than
a consequence of the inherent qualities of the
deviant act.[28]

The new perspective on deviance was quickly
applied to the mentally handicapped. In an early
collection of papers edited by Becker, Dexter
discussed the politics of stupidity and argued that
the mentally handicapped suffered especially badly
from a societal reaction,

> There is ... the experience which may be ob-
> served over and over again of the denial of
> employment, of legal rights, of a fair hearing,
> of an opportunity, to the stupid because they
> are stupid (e.g., have a low I.Q. or show poor
> academic performance), and not because the
> stupidity is relevant to the task, or claim, or
> situation.[29]

Dexter argued that the mentally handicapped were
discriminated against because they challenged the
basic values of industrial society such as the importance of intellectual excellence.

> But the stupid who get along well cast doubt on
> the alleged secular justification of the
> system - that it helps people succeed. It is
> repulsive for some to believe that mental
> defectives can support themselves, no matter
> how much evidence is amassed to this effect,
> because, if so, how can we justify the discom-
> forts and sacrifices and anguish of schooling?
> And when a scholar reported that some defec-
> tives have been more successful than non-
> defective counterparts, it is not surprising
> that she received fifty or so scurrilous
> attacks; she was denying the sacred.[30]

The societal reaction perspective on mental retardation found its clearest expression in the work
of Mercer. Mercer was involved in a major programme
of research in mental retardation funded by the
National Institute of Mental Health in California.
Mercer joined the project to study the families of
the mentally retarded and to conduct research into
the problems of the mentally retarded responding to
the stress and normal crises of life in a community
setting. The research rapidly ran into the problem
of defining who the mentally handicapped were and
like many studies of deviance transformed into a
study of the ways in which mental retardation was
created by various agencies.
    Mercer started by identifying two separate
perspectives on mental retardation, the clinical
perspective and the social system perspective:

> The clinical perspective classifies mental
> retardation as a handicapping condition, which
> exists in the individual and can be diagnosed
> by clinically trained professionals using
> properly standardized assessment techniques.

The social system perspective classifies mental
retardation as an acquired status. Like any
social status, that of mental retardate is
defined by its location in the social system
vis-a-vis other statuses, and by the role
prescriptions that define the type of performance expected of persons holding the status.[31]

The implications of the social system perspectice
were, as Mercer made clear, radical.

If a person does not occupy the status of
mental retardate, is not playing the role of
mental retardate in any social system, and is
not regarded as mentally retarded by any of the
significant others in his social world, then he
is not mentally retarded, irrespective of the
level of his IQ, the adequacy of his adaptive
behavior, or the extent of his organic
impairment.[32]

From this point of view activities of agencies such
as the Board of Control in Britain who actively
sought out mental defectives in the 1920s and
1930s were not responses to a pre-existing problem
but were active measures that in some senses created
the problem and created mental deficiency.
Mercer's research found that state schools
played an important part in the process of identifying and labelling mental retardates in California.
The behaviour and skills of the children played a
part in the process of labelling, but equally
important was the child's social status. Children
with the same skills but different social backgrounds could be labelled and treated in very
different ways. The closer a child's background was
to the dominant 'anglocentric' or white Anglo-
Saxon Protestant culture the less likely was that
child to be labelled mentally retarded. Mercer
argued that existing diagnostic patterns, especially
I.Q. tests, discriminated against minority groups.

We found that becoming a social retardate in
the public schools is a complex social process,
which hinges on a series of crucial decisions
made by teachers, principals, and psychologists. Some children are exposed to a much
higher risk of achieving the status of mental
retardate than others... Those who failed the
IQ test were disproportionately from lower
socio-economic levels and ethnic minority

groups... Children whose backgrounds do not
conform to the modal sociocultural config-
uration of the community are exposed to a
higher risk of being labeled mentally retarded.[33]

Mercer's study had a number of policy implications. Mercer noted that individuals were
labelled mentally retarded for a number of different
reasons. However official agencies tended to treat
this heterogenous group of individuals as if it were
homogenous. For example education programmes were
based on the assumption that all individuals
classified as mentally retarded had a low potential
for learning. Mercer's recommendations drew on the
contemporary civil rights movement. She emphasised
the civil rights and liberties of citizens, whether
they are handicapped or not and emphasised the right
of individuals to have equal opportunities and equal
treatment. Specifically Mercer argued that individuals had the right not to be classified as mentally
retarded merely because their social background
happened to be different from that of the dominant
social group. Labelling and classifying the mentally retarded should not be based on one single
assessment such as the I.Q. test but should be
based on a variety of procedures. Individuals
should only be classified as mentally retarded if
all the assessment procedures indicated they should
be. The research team experimented with this type
of pluralistic evaluation and found that it halved
the number of children classified as mentally
retarded and reduced the social discrimination
against minority groups. The concept of pluralistic
evaluation was adopted as part of the Californian
legal system in 1971.[34]
The right of individuals not to be labelled
mentally retarded was the dominant theme in Mercer's
study. However there were associated rights for the
residual group of individuals who are labelled
mentally retarded. Mercer did not discuss these in
detail but emphasised that individuals labelled
mentally retarded should not experience a disadvantage as a result of the labelling. They should have
treatment and facilities appropriate to their
circumstances which should be designed to help them
return as fast as possible and as near as possible
to normality. They should not experience treatment
and facilities that were inferior to those
experienced by other people and which could
emphasise and maintain their status as retarded

individuals.

The societal reaction approach to deviance found a sympathetic audience in British research circles. For example, Peter Townsend in his Foreword to Pauline Morris's Put Away argued that the process of classifying mental handicap was dependent on social and cultural factors and I.Q. tests were not culture free and children of middle class parents had an 'unfair advantage' when tested. He went on to argue that many people classified as 'subnormal' and 'severely subnormal' had either not been properly assessed or tested or 'their intelligence test scores considerably exceed the limits normally accepted for purposes of definition by psychologists'.[35] Although Townsend defined community care as small scale provision within the community he was also aware of and advocated the need to maintain the civil liberties of individuals by integrating them within normal society.

> In appreciating what the imprecise criteria of subnormal intelligence, personal incapacity and deviance contribute to our concept of mental handicap we can perhaps see the need to revise our standards of humanity and justice. For the significance of this analysis is much more than semantic. It implies that there may be persons who are deprived of full civic rights and responsibilities and even in some cases of their personal freedom because their ability to read and write has not yet been perceived, their relatively adequate intelligence has not been measured (or has not been measured efficiently), their behaviour is found to be morally repugnant or they are an embarrassment in school. It also implies that any physical segregation, even of people of extreme handicap, may be improper.[36]

In policy terms, the societal reaction school stressed the discriminatory nature of labelling and the deprivation experienced by the mentally handicapped in various segregated facilities. The emphasis was on desegregating the mentally handicapped and integrating them within the normal services. This movement has taken many forms and one pervasive name for desegregation is normalization. In the United States this movement was associated with the writing of Wolfensberger and with the work of Eastern Nebraska Community Office of Retardation (ENCOR).[37]

Wolfensberger's starting point was deviance. He argued that societies could manage deviance in four ways: through the 'destruction of deviant individuals, their segregation, reversal of their condition or prevention thereof'.[38] He argued that the first two techniques were unacceptable and harmed the mentally handicapped whereas the prevention and reversal of deviance were acceptable, and desirable goals for society and the basis of normalization. Normalization involved altering both the deviant individual and his or her social environment so that the deviant person no longer appeared to be deviant. In England the concept of normalization formed the basis of a series of publications by the Campaign for Mentally Handicapped People. An early pamphlet written by Kendall and Moss set out many of the arguments for desegregation and for integration. Kendall and Moss argued that existing segregated services stigmatized the mentally handicapped and created perceptions of the handicapped as deviant and abnormal.

> A cause and consequence (of segregated ser-
> vices) has been the stigma attached to the
> mentally handicapped and the separate insti-
> tutions for them... Isolation and stigma help
> the non-handicapped to lose sight of the
> essentially common features that they share
> with the handicapped - common needs, feelings,
> reactions, behaviours, worth and humanity;
> instead, differences are searched for and
> stressed. When faced by the comparatively rare
> sight of a mentally handicapped child, the non-
> handicapped will often see the handicap before
> the child, and intepret all the child's actions
> in terms of the handicap.[39]

Associated with the stigmatization of the mentally handicapped within segregated services was the inferior quality of services. The mentally handicapped were deprived of services and resources when compared to other people.

> The past record of segregated services for the
> mentally handicapped also provides a strong
> case against the continuation of segregation,
> with educational and residential standards
> often grossly inferior to those for non-handi-
> capped children. This is hardly surprising -
> separate services for stigmatised, minority
> groups are invariably inferior, the inferiority

and separation feeding on one another.[40]

Kendall and Moss argued that, with suitable preparation, mentally handicapped children could and
should use the same educational and residential
facilities as other children. The integration would
allow mentally handicapped children access to the
superior facilities of ordinary children and would
help the mentally handicapped children to live and
be accepted in a normal environment.

> For the handicapped child, integration offers
> the opportunity to gain self-confidence and
> social skills for dealing with the outside
> world and non-handicapped people... Inte-
> gration should offer a more normal environment,
> and more relevant and wider social experiences
> ... It should also enable the mentally handi-
> capped to feel part of, and be part of, their
> local neighbourhoods.[41]

The pamphlet by Kendall and Moss was followed
by a series of pamphlets published by the CMH
advocating integration and normalization. For
example in 1974 the CMH published the results of its
investigation into the integration of education and
residential care. The investigation showed that the
general practice within local agencies was to segregate facilities although there were a few examples
of agencies that deliberately integrated facilities.
The authors of the report suggested that, handled
properly, the integration of the mentally handicapped yielded considerable benefits for the
mentally handicapped. The authors ended the
pamphlet with a plea that the option of integrating
the mentally handicapped should be placed on the
policy agenda.

> We must appreciate that there is a crucial
> choice to be made, that there is a strong case
> for integration and a case to be answered
> against segregation. But before we can make
> the right choice, strike the right balance we
> need to explore and know more. We must decide
> how far the essence of being labelled 'mentally
> handicapped' must continue to be segregation.[42]

Policy statements on community care by central
government departments and various working parties
and committees have since the mid 50s stressed the
importance of integration of the mentally handi-

capped within services provided for other client
groups. However there has been an important change
in emphasis. Early policy statements such as the
Report of the Royal Commission on the Law relating
to Mental Illness and Mental Deficiency and the
White Paper Better Services for the Mentally
Handicapped had a weak version of integration. They
stressed the rights of mentally handicapped people
to use services provided for the general population
but the bulk of practical recommendations were
related to the development of specialist facilities.
For example one of the White Paper's main principles
was that:

> Mentally handicapped children and adults should
> not be segregated unnecessarily from other
> people of similar age, nor from the general
> life of the local community.[43]

However the detailed proposals of the White Paper
related to specific targets on building, staff and
places in specialist facilities.
  More recent policy statements have provided a
stronger definition and have suggested not only that
the mentally handicapped could be integrated within
facilities provided for other client groups but that
they should. For example within the education
services the Warnock Committee recommended the
integration of children with special needs into the
mainstream of education.[44]
  The Jay Committee was influenced by concepts of
integration and normalization and the view of
community care as integration of the mentally handicapped was clearly developed within the committee's
report. Previous reports started with a review of
current services and practices and then made
suggestions for incremental changes in the pattern
of service provision. The Jay Committee took a more
radical approach and started with a discussion of
the rights of mentally handicapped people in the
form of a philosophy and model of care. The first
principle emphasised the right of individuals to a
normal life. 'Mentally handicapped people have a
right to enjoy normal patterns of life in the
community.[45]
  The service principles based on the rights of
handicapped people stressed the view of community
care as the integration of the mentally handicapped
within the community.

  The two groups of principles (on a normal

51

lifestyle and on individuality) ... involve
value judgements about the human rights of
handicapped people in society... It is important that the service system we develop should
not be based on historical accident, that it
should facilitate rather than hamper the
integration of handicapped people into society,
and should help the community to accept
differences in their peers rather than reinforce
prejudices. For these reasons we believe that:
Mentally handicapped people should use
normal services wherever possible.
Special provision tends to set apart those
who receive them and may therefore
increase the distance between mentally
handicapped people and the rest of
society...
'Specialised' services or organisations
for mentally handicapped people should be
provided only to the extent that they
demonstrably meet or are likely to meet
additional needs that cannot be met by the
general services... Wherever possible
the special services should be delivered
in integrated settings. In the past such
services have often been specialised only
in name, they have not met defined special
needs...
Finally, if we are to establish and maintain high quality services for a group of
people who cannot easily articulate and
press their just claims, we need someone
to incercede on behalf of mentally handicapped people in obtaining services.[46]

As we have already noted in the previous section the Jay Committee had other definitions of
community care, e.g. as care in small residential
units in the community. The committee was aware of
the contradictions between the different definitions
and found them difficult to resolve. For example in
discussing the most severely handicapped individuals
the committee was divided between members who wanted
to categorise or identify 'special groups' or sub-
classes of the mentally handicapped and members who
wanted to see each mentally handicapped as a unique
individual with special needs and any classification
would be artitrary and have undesirable consequences.
The committee resolved this disagreement by agreeing
to avoid 'categorisation of special groups'.[47]
Other disagreements were not resolved so amicably.

The trade union representative on the committee
refused to sign the main report as he believed its
recommendations would devalue the status of his
members - nurses in mental handicap hospitals, who
provided the bulk of the segregated services.[48]

Comment
   The conception of community care as integration
of the mentally handicapped within the community has
a similar background to the concept of community
care as provision within small scale residential
facilities in the community. Academics and
researchers, who examined existing service provision
and organisational practices in the 1950s and 1960s,
challenged the basis and assumptions of these organisations. Sociologists, using a societal reaction
view of deviance, argued that deviance was not an
innate characteristic of individual deviant but a
result of a complex set of social processes.
Agencies didn't discover mental handicap, they, in
some ways created it.   Furthermore the process of
labelling individuals as deviant could and did
create further disabilities for the deviants through
the associated process of stigmatisation. Deviants
were separated from the rest of society and given an
inferior and subordinate position from which it was
difficult to escape.
   The implications of this view was that, as far
as possible, individuals should not be labelled
mentally handicapped. However, if they were then
they should not be excluded from the services
received by the rest of the population but should
benefit from these services. The extra services
they received should enable them to return as
quickly as possible and as far as possible to the
life enjoyed by the rest of the population.
   It is possible to identify this definition of
community care within policy documents but the
precise meaning and significance attached to it has
changed. In early reports a fairly weak interpretation can be found. The mentally handicapped
were not to be excluded from services provided for
the rest of the population. In later statements the
interpretation is stronger. Community care was not
just removal of barriers to use of services but a
positive attempt to integrate the mentally handicapped within the community and detailed proposals
were given for this integration.
   This meaning of community care co-existed with
other definitions within reports. Sometimes the

co-existence led to explicit disagreements and
difficulties as in the case of the Jay Committee but
more usually the various meanings co-existed and the
contradictions were unresolved.

COMMUNITY CARE AS CARE BY THE COMMUNITY

It is possible to identify a third meaning of
community care within official reports. Community
care is also identified as care by the community,
i.e. support for the mentally handicapped people
and their families from the community, relatives,
friends and neighbours. Again this definition can
be traced to sociological research; in this case
community studies.

At the end of the 19th century commentators on
society detected the collapse of traditional forms
of social organisations, especially locally based
communities, and their replacement by associations
of individuals held together by mutual interests.

Tönnies, a German sociologist, contrasted
traditional communities with modern associations.
He argued that the community or, in his terms,
Gemeinschaft, provided an intimate satisfying
experience for its members whereas the association
or Geselleschaft was merely a combination of individuals held together by self-interest. He
contrasted the two in the following way:

> Gemeinschaft (the community) is old;
> Gesellschaft (the association) is new as a name
> as well as a phenomenon. All praise of rural
> life has pointed out that the Gemeinschaft
> among people is stronger there and more alive;
> it is the lasting and genuine form of living
> together. In contrast to Gemeinschaft,
> Gesellschaft is transitory and superficial.
> Accordingly, Gemeinschaft should be understood
> as a living organism, Gesellschaft as a
> mechancial aggregate and artifact...
> Gesellschaft, an aggregate by convention and
> law of nature, is to be understood as a
> multitude of natural and artificial individ-
> uals, the wills and spheres of whom are in
> many relations with and to one another, and
> remain nevertheless independent of one another
> and devoid of mutual familiar relationships.[49]

There is in Tönnies' writing, as in many of his
contemporaries a strong element of romanticism and

an assumption that industrialisation had disrupted
the fabric of society and destroyed traditional
communities and in some way impoverished the
experience of individuals. Traditional communities
were seen as caring, whereas modern society was seen
as a collection of individuals, a crowd of strangers
in which each individual is only concerned with his
or her self-interest.

In the 1930s and 1940s sociologists, especially
in the USA, began to study communities. The
technique was pioneered by the Lynds in their study
of Middlestown[50] and their study set the trend for
subsequent community study. It was an attempt to
objectively describe a community and was:

> the first scientific and ostensibly uncritical,
> objective description of small-town life. Here
> for the first time, without reformist overtones
> and without dramatization, was a mirror held
> up to the ordinary American.[51]

The community study formed a recognisable type
of investigation. These studies tended to show that
the sharp division made by Tönnies between community
and association was artificial. Neighbourhoods were
not usually made up of strangers but contained
social networks. Neighbourhoods could and did provide networks of support. Indeed more care and
support was provided by these networks than by
formal agencies funded by the state. For example in
the USA Whyte studied an Italian slum and identified
important mechanisms of social cohesion and mutual
support. One such mechanism was the gangs to which
most young men belonged. He described the mechanism
of mutual support in gangs in the following way:

> The stable composition of the group and the
> lack of social assurance on the part of its
> members contributed towards producing a very
> high rate of social interaction within the
> group. The group structure is a product of
> these interactions. Out of such interactions
> there arises a system of mutual obligations
> which is fundamental to group cohesion ...
> (when conflict developed) actions which were
> performed explicitly for the sake of friendship
> were revealed as being part of a system of
> mutual obligations.[52]

In England, Young and Willmott conducted a
major study of family and kinship in East London in

a traditional working class area, Bethnal Green, and
in a new housing estate, Greenleigh. Bethnal Green
was a community. Individuals were born into it,
lived in it and died in it. They identified with it
and were bound to it by a whole range of relations:

> The view we have formed and tested more or less
> daily for three years is that very few people
> wish to leave the East End. They are attached
> to Mum and Dad, to the markets, to the pubs and
> settlements, to Club Row and the London
> Hospital ... (people) are tied to the district
> by time... People do not, after marriage,
> throw off the past which contains their former
> family and friends. They combine past and
> present. They continue to belong to the same
> community.[53]

Young and Willmott identified the relationship
between mothers and daughters as the key element in
maintaining the cohesiveness of the community and
argued that this bond tended to link three genera-
tions together in a mutually supportive network:
'In a three-generation family the old as well as the
young both receive and give services; the aid is
reciprocal'.[54]
    Young and Willmott examined the family life of
individuals who had been rehoused in a new housing
estate on the outskirts of London - Greenleigh.
They argued that the transfer broke traditional
community ties and relations. They described the
social consequences of the transfer in the following
way:

> The relatives of Bethnal Green have not, there-
> fore, been replaced by the neighbours of
> Greenleigh. The newcomers are surrounded by
> strangers instead of kin. Their lives outside
> the family are no longer centred on people;
> their lives are centred on the house.[55]

Young and Willmott argued that the migration dis-
located the structure of family relations and therefore impaired the caring capacity of the community.

> It seems that when the balance of a three-
> generation family is disturbed, the task of
> caring for dependents at both ends of life,
> always one of the great and indispensable
> functions of any society, becomes less
> manageable.[56]

To maintain the caring capacity of the
community, Young and Willmott recommended that
planners should not disrupt traditional communities.
Existing houses should, as far as possible, be re-
furbished otherwise communities should be rehoused
en bloc so that social relations were not disrupted.
The community studies showed that networks of
mutual support did exist within industrial society.
However the studies also suggested that these networks were restricted. Some people could draw on
better networks and some neighbourhoods were more
supportive. The caring capacity of the community
had to be enhanced so that the community could
really care.
Parallel to sociological studies of communities
which identified and examined networks of social
relations within communities were epidemiological
surveys which studied the nature and distribution of
health problems within social groups. The epidemiological studies reinforced the sociological
studies by focussing on and stressing the importance
of the community in the creation and management of
health problems.
Armstrong has argued that the development of
routine surveys of the health of communities was
associated with the development of the dispensaries
or health centres in the 1920s. For example the
Peckham health centre was opened in 1926 and re-
opened in 1935.[57] The health centres had a radical
impact on the conception of disease and disability.
Whereas disease and disability had been viewed as a
biological malfunction of the body experienced by a
few individuals, disease and disability came to be
seen as processes affecting the whole community.
There was no clear divide between the normal and
abnormal and therefore everybody was potentially
diseased or disabled.

> Surveillance discovered disease in the com-
> munity and this discovery necessitated further
> surveillance. In effect, the Pioneer centre
> destroyed the distinction between those who
> were healthy and those who were diseased.
> Whereas for traditional hospital medicine,
> illness was a deviant status, to the Dispensary,
> as found at Peckham, it was normal. If every-
> one had pathology then everyone would need
> observing. Thus of everyone attending the
> health centre only 7% were found to be truly
> healthy.[58]

57

Epidemiological studies became a major part of medical science after the Second World War and these confirmed the importance of the community in both creating and managing health problems. Whereas community studies indicated the nature and poss- bility of changing and improving local communities, epidemiological studies indicated the importance of controlling disease by controlling the community.[59]

An interesting example of the assumptions on which care by the community is based can be found in Curtis' publications in the USA.[60] Curtis' start- ing point is the collapse of traditional networks of social support.

Less than a century ago, the social structure of community and neighbourhood towered above all other forces to create the environment in which primary relationships were carried out. With the eclipse of community, group structures have come to dominate collectively our social networks.[61]

Curtis argued that the existing pattern of service development did little to enhance the caring capacity of the community because services were dominated by professionals who only treated the individual who presented the problem. The social networks within which these individuals were en- meshed were disregarded. The role of the whole network in creating the problem or their potential for solving it were not considered. Curtis was concerned that this narrow response to problems was found not only in traditional institutions but also in the new 'community services' that were supposed to replace them. The development of community services was merely creating a parallel system of care based on the same assumptions and competing for the same resources as the institutions. He des- cribed the situation in the following way:

The evidence that institutions have not been replaced as the major focus of mental health care is clearly demonstrated by the way state mental health funds are currently divided between institutions and community centers. The institutions still consume the lion's share of mental health resources. In addition, there are very few linkages between state hospitals and community centers. As a consequence we now have two parallel underfunded mental health systems. Of course, competition for funding

between the two is heightened during a period
of limited growth. This dual system is an
excellent example of how investments in professional care can sometimes be just as harmful
as helpful. The 'family' of mental health
professionals, scattered without direction
across two approaches to service delivery often
works at cross purposes with the same individuals and families, and within the same
communities.[62]

Curtis argued that the emphasis of intervention
and activity should shift from the person who
presented the problem to the whole network of
relations. The community rather than the professional was the healer and possessed the resources
for healing. Curtis contrasted the traditional
approach with his approach in the following way:

The traditional approach to professional care
begins at intake: A single individual is
admitted, and the case record, which describes
the client in detail, reports the planned
behavioral change... If mental health professionals defined every new individual coming
into a center as a member of a network, and
the network itself became the client instead
of the single 'sick' person, there could be
three or four or a dozen more people to work on
the problem. Many of these people could work
on resolving the problem during each week,
rather than having just two people (the client
and the professional) working on a solution for
an hour or two each week.[63]

Curtis emphasised self-help and mutual help in
the community which could be fostered and enhanced
by professional support. The individual should be
maintained in his or her community as long as possible and if this was not possible then a network of
mutual support was to be created:

For those who have already become dependent on
a professional residence or for those who must
be removed from their home, alternative households could be created which maximize
reciprocal investments. A geographic area
should be dotted with a network of small group
residences, cooperative apartments, and foster
or adopting parents, who expect each resident
to move toward independence as quickly or as

ɔletely as possible.[64]

England the Mutual Aid Centre was set up to foster the development of community self-help. The programme for the Centre was laid out in a pamphlet written by Young and Rigg. The starting point was the selfishness of modern society,

> ... at its worst modern society seems to be only a well-heeled mob, with anything deserving the name of altruism not extending much beyond the bounds of individual families.[65]

Young and Rigg wished to enhance the caring capacity of the community by developing a network of mutual aid of self-help groups through which the skills and knowledge of the community could be mobilised.

> (The) bond of common experience is one which characterises all true self-help groups. The most fundamental distinction between these and other groups is that those who are helped are also the helpers... When outsiders offer help they are more likely to offer pity as well... The willpower of a group striving towards a goal together is far more effective than that of an individual.[66]

These concepts of care by the community were also evident in sociological studies of care for the mentally handicapped, e.g., Bayley's study of the care of the mentally handicapped in Sheffield at the end of the 1960s. Bayley recognised the ambiguity of the concept of community care. His book started with the following paragraph:

> Care IN the community or care BY the community
> Community care has become part of the jargon of our day. It is used to cover a wide range of care and an equally wide variety of under-standings of community.[67]

Bayley defined community care as care by the community:

> The futility of even thinking of creating a service apart from the community (in the micro-cosmic sense) is shown by the elderly. Over 94 per cent live at home and the vast majority live at home because they want to. Here, as

clearly as in any branch of the social services, we can see that the community caring at the small-scale, face-to-face level is and must be the basis on which all services depend.[68]

In his study Bayley found that official agencies such as local authority social services departments were trying to replace rather than supplement the caring capacity of families and the community. Bayley recommended a major revision of policy and practice:

> The radical implications of a policy of com-
> munity care find little place in the way the
> social services operate... The assumption
> about the way the social services should op-
> erate still appears to be that, first of all,
> the social services will try to help a certain
> group of people, and then the general public
> should be asked to help the social services.
> Such an understanding seems implicit in the
> 1971 White Paper <u>Better Services for the
> Mentally Handicapped</u>... The position of these
> families (in the Sheffield Study) shows that
> this approach is the wrong way round. It is
> not a question of the community 'supplementing
> official services'; it is a question of the
> official services helping and enabling the
> community to do better the caring it does
> already, with more help and less strain on
> individual members of it.[69]

As Bayley points out it is difficult to identify, in early reports, the conception of community care as care by the community. It finds its first major statement in the Report of the Seebohm Committee. The Seebohm Committee reported in 1968 and recommended the formation of integrated social service departments within local authorities. One major function of these new departments and the social workers they employed was to mobilise the caring capacity of the community. The committee defined community in the following way:

> The term 'community' is usually understood to
> cover both the physical location and the common
> identify of a group of people... The notion
> of a community implies the existence of a net-
> work of reciprocal social relationships, which
> among other things ensure mutual aid and give
> those who experience it a sense of well-being.[70]

61

The committee suggested that many social problems arose because of malfunctioning of the
community. Either there was little sense of
community and little pressure of the community on
individual deviants or, in some cases, the community
itself was deviant.[71] The social services departments had to engage in social engineering or
community development to create the right sort of
community:

> (there is a) need for the personal social
> services to engage in the extremely difficult
> and complex task of encouraging and assisting
> the development of community identity and
> mutual aid, particularly in areas characterised
> by rapid population turnover, high delinquency,
> child deprivation and mental illness rates and
> other indices of social pathology. Social work
> with individuals alone is bound to be of
> limited effect in an area where the community
> environment itself is a major impediment to
> healthy individual development... A clear
> responsibility then should be placed upon the
> social service department for developing
> conditions favourable to community identity and
> activity.[72]

The desire to foster and mobilise community
participation and involvement was a major part of
successive government initiatives in the 1970s.
These included educational priority areas of the
Department of Education and Science, Community
Development Projects of the Home Office and the
Good Neighbour campaign initiated by the DHSS.
These initiatives have had relatively limited impact
on the structure and organisation of formal services
and have generally been abandoned fairly rapidly.
However Bayley, in a review of community oriented
systems of care, was able to identify and document a
series of local initiatives.[73]
The conception of community care as care by the
community did appear in the Jay Report but it was
the least developed of the three versions of community care. One of the committee's three underlying principles related to this conception:
'Mentally handicapped people will require additional
help from the cummunities in which they live'.[74]
And this principle was developed in the committee's
discussion of service principles: 'Existing networks of community support should be strengthened by
professional services rather than supplanted by

them'.[75] The committee also argued that 'local
community networks' could provide 'the understanding
and support which the professionals cannot always
provide'.[76] Although the committee obviously
favoured community involvement and care by the community, the terms of reference of the committee
restricted it to a consideration of residential
facilities. The concrete proposals for mobilising
the community were limited. For example the committee devoted three paragraphs to a discussion of
the use of volunteers as a means of mobilising
community involvement but only in relation to
residential units.[77]

   The latest policy statement by the DHSS on
services for mentally handicapped people was rather
more explicit than the Jay Report. The need to
mobilise the community is acknowledged and a
specific mechanism is advocated, self-help groups.
However the impact of the discussion is rather
limited as it segregated from the discussion of
routine services and placed in a separate section on
the role of the voluntary and private sectors.[78]

Comment
   As with other conceptions of community care,
the view of community care as care by the community
can be traced back to sociological studies, in this
case various types of community studies. One type
of study showed that in industrial society networks
of mutual support did exist. However these networks
were variable in extent and function and needed to
be reinforced or systematically fostered. The other
type of study indicated that the community played
an important part in the development and management
of illness and disability. There was a symptom iceberg and the formal services only dealt with the tip
of the iceberg. The amount and type of problems
that were referred to formal services depended on
social processes within the community rather than on
the nature and structure of the formal services. To
control disease or deviance it was important to
control the community.
   The importance of the community in both
creating and managing disability led to an obvious
concern with improvements in the structure of the
community. Various government departments have
manifested an interest in community development.
However no agreed or proven technology exists for
this type of social engineering. Many reports
recommend more community involvement but it often
remains, as in the Jay Report, at the level of vague

generality rather than concrete proposal.

CONCLUSION

We have in this chapter identified three major
perspectives on community care. One perspective
draws on the anti-institution literature and community care is seen as care in small residential
units in the community. The second perspective draws
on deviance theory and community care is seen as
desegregation and as an attempt to integrate the
mentally handicapped within the community. The
third perspective draws on different types of community studies and is seen as care by the community
through the mobilisation of social networks to care
for mentally handicapped people.

We have shown that all three perspectives can
be identified within official reports. The dominant
perspective in these reports has been the view of
community care as care within small residential units
provided by personal social services as opposed to
the traditional pattern of care in large scale
institutions provided by the NHS. Other perspectives appear but detailed analysis and specific
proposals tend to be based upon the dominant
perspective.

The present situation has undesirable consequences. There is considerable confusion about the
precise meaning of the concept of community care.
The policy means different things to different
people - policy-makers, service providers and the
relatives of mentally handicapped people are often
at cross purposes. The current slant of policy is
more preoccupied with the problems of institutions
than with the problems of the mentally handicapped
people themselves. For example the DHSS review of
community care emphasised the benefits to existing
agencies of community care for mentally handicapped
people:

> Services for mentally handicapped people may
> give the most straightforward illustration of
> the benefits to be gained from a shift in the
> balance of care between the NHS and the PSS:
> the NHS is relieved of the responsibility of
> providing residential care for the majority of
> them; the services are better suited to the
> predominantly social needs of mentally handi-
> capped people; and there may be an overall
> saving.[79]

In the rest of this book we shall examine what current policies of community care for the mentally handicapped mean for the 120 mothers with severely mentally handicapped children. We shall show that current policies offer some but not a lot of help to the mothers we talked to and in the conclusion we shall suggest ways in which, for mothers caring for mentally handicapped children, the policy can be given more substance and reality.

NOTES

1. E. Goffman, Asylums, New York, Doubleday, 1961.
2. Lady Marjory Allen of Hurtwood, Whose Children? Simpkin Marshall, 1945.
3. R. Barton, Institutional Neurosis, John Wright, Bristol, 1959.
4. P. Townsend, The Last Refuge, Routledge and Kegan Paul, 1962.
5. T. Morris and P. Morris, Pentonville: A Sociological Study of an English Prison, Routledge and Kegan Paul, 1963, especially Chapter 12.
6. P. Morris, Put Away: A Sociological Study of Institutions for the Mentally Retarded, Routledge and Kegan Paul, 1969.
7. R.D. King, N.V. Raynes and J. Tizard, Patterns of Residential Care: Sociological Studies in Institutions for Handicapped Children, Routledge and Kegan Paul, 1971.
8. The DHSS was aware of the widespread short-comings in mental handicap hospitals. See for example R. Crossman, The Diaries of a Cabinet Minister, III, 1968-1970, Hamish Hamilton and Jonathan Cape, 1977, p. 411.
9. Morris, Put Away, p. 315.
10. P. Townsend, 'Foreword: Social Planning for the Mentally Handicapped', in Morris, Put Away, p. xxviii.
11. King, Raynes and Tizard, Patterns of Residential Care.
12. J. Tizard, Community Services for the Mentally Handicapped, Oxford University Press, 1964.
13. ibid., pp. 133-34.
14. Royal Commission on the Law relating to Mental Illness and Mental Deficiency, 1954-1957, Report, Cmnd. 169, H.M.S.O., 1957, para. 618.
15. ibid., para. 616.
16. DHSS, Better Services for the Mentally Handicapped, Cmnd. 4683, H.M.S.O., 1971, para. 114.

17. ibid., paras. 51 and 68.
18. ibid., p. 42.
19. Report of the Committee of Enquiry into Mental Handicap Nursing and Care, Chairman Peggy Jay, Vol.I, Cmnd. 7468-I, H.M.S.O., 1979.
20. ibid., para. 135.
21. ibid., paras. 114 and 143.
22. ibid., para. 144.
23. ibid., para. 147.
24. DHSS, Report of a Study on Community Care, DHSS, 1981, para. 1.1.
25. ibid., para. 2.1.
26. ibid., para. 1.7.
27. H. Becker, Outsiders: Studies in the Sociology of Deviance, The Free Press, New York, revised ed. 1973, (first edition published 1963) p.9.
28. ibid., pp. 34-35.
29. L.A. Dexter, 'On the Politics and Sociology of Stupidity in our Society', in H.S. Becker (ed.) The Other Side: Perspectives on Deviance, The Free Press, New York, 1964, p. 40.
30. ibid., pp. 43-44.
31. J.R. Mercer, Labeling the Mentally Retarded: Clinical and Social System Perspectives on Mental Retardation, University of California Press, Berkeley, California, 1973, p. 2.
32. ibid., p. 28.
33. ibid., p. 120.
34. California Senate Bill 33, 1971, cited in Mercer, Labeling the Mentally Retarded, p. 123, see also Chapter 17, Sociocultural Pluralism.
35. Townsend, Foreword, p. xvi.
36. ibid., p. xxiii.
37. D. Thomas, H. Firth and A. Kendall, ENCOR - A Way Ahead, Campaign for Mentally Handicapped People, 1978.
38. W. Wolfensberger, The Principle of Normalization in Human Services, Leonard Crainford, Toronto, 1972, p. 24.
39. A. Kendall and P. Moss, Integration or Segregation? The Future of Educational and Residential Services for Mentally Handicapped Children, Campaign for the Mentally Handicapped, 1972, p. 7.
40. ibid., p. 7.
41. ibid., p. 8.
42. Campaign for the Mentally Handicapped, Integration or Segregation - The Choice in Practice, Campaign for the Mentally Handicapped, 1974, p. 42
43. Better Services for the Mentally Handicapped,

para. 40ii.
44. Special Educational Needs: Report of the Committee of Enquiry into the Education of Handicapped Children and Young People, Cmnd. 7212, H.M.S.O., 1978.
45. Report of the Committee of Enquiry into Mental Handicap Nursing and Care, para. 89a.
46. ibid., para. 93.
47. ibid., para 98.
48. ibid. Minority Report by Mr. D.O. Williams, pp. 157-60.
49. F. Tönnies, 'Gemeinschaft and Gesellschaft' in C. Bell and H. Newby (eds.), The Sociology of Community, Cass, 1974, pp. 8 and 10.
50. R.S. Lynd and H.M. Lynd, Middletown: A Study in Contemporary American Culture, Constable, 1929.
51. J. Madge quoted in Bell and Newby, The Sociology of Community, p. xliv.
52. W.F. Whyte, Street Corner Society: The Social Structure of an Italian Slum, University of Chicago Press, 2nd ed., 1955, pp. 256-7.
53. M.D. Young and P. Willmott, Family and Kinship in East London, Routledge and Kegan Paul, 1957, pp. 155-6.
54. ibid., p. 160.
55. ibid., p. 127.
56. ibid., p. 164.
57. D. Armstrong, Political Anatomy of the Body: Medical Knowledge in Britain in the Twentieth Century, Cambridge University Press, 1983, Chapter 4.
58. ibid., p. 37.
59. ibid., Chapter 10.
60. W.R. Curtis, The Future Use of Social Networks in Mental Health, Social Matrix Research Inc., Boston, Mass., 1979.
61. ibid., p. 26.
62. ibid., pp. 5-6.
63. ibid., p. 9.
64. ibid., p. 35.
65. M. Young and M. Rigg, Mutual Aid in a Selfish Society, Mutual Aid Press, no date, p. 8.
66. ibid., p. 26.
67. M. Bayley, Mental Handicap and Community Care: A Study of Mentally Handicapped People in Sheffield, Routledge and Kegan Paul, 1973, p. 1.
68. ibid., p. 13.
69. ibid., p. 310.
70. Report of The Committee on Local Authority and Allied Personal Social Services, Cmnd. 3703,

     H.M.S.O., 1968, para. 476.
71. ibid., para. 477.
72. ibid., paras. 477 and 483.
73. M. Bayley, <u>Community-orientated Systems of Care</u>, The Volunteer Centre, 1978.
74. <u>Report of the Committee of Enquiry into Mental Handicapped Nursing and Care</u>, para. 89c.
75. ibid., para. 93b.
76. ibid., para. 107.
77. ibid., paras. 317-319.
78. DHSS, <u>Mental Handicap: Progress, Problems and Priorities</u>, DHSS, 1980, para. 9.39.
79. DHSS, <u>Report of a Study on Community Care</u>, para. 7.5.

Chapter 3

THE NORTH HUMBERSIDE STUDY

INTRODUCTION

There has been a radical change in official
attitudes to mentally handicapped people and their
families. In the 1950s the basis and prime focus of
services for mentally handicapped people was the
mental handicap hospital and many parents were
advised, when their child was classified as 'severely
subnormal', to 'put their child away or have
another one'. In the 1970s the emphasis changed.
Mental handicap hospitals were relegated to a
service backwater. The prime place of care was now
the community and the family. Parents are now
advised to 'take their child and treat him or her as
normal'.
There are probably 70,000 adults and 50,000
children in England and Wales who are severely
mentally handicapped. The overwhelming majority of
the children live at home and are cared for by their
families. Despite a well established policy of
community care we know very little about the daily
lives of these families. Yet a constructive and
sensitive service based upon support within the community must be based on the problems and needs as
experienced by individuals and families. The only
way to obtain this type of information and to make
community care more than a useful piece of political
rhetoric is to talk to the families.
Researchers have talked to families but a lot
of the studies pre-date recent policy developments
or focus on one limited aspect of family life. For
example Tizard and Grad's classic study[1] was conducted nearly 25 years ago. On the other hand
Wilkin's interesting and useful study of families
with a handicapped child focussed on the reasons why
some families sought long-term residential care for

69

their children whereas others did not.[2]

In this chapter we shall discuss our survey of 120 mothers of mentally handicapped school children living in North Humberside. We shall discuss who we talked to, where they lived and the type of things we talked about.

TALKING TO MOTHERS

Community care is often seen as family care. In practice care by the family is usually care by the active woman in the household - the mother. Talking to mothers did not reflect a feeling on our part that mothers ought to play a dominant part in caring for children or dependent members of the household, rather it reflected the reality of the situation, mothers played a dominant role in caring and were helped and supported in varying degrees by other members of the household.

The position of women in society has changed since the end of the Second World War. The number of women in employment outside the home has risen rapidly[3] and there have been important changes in the social and legal status of women.[4] However, as Farmer points out, the new wage-earning role of women does not replace their traditional home-making role, it is an additional role which frequently conflicts with the traditional role.[5] The domestic division of labour has remained unchanged in spite of the wider changes in society. Therefore the extra burden that caring for a mentally handicapped child imposes on the family is likely to fall on the mothers and we felt it was essential to concentrate on the mothers' perception of the situation.

THE MOTHERS WE TALKED TO

It is not possible for a single researcher to talk to all the mothers of all the mentally handicapped children. We had to decide which mothers we wanted to talk to. We decided to talk to mothers whose experiences were fairly recent and limited to the new era of community care. But we were interested in mothers who had a clear experience of the services and whose child were clearly defined as mentally handicapped. Therefore we decided to talk to mothers with school age mentally handicapped children. Of the 120 mothers we talked to 13 had a mentally handicapped child under 5, 31 had a mentally handicapped child between 9 and 12, and 41 had a mentally handicapped child aged over 13. The youngest child was 3 and the oldest 17.

It was important to obtain a representative group of mothers so that information from our study would not have any particular bias. We decided to select mothers from a service utilised by the over-whelming majority of mentally handicapped school children, the special school. We sent letters to all the parents (206) of children in three special schools in North Humberside. Two of these schools served the city of Hull and the third served the rural areas of North Humberside. Overall 124 mothers indicated that they were willing to talk to us and 120 eventually did.

These 120 mothers came from a variety of back-grounds. Using the Registrar General's Classi-fication of Occupations and classifying our mothers according to their husband's occupations our sample broadly followed the overall pattern of socio-economic classes in the population. Compared to the national average the intermediate class, e.g. managers, schoolteachers and nurses, were over-represented, and the skilled manual, e.g. bus-driver, butcher, coal-face worker, carpenter, under-represented. Excluding 21 mothers who did not live with a husband, 45 families were classed as middle class (Classes I, II and III non-manual) and 54 as working class (III manual, IV and V). (See Table 3.1).

Table 3.1   Socio-economic classes of mothers interviewed[6]

Class (OPCS classification)	Number	%	Nationally (1971)
I (Professional)	4	4	5%
II (Intermediate)	30	30	18%
III (Skilled non-manual)	11	11	12%
III (Skilled manual)	27	27	38%
IV (Partly skilled)	23	23	18%
V (Unskilled)	4	4	9%

THE ISSUES WE TALKED ABOUT[7]

Having selected our 120 mothers with school age severely mentally handicapped children, the next step was deciding the type of issues we wanted to talk about. We were interested in the daily care of the child, especially the problems that the mother encountered and the sources of assistance. A starting point was the child, with his or her handicaps. We started by talking about the initial recognition of handicap, the effect this had on the mother and the sources of advice and help that were available. Then we discussed the current situation, especially the ability of the child to perform the activities of daily living, communicate and whether there were any specific problems. These topics allowed us to explore the mother's perception of her child's handicap and the care problems these created for her.

In the rest of the interview we explored the family response to this situation. The next topic of discussion was the internal structure of the household and the support the mother could obtain inside the household. We asked about other brothers and sisters and we asked about the help that mothers received with specific activities such as washing and dressing. We than talked about the informal support available outside the household, especially from relatives, neighbours and friends. This led us to a discussion on the assistance mothers received from formal services such as the hospital services and social services. Finally we talked about the support mothers received with specific caring activities.

Overall our topics provided us with a way of exploring with mothers the reality of their situation, including their past experiences, their current problems and the support they received from other members of the household, from relatives and friends and formal services. This type of information enabled us to identify the main areas of difficulty encountered and the main shortcomings in the support network.

CONCLUSION

In this chapter we have briefly discussed our study of 120 mothers in North Humberside who have severely mentally handicapped school children. We believe that mothers provide the main bulk of care and support for these children and they therefore formed the focus of our study. In the subsequent chapters of this book we shall discuss our findings following broadly the pattern of our talks with the mothers. In the next chapter we discuss the variety of problems faced by different families in terms of the different types of disability of the children in

our study. In Chapter 5 we discuss mothers' initial
encounters with the services, especially the ways in
which they become aware of the handicap and the
initial advice they were offered. In Chapter 6 we
look at the routine of daily care inside the household and examine the problems of care and divisions
of activities. In Chapter 7 we discuss the sources
of informal support available from outside the
family. In Chapter 8 we examine the support mothers
received from various agencies. In Chapter 9 we
illustrate some of the themes running through our
previous discussion by focussing on the problems
experienced by two mothers, the contrasting resources
available to these mothers and the contrasting
strategies these two mothers use to deal with their
problems.

NOTES

1. J. Tizard and J.C. Grad, The Mentally Handicapped and their Families: A Social Survey,
   Oxford University Press, 1961.
2. D. Wilkin, The Severely Mentally Handicapped
   Child in the Family: Support and Decisions
   relating to Long Term Care, Unpublished Ph.D.
   Thesis, University of Manchester, 1977. Subsequently published as D. Wilkin, Caring for the
   Mentally Handicapped Child, Croom Helm, 1979.
3. J.A.S. Robertson and J.M. Briggs, 'Part-time
   working in Great Britain', Department of
   Employment Gazette, 87, 7, 671-7, 1979.
4. For example Sex Discrimination Act, 1975, C. 65,
   Elizabeth 2, 1975.
5. M. Farmer, The Family, Longmans, 1979, 2nd ed.,
   p. 71.
6. We draw our national figures from Inequalities
   in Health, Report of a Research Working Group,
   DHSS, 1980. This report also has a useful
   discussion of the concept of class and its
   inadequacies.
7. In this chapter we have omitted most of the
   technical discussion about how we went about the
   research. For a full account see S. Ayer,
   Family Care for Severely Mentally Handicapped
   School Children, unpublished Ph.D. Thesis,
   University of Hull, 1982. Copies available on
   loan from University Library or from Dr.
   Alaszewski, I.H.S., Hull University.

Chapter 4

MEASURING DISABILITY

INTRODUCTION

     The problems mothers encounter in caring for
their handicapped children are likely to be related
to the nature and extent of their child's disability.
In government policy, official publications and the
procedures of agencies concerned with the services
for the mentally handicapped, all children suffering
from mental handicap tend to be treated as if they
are the same and have the same type of disability.
In reality the variation between children classified
as mentally handicapped is likely to be far greater
than the variation between other children of the
same age. This means that their needs are likely to
be extremely varied as are the problems their
mothers encounter in providing for these needs. An
essential preliminary to discussing the nature of
family life, is an assessment of the nature and
meaning of disability of the children whose mothers
we talked to.
     In the first section of this chapter, we discuss
the problems of assessing mental handicap and
associated disability and the methods we used to
assess the children in our study. In the second
section we discuss the nature and type of disabilities of the children in our study. In the
final section we concentrate on one specific area
of disability that creates special problems for
mentally handicapped children and their families,
incontinence.

MEASURING DISABILITY

     In every day conversation the word disabled
refers to an individual who is impaired when

74

compared to the majority of the population and is at
a disadvantage in performing the activities of
everyday life.[1] Disability can be seen as a kind of
deviance in which the disabled individual deviates
in some specific way from a population norm. As
with other forms of deviance measurement or assessment is difficult. It depends very much on social
context, especially the type of activities involved
and what is normal or expected of a competent individual in a particular situation. Thus in assessing
the disability of the children in our study we had
serious problems and in this section we shall
describe the nature of these problems and how we
dealt with them.

Handicap or disability?
     Attempts to describe or classify the mentally
handicapped have a long history and broadly two
approaches can be identified. The first approach
focuses on the individual's handicap. Researchers
and practitioners have tried to directly measure
the physical and/or mental incompetence of the
individual separated from the social context in
which the individual functions. The second approach
focuses on the individual's disability. Handicap is
assessed indirectly in terms of individual's
difficulties in performing specific activities.
Although most classifications of the mentally handicapped use a mixture of approaches we shall consider
the two approaches separately.
     The major approach to the direct assessment of
mental handicap has been the assessment of the
intelligence of individuals. This approach has led
to a vast technology of IQ (Intelligence Quotient)
testing. Although the IQ testing of the mentally
handicapped has been severely criticised[2] and is now
out of fashion, psychological tests in general and
IQ tests in particular remain one of the major ways
of describing mental handicap.
     Intelligence tests aim to measure intellectual
abilities in certain areas of intellectual function-
ing and by doing so predict an individual's ability
to perform essential functions involved in leading
an independent life in the future. Although they
aim to measure ability of individuals independently
of cultural background and context, they are, in
practice, heavily influenced by these cultural
factors. The tests are often designed by people
coming from white middle-class literate backgrounds
and are based on assumptions and skills most clearly

found in this particular social context.

The tests tend to exaggerate the incompetence of mentally handicapped children. Any individual test is calibrated in terms of the range of performance of a group of individuals of a specific age. Fast learners, who are ahead of their peers, tend to do well on IQ tests, whereas slow learners are behind their peers and do badly. However IQ tests are not interpreted in terms of speed of learning but in terms of absolute intellectual capacity. Many slow learners take longer to achieve full intellectual development but in many cases their intellectual skills, when fully developed, are not substantially different to those of faster learners. Mentally handicapped children are generally slow learners and therefore IQ tests can seriously underestimate their potential level of development.[3]

The use of IQ tests to assess mental handicap is one example of the clinical approach to mental handicap.[4] In contrast to clinical and other approaches that focus on the individual, there is the social system or societal reaction approach, discussed in Chapter 2. This approach focusses on the way in which disability is related to, indeed in some ways, created by the social environment in which the individual lives.

The societal reaction approach emphasises the social environment in which the individual's handicap manifests itself as a disability. The disability is not a static objective aspect of the individual but is actively defined by the individual and those around him. It is a form of deviance and as such fits in with Becker's general discussion of the way deviance is created and defined in society[5] which we discussed in Chapter 2.

In our assessment of disability we adopted a social systems perspective. We were not interested in an objective assessment of the child's mental handicap. Rather we were concerned with the problems which mothers had to deal with when caring for their mentally handicapped children. We were primarily interested in the disabilities of the children in the domestic context. In assessing the disabilities of the children in our study, we focused on their abilities to perform everyday living activities, especially in the house, of the sort that would be encountered by ordinary children as part of their everyday life. An inability to complete a specific item would indicate an area of dependency in which the child had to rely on his mother and others for assistance.

Developing a measure of disability
        In doing research it is usually best to draw
on the experience of previous researchers. We
started to develop our methods for assessing disability by looking at existing measures. Kushlick
and his colleagues in the Wessex Region have developed two scales for assessing mental handicap. Both
are rather crude and tend to mix handicap and
disability. The Social and Speech Incapacity (SPI)
scale assesses individuals according to behaviour,
mobility and ambulance. Whereas the other scale is
based on Speech, Self-help and Literacy.[6] Wing and
Gould have suggested that the results of these
assessments are extremely difficult to interpret.
In their study of adult mentally handicapped residents at St. Ebba's Hospital, Wing and Gould
completed the SPI and their own Handicap, Behaviour
and Skills (HBS) scale for 611 adults.[7] They point
out that the Wessex scale group individuals within
4 categories. Some of the items which make up the
scale such as 'behaviour disordered', are difficult
to define.
        However the difficulties with these scales
relate not to specific technical problems that can
be overcome by technical refinement but to their
purposes. They are general descriptions. They do
not describe the consequences of handicap for the
individual or for people providing daily care. Even
when social information is used the aims are a de-
contextualised description. We were interested in
the meaning of handicap within the specific context
of the home.
        We therefore decided to develop our own scale.
Our assessment was not based on the children's
clinical condition or on the level of intelligence
but on the context of disability and the limitations
that the disability placed on the child's ability
to perform everyday activities in their own homes.
Our assessments were intended to describe the
disability, especially the problems involved in the
day-to-day care of the children. We assessed the
children by talking to their mothers about their
abilities to perform specified everyday activities.
        All children are dependent on adults for some
or all the basic necessities of life. Relations
with these adults are essential for a child's
survival as a social being. The maintenance of
these relationships depends on certain basic
assumptions about the child. The growing child
after 'babyhood', is expected to:

1. maintain an effective independent existence in
    regard to the most immediate physical needs of
    his or her body, including feeding, washing,
    dressing and personal hygiene;
2. move around effectively in his or her environ-
    ment;
3. occupy his or her time in a fashion appropriate
    to his or her sex, age and culture, including
    carrying out physical activities such as play or
    recreation; and
4. participate in or interact with and maintain
    social relationships with members of his or her
    family and others.

To assess the meaning of disability we talked
to the mothers about their children's abilities in
these areas in relation to their particular home and
families. Table 4.1 indicates the area we covered
with the mothers. We focused heavily on the
children's ability to maintain an independent
existence and to perform the basic activities of
everyday life such as eating, controlling their
bowels and bladder, using the toilet, bathing and
dressing. However we also included questions on the
three other areas of development. The child's ability to move effectively around in his environment
was assessed by talking to mothers about how the
child moved around the house. Participation or
interaction with members of the family was assessed
in terms of communication skills such as speech and
comprehension. The child's ability to occupy
time in an appropriate fashion was assessed in
terms of the supervision required (see Table 4.1).
Although it is fairly easy to discuss with
mothers the specific disabilities their children
experience, it is difficult to compare different
children and their disabilities. We decided to
adopt a fairly straightforward approach and give
individual scores to different areas of activity. A
child, who could perform a particular activity or
had a particular skill, was given a score of zero
for this item. A child, who could perform an
activity with help, was given a score of one. A
child, who relied completely on his mother for the
performance of an activity, was given a score of
two. The scores from the different items were then
added together to form one single scale of disability. An overall incapacity score of zero indicated that the child had no disability in terms of
the items we asked about. Whereas an overall incapacity score of 18 indicated the child was totally

Measuring Disability

Table 4.1 Assessment of Disability

Activity (Type of skill or ability)	Examples of how individual children experienced problems with this skill	Assessment Category (and score given)	
DRESSING	able to dress without help	Little/no incapacity	0
	able to dress himself but unable to tie shoe laces	Moderate incapacity	1
	unable to dress	Severe incapacity	2
BATHING	able to bath and wash without help	Little/no incapacity	0
	takes unreasonable time to wash or unable to bath or wash	Severe incapacity	2
EATING	able to feed himself without help	Little/no incapacity	0
	causes undue disturbance by messy eating or takes unreasonable time to finish eating if left to himself or his food has to be specially prepared after it has left the kitchen	Severe incapacity	2
TOILETING	can toilet himself without help	Little/no incapacity	0
	needs help with clothes or has to be cleaned after he's been to toilet	Moderate incapacity	1
	unable to use toilet himself	Severe incapacity	2
INCON-TINENCE	fully continent day or night	Little/no incapacity	0
	occasional wetting or soiling by day or by night	Moderate incapacity	1
	soiling by night or by day, wetting during the day occurs frequently	Severe incapacity	2

WALKING	able to walk upstairs and elsewhere by himself	Little/no incapacity	0
	not able to walk upstairs by himself but with help able to walk upstairs and elsewhere	Moderate incapacity	1
	unable to walk by himself at all	Severe incapacity	2
COMMUNI-CATION	can speak in sentences	Little/no incapacity	0
	frequently uses single words: 'tea', 'stop', 'take'	Moderate incapacity	1
	has no speech at all	Severe incapacity	2
COMMUNI-CATION (compre-hension)	can hold intelligent conversation	Little/no incapacity	0
	understands only simple instructions: 'sit down', 'give me'	Moderate incapacity	1
	has no understanding at all	Severe incapacity	2
SUPER-VISION	can be left to play by himself unwatched, no danger to self/others	Little/no incapacity	0
	hits out/attacks others, damages furniture, rest-less, injury to himself, picking at sores, head banging, danger to self/others	Severe incapacity	2

disabled in terms of these items.

We worked out an incapacity score for each child and as Table 4.2 indicates there was a wide range of disability.[8] 27 children had very little disability. 19 children were almost totally dis-abled. The majority of children fell in the inter-mediate group and were either moderately (38) or severely disabled (36) children.

This method of assessing the children's disa-bilities was simple but crude. As the mothers' experience of caring for her mentally handicapped child at home was the focus of our study it was important to assess the child's ability in terms of what the child's mother said he or she could do in

80

the home.[9]

Table 4.2 Classification of the Children's
Disability

Degree of Disability	Score Band	No.	%
Little or no disability	0-3	27	22.5
Moderate disability	4-8	38	31.7
Severe disability	9-13	36	30.0
Very severe disability	14-18	19	15.8

Children as they get older develop and their ability to do things for themselves improve. It is important therefore to relate the child's disability to age. Looking at groups of items on the scale the developmental aspect can clearly be seen (Table 4.3). Older children had on average, lower scores and lower levels of disability as assessed by this disability scale.

Table 4.3 Relationship between Age and Incapacity
Score

Categories of Index (possible range of scores)	Children aged under 5 years	Children aged between 5 and 8 years	Children aged 8 years and over	All ages
Personal care/ ability (0-8)	6.84	5.05	4.08	4.52
Incontinence (0-2)	1.76	1.05	0.88	1.00
Mobility (0-2)	0.76	0.17	0.36	0.33
Communication (0-4)	2.23	1.35	1.57	1.61
Supervision (0-2)	1.23	0.58	0.57	0.65
Overall score (0-18)	12.84	8.23	7.50	8.18

Looked at from the point of view overall scores (Table 4.4) a similar result emerges. Very few (15%) of the children under 5 years old were classified as having either little or moderate disability. In contrast most (62%) of the children over 8 years old were classified on our scale as having little or no disability.

Table 4.4   Relationship between age and degree of disability

	Children aged under 5 years	Children aged between 5 and 8 years	Children aged 8 years and over	All ages
Little disability (0-3)	0	5	22	27
Moderate disability (4-8)	2	11	25	38
Severe disability (9-13)	6	11	19	36
Very severe disability	5	4	10	19
All	13	31	76	120

Summary. Our study is concerned with assessing the impact of a mentally handicapped child on family life and especially on mothers. Since the problems of caring are likely to be related to the extent of the child's disability and since the range of disabilities amongst mentally handicapped children is likely to be far greater than the range amongst other children, we felt it was important to assess the nature and extent of disability amongst our group of children. We felt it was neither desirable nor possible to have an objective assessment of the children's handicap, instead we developed our own measures of disability based on the mother's accounts of the skills and problems their children had in performing the activities of everyday life in the house. Using our assessment we were able to show there was considerable variation between the children. Some children were, according to our assessment, totally disabled. Whereas others had virtually no disability. As expected the level of disability varied with age. The very severely disabled children were concentrated in the lowest age group and the least disabled in the oldest.
        Any scale which reduces a child's disability to a single score is, by definition, crude, and may be misleading. To understand what these scores may mean we shall in the next section consider the cases

of eight children.

THE MEANING OF OUR DISABILITY SCORES: EIGHT CASES

    To show how our disability scores can be used
to assess the individual children, we shall discuss
eight individual cases. We have selected two cases
from each category and tried to take account of the
developmental aspect by considering a younger and an
older child.

Allen - A younger child with little disability (age 6 years)

Personal care ability	0
Incontinence	0
Mobility	0
Communication	0
Supervision	0
Dependency Score	0

    Allen AE is a 6 year old Down's Syndrome boy.
He is the AE's only child. At the time of the
interview Allen was 'going through a funny phase'.
He has been ill with chest infection. Mrs. AE said
that he had become very noise conscious and slept
badly because he was ill. He tended to pick his
nails and his two big toe nails were sore. As Mrs.
AE said: 'normally Allen is very sociable and loves
to play with other children. He is cheeky and a
chatty type. He can play with his toys for hours
and will be no bother. He has always gone to bed
perfectly well - you could just pop him in bed and
say "good night cherub"'. Mrs. AE was determined to
make Allen as self sufficient as possible 'so that
he's not going to be too much a burden on society in
the future'.
    Mrs. AE described Allen as 'a very capable boy'.
He could feed, wash, dress and toilet himself as
well as most children of his own age. He had been
dry since he was four years old. Mrs. AE did not
like the way children like Allen are treated:

> Medical people tend to group these children as
> a block and I don't think you can do that
> because they are all individuals with indi-
> vidual problems as any other child. I just
> wish they wouldn't group them in a block and
> say all Mongol children do this, that and the
> other because I haven't found that to be so.

Mrs. AE was worried about what might happen to Allen when she was too old to care for him at home. 'Allen is such a capable child and I can't for the life of me see him in an institution as such. My ideal for him would be where he could have his own room under general supervision and be as individual as possible because he can do things for himself'.

Hilda - An older child with little disability (age 14 years)

Personal care ability	0
Incontinence	0
Mobility	0
Communication	0
Supervision	0
Dependency Score	0

Hilda was a plump 14 year old with a prim ladylike manner and shy smile. Mrs. AO said she was determined to bring Hilda up 'like an ordinary kid'. Hilda took special lessons 'to improve her speech and manner and learn to read and count'. At the interview Hilda was eager to demonstrate her reading skills to the interviewer. She could read simple words correctly and fluently, albeit slowly.

Mrs. AO was proud of Hilda's accomplishments. Hilda had washed, dressed and fed herself and was toilet trained from the age of 4. In recent weeks she had learned to make minor purchases: 'she can bring back correct change for 50p'. Mrs. AO summed Hilda up in this manner: 'I've trained her, it hasn't been easy but she is now very independent, very sensible in a lot of ways ... it's such a shame really that she's Mongol'.

Elizabeth - A younger child with moderate disability (age 8 years)

Personal care ability	4
Incontinence	2
Mobility	1
Communication	1
Supervision	0
Dependency Score	8

Elizabeth was the youngest of Mrs. AL's three children. She was a pretty blond girl of 8 and looked rather small for her age. Her mother described her as 'very mentally backward' and said Elizabeth would never be able to look after herself. Elizabeth was not toilet trained. She wet and soiled herself every night. Mrs. AL said Elizabeth couldn't be taken anywhere because of her incontinence. 'It's awfully embarrassing if you've to carry soiled drawers with awful smell'.

Elizabeth was clumsy and unsteady on her feet. She had to be bathed and dressed but could feed herself. She understood what was said to her but could only use single words. Her mother described her personality as very pleasing and loving. 'If you tell her off she'll come to you and say "sorry", "sorry". She liked watching television and is fond of music'.

Alice - An older child with moderate disability (age 15 years)

Personal care ability	4
Incontinence	0
Mobility	1
Supervision	2
Dependency Score	7

Alice was 15 and the youngest of seven children. At the time of the interview Mrs. HA had been a widow for 5 years and lived with her children in an overcrowded council house. Alice had suffered from cerebral palsy since birth. Alice was hemiplegic (paralysis affecting one side of her body) and could walk only with support. She had to be bathed, dressed and toileted, but she fed herself and was dry at night. She had frequent epileptic fits. Television, anything zigzag, striped or spotted could trigger a fit. She needed constant attention. Mrs. HA said: 'I always have to be around to make sure she isn't in danger because even though all the family know that she can have a fit at any time, they take it for granted that I'm here. And I'm always here. I don't go out except when she's at school'.

Alice's mother described her as a girl with a split personality, very good at school but violent tempers at home - smashing window panes when she didn't get her way, but she could be a friendly child when her mood was right.

Patricia - A younger child with severe disability (age 4 years)

Personal care ability	7
Incontinence	2
Mobility	1

```
Communication          2
Supervision            0
Dependency Score      12
```

Patricia AN was the youngest of three children.
She looked somewhat younger than her 4 years. She
suffered from epilepsy but had not had a fit for
nearly six months. Patricia had to be washed,
dressed and fed. 'It's impossible to eat as a
family. She's a little horror at meal times', is
the way Mrs. AN describes Patricia's food-throwing,
tablecloth pulling and head-banging tantrums.
Patricia's toileting habits were said to be
improving - she didn't like to be wet and 'pulls a
funny face' when she wanted the pot and hid her face
when she wet herself. Mrs. AN still had serious
problems with toileting. 'You can't take her out,
she'll wet herself and then create a scene'.
Patricia's moods were an important factor in assessing her ability to communicate. She had no understandable speech but she would obey simple commands.
When she was in a bad mood 'she doesn't take a blind
bit of notice'. Patricia would listen to music and
watch television especially advertisements.

Toni - An older child with severe disability (age
       13 years)

```
Personal care ability   7
Incontinence            2
Mobility                0
Communication           2
Supervision             2
Dependency Score       13
```

Toni was described by his mother as very
'badly retarded'. He was a tall, big and strong
adolescent. Mrs. MA said he was not able to do
much for himself. He had never been successfully
toilet-trained 'after years of effort'. He wet and
soiled himself both day and night. At the interview
Toni was sitting on a heavy blanket on a settee
'just in case'. Mrs. MA described the situation
this way: 'You can't take him anywhere, he'll be
dirty in no time and it's embarrassing. I can't go
out because I can't let anybody babysit. I don't
think it is right to ask anybody to clean him. The
house always smells no matter what you spray'.
Toni was washed several times a day. Dressing
was a problem. He tended to put clothes on back to
front and to put his arms in his leg holes. He

could take his clothes off, but his parents had to
be quick or he could rip the buttons off as well.
He had no understandable speech, except odd words
but he understood a lot and cooperated most of the
time. Television was his whole life and he had to
be watched or else he tore the set apart. Toni was
very loving and affectionate to those he liked.
Mrs. MA said: 'Toni is like a dog in that he knows
who likes him and who dislikes him'.

Angela - A younger child with very severe disability
            (aged 5 years)

Personal care ability	8
Incontinence	2
Mobility	2
Communication	4
Supervision	2
Dependency Score	18

Angela was the second of the QA's three children. Now 5 years old she was the surviving twin
(the other being still-born after a premature
birth). She had severe cerebral palsy with athetoid
(random muscular) movements. Mrs. QA described her
as 'mentally handicapped with poor vision and very
little hearing'. Angela had frequent epileptic fits.
She had a padded helmet to prevent her hurting her
head. With the help of physiotherapists she was
acquiring better head control and longer periods of
sitting up.
Angela was very awkward to bath and dress: 'We
use a special bath, it is fitted over the big one.
My husband baths her and I bring her down to dry
her'. Feeding was another problem. 'It takes over
two hours to feed her. She can be very tempera-
mental and difficult stiffening and spitting out
food and drink'. With no control over her bladder
and bowels, she was constantly wet and dirty.
She understood very little, though she showed
social awareness. For example, she greeted the
interviewer with shouts of 'hello! hello!' (the only
word she can speak). She had no understanding of
the danger involved in touching a hot stove, playing
with sharp knives or dipping her hand into hot tea.

Neil - An older child with very severe disability
          (aged 8)

Personal care ability	8
Incontinence	2

Mobility	2
Communication	4
Supervision	2
Dependency Score	18

Neil was the younger of the PA's two children. Following a precipitated delivery before the arrival of the midwife he was concussed at birth resulting in quadriplegia, paralysis affecting his whole body. His limbs were normally contracted, but he sometimes made uncontrolled movements of his legs and arms (athetoid movements) particularly when he was excited. Neil had good eyesight and hearing. He smiled loudly and displayed many facial expressions. He made sounds as if he was attempting to speak.

Mrs. PA said bathing, washing and dressing were a problem. 'You've got to watch there aren't any buttons at the top, he bites them, it's just like having a baby, he has no understanding. Feeding was another problem: 'everything is mashed, of course. He makes himself sick by sticking his fingers down his throat. It is difficult to feed and make him retain his feed'. He was doubly-incontinent and had to be changed every two hours. 'It's the nappies, there is always nappies, week after week, you have to keep washing them all the time'. Neil was growing bigger and bigger and Mrs. PA said: 'The constant lifting of heavy, awkward, totally dependent doubly incontinent child who can do virtually nothing for himself is becoming an impossible burden'.

Neil enjoyed simple stories about domestic events read from books, and the radio and television programmes. Stories from 'Listen with Mother' on records give him great pleasure provided Mrs. PA was nearby to keep his attention focused. Neil was described as an immensely warm and affectionate child.

Summary
The contrast between these eight children in terms of what their mothers perceive to be their child's degree of dependence on them illustrates that terms used by agencies such as mentally handicapped refer to children of widely ranging abilities. Rather than being a homogenous group their disabilities range from some children who are virtually helpless, wheelchair-bound and bedfast to children whose abilities for self management and care overlap those of non-handicapped children. Many severely

mentally handicapped children differ from non-
handicapped children not because they are dependent
but in the degree to which they are dependent. It
also illustrates the difficulties involved in referring to families with such children as an homogenous
group. Each family is unique in terms of the
problems it faces and the ways in which it copes
with them. As has been suggested earlier, it is out
of these perceived problems that these mothers
develop their own definition of mental handicap.

The purpose of our assessment is to develop a
way of describing different children and the problems of caring for them. To illustrate the meaning
and utility of the information we collected on disability, we shall in the last section of this
chapter focus on one area of self-help that can
cause special problems for mentally handicapped
children and their families - incontinence.

INCONTINENCE: A FORM OF DISABILITY

One of the commonest daily care and management
problems which mothers mentioned was incontinence.
67 mothers (55.8%)[10] said their child was constantly
wet or dirty. Incontinence created many intractable
problems. Its consequences were pervasive and
affected most areas of the children's life and care.
Most children, who were incontinent, could not bath
or dress themselves. Incontinence meant they had to
be changed and bathed more frequently. Incontinence
not only increased the physical burdens of care, but
it also had social and financial consequences for
the families of handicapped children. Severe incontinence has been identified as one of the factors
in the decision made by parents to seek long-term
care for their children.[11]

Yet it is remarkable how little attention has
been given to a problem which presents such a
burden to families. Some of the studies of families
with handicapped children mention incontinence.
Bayley studying[12] severely mentally handicapped
people in Sheffield found that 47% of the severely
handicapped children living at home were incontinent and Wilkin[13] reported that 42% of the severely
mentally handicapped children he studied were
frequently incontinent during the day. Bradshaw[14]
found that 73.6% of mentally and physically handicapped children (over 4 years of age) whose parents
received assistance from the Family Fund were incontinent. The problems of incontinence among adults

at home have been the subject of a study by the
Disabled Living Foundation.[15]

In some ways the mothers in our study were well
prepared to deal with the problems associated with
incontinence. The overwhelming majority had the
basic equipment, such as bathrooms, washing machines,
to deal with these problems (see Table 4.5).

Table 4.5   Lack of Basic Facilities

	Families without this facility	% of total sample
Bathroom	2	2
Hot water	3	2.5
Inside WC	7	6
Washing Machine	5	4
Spin Dryer	9	7.5

There is no doubt that availability of these
facilities has gone some way to reduce the physical
burden of coping with the severely mentally handicapped and incontinent child. This is borne out by
the mothers' experience. Mothers were asked what
difficulties their child's incontinence created. No
mother mentioned lack of any of these facilities as
contributing to the problems of coping with the
child's incontinence.

However, mothers mentioned a range of physical,
social and financial problems which their child's
incontinence created. These included the problems
of lifting and carrying the child (48%), damage to
furniture (58%), the difficulty of drying clothes
(63%), the extra washing (64%), the extra expenses
especially of clothes (66%), the smell in the house
(69%) and restrictions on work and social life (78%).

Lifting and Carrying. Thirty-two (47.8%) mothers
who had an incontinent child mentioned lifting and
carrying as a major problem. The problem was
related to overall levels of disability. 50% of
mothers whose child we classified as very severely
disabled mentioned it, compared to 37.5% of mothers
of the severely disabled children and 12.5% of
children with moderate or little disability. The
burden of lifting and carrying was related to
housing conditions. A heavy non-ambulant child in
a house with no easily accessible lavatory (e.g.
the lavatory and bathroom is upstairs and there is
no stair-lift) created a greater problem as the

child had to be carried to toilet and/or bathroom
when necessary.

Extra Domestic Chores. The care of most disabled
children creates extra laundry. This extra laundry
may be created by constant dribbling and crawling,
but a major cause is incontinence. Forty-three
(64.2%) mothers with an incontinent child mentioned
incontinence as the main cause of their extra
laundry. Again more mothers (62.8%) of children
with severely disabled children reported that their
children's incontinence created extra laundry
compared with 37.2% of mothers of children with
little or moderate disability.

The extra laundry was caused by numerous
changes of clothes, the frequent washing of sheets,
bedding, nappies and pants. It was an expensive,
time-consuming and exhausting chore especially if
the family had inadequate washing and drying
facilities. With the need for constant change of
clothes it was not surprising that most mothers
(68.2%) of severely disabled children found the
expenses arising out of buying clothing difficult
to bear.

It was difficult to assess in our study the
extent to which the burdens of incontinence could be
relieved if these mothers were provided with extra
laundry facilities. However, many mothers said the
expenses of the equipment and the physical burdens
of washing could be reduced by additional improvements to housing conditions. Five families had made
alterations to their houses to make it easier to
look after their child. Two families had built an
extra bathroom and three had built an extra toilet.

Restrictions on Social Life. Most mothers mentioned
the social restrictions associated with their
child's incontinence. Fifty-two mothers (77.6%)
with an incontinent child said their child's incontinence restricted their work and their social life.
Apart from the practical difficulties which
increased as the child grew older, bigger and
heavier, many mothers said that incontinence became
less and less socially acceptable as their child
grew older.

One mother related her experience with her 16
year old incontinent son in this way:

It was terrible. You could never take him out.
When you were in town you could suddenly find
that he was dirty and then you had to rush
home. I knew every toilet in Hull and
Scarborough, you know. I always took a spare
change of clothes. I used to take him down
the toilet and clean him up and change him with
all the dirty clothes out in the street. Oh,
it was awful you just couldn't travel with him.
Now I simply don't bother to take him out. I
simply don't go out.

The child's incontinence was also a factor in
preventing many mothers taking up paid employment
outside the home. As many as 68 mothers (56.7%)
said their child restricted them from working.
There was a strong desire among many survey mothers
to work outside the home.[16]
    Researchers have found that mothers with incon-
tinent children are likely to suffer from stress.[17]
The stress of coping with Matthew, a 9 year old
severely incontinent boy, became too much for Mrs.
M so she went to see her doctor. She said:

The doctor told me to find a job because he
said it would help me with my nerves. But, of
course, it is impossible to find one because
of Matthew. It's a vicious circle.

For most mothers coping with their incontinent
child was a daily problem. Mothers of younger
children tended not to identify their child's incontinence as a major problem. However some mothers of
younger children expressed anxiety about whether
they could cope in future when the child grew
bigger, stronger and heavier while they became older
and weaker. The height and the weight of many
children inevitably made activities such as bathing,
dressing and changing nappies a great deal more
arduous after the age of five. For study mothers of
older, heavier and incontinent children, life inside
and outside of the home revolved around the problems
of changing nappies, washing, getting rid of offen-
sive smells and finding toilets. The degree of
overall disability was important. More mothers
(73.1%) of children with severe disability found
their life restricted than mothers with children
with little or moderate disability (26.9%).
    Support or advice were available but mothers
frequently did not know about it. Many mothers with
an incontinent child lacked knowledge about basic

items for coping with severe incontinence. Almost 88% of study mothers did not know about the home help service. 70% did not know that they could obtain help with home adaptations. Another 70% of study mothers also said that they did not know that they could obtain help for the purchase of aids and appliances - for example, in replacing furniture or floor coverings - and nearly 40% did not know they could obtain disposable nappies.

There was no evidence to suggest that mothers of children with severe disability or of younger children whose need for assistance was greater had any greater knowledge about the availability of assistance. Similarly, there was no evidence to suggest that middle class families had greater awareness of the available help than working class families. This suggests that the lack of awareness of these basic items which can help mothers of incontinent children cope with their child's incontinence is a widespread problem and is not confined to any particular category of parents of severely mentally handicapped school children.

Mothers obtain information in a haphazard fashion - one mother described the process in the following way:

> My sheets, blankets and mattresses were ruined, we had to renew them all every so often. I rang up in desperation to the school and the secretary said I should have them from my district nurse.

This mother was eventually put in touch with the health visiting service and she was able to obtain a regular supply of disposable nappies from the local health centre. She commented: 'They saved not only money but the time I spent for washing. I used to wash every day of the week'.

As this mother's experience shows, the lack of a family adviser meant that many mothers had to depend on a multiplicity of sources for basic information about the services they could call on. It was often so difficult to obtain items that many mothers did not bother. One mother preferred to spend over £4 a week on disposable nappies than obtain them free from the health authority.

Summary. Incontinence was a major problem for many of the mothers in the present study. The physical burden of caring for the severely incontinent and

mentally handicapped child increased as the child
grew bigger and the mother grew older. The older
and more disabled the child, the more difficult
were the problems. The constant care involved and
the social disapproval of incontinence - particularly in an older child - meant that many study
mothers could not rely on substitute care. Many had
difficulty in obtaining suitable babysitters. Many
of the study mothers were thus restricted in their
ability to go out to work and in their social life.
A recent study in the County of Avon reported
similar findings.[18]
      In spite of the general improvements in housing
conditions and the availability of items such as
washing machines and spin dryers the care of these
children still involved many extra expenses for
many families. In the majority of cases the study
families bore extra expenses because they did not
have adequate knowledge of the full range of supporting services which were available. As we shall
show in later chapters of this book a lack of awareness of available benefits and help in general was
a common finding throughout the survey and has been
widely reported by other researchers.

CONCLUSION

      In this chapter we have been concerned with the
study children's disabilities. Society's attitudes
to the severely mentally handicapped are complex
and contradictory. In theory, society now accepts
the mentally handicapped as fellow human beings with
the same rights as the able-bodied. In practice,
society tends to segregate them not only in institutions, but also by accepting a stereotype of
mentally handicapped persons which tends to set
them apart from the able-bodied. We have concentrated on identifying the children's general
disability and examining one particular disability -
incontinence.

Measuring Disability. We used the children's
abilities - as judged by their mothers - to perform
basic tasks necessary for daily living as a robust
assessment of their disabilities. The operational
definition we used demonstrates the variability of
conditions included in the category 'severe mental
handicap'. At one end of the scale were 19 children
who were very severely disabled. These children

were unable to feed, toilet, wash or dress themselves. Most of them were severely incontinent.
Many needed constant supervision both day and night.
Few were able to walk and hardly any of them was
able to communicate beyond the use of single and
odd words. At the other end of the scale were 27
children with little or no disability. 9 of these
had acquired complete independence in basic living
activities.

Measurement of mental handicap had traditionally been associated with large scale institutional
care. The researchers either wanted to assess the
individuals already 'warehoused' in the institutions
or they wanted to ensure a better classification and
allocation of individuals in the institution. The
current policy towards care within ordinary domestic
situations must include a realistic attempt to
examine the consequences for the daily life of the
family. An important step towards this should be a
search for a wider criteria of disability to include
the perceptions of parents upon whom the main responsibility for care fall. The index developed for
this study represents part of that search. It was
developed as a means of examining and analysing the
consequences which mental handicap had for the
families studied.

When examining the present method its limitations should be borne in mind. The sample was not
randomly selected. The results may not be entirely
representative of all severely mentally handicapped
school children and their families. However, the
present attempt provides a means of assessing the
different problems encountered by people grouped as
severely mentally handicapped. Its advantage over
the other methods of defining mental handicap is
that it lays stress on the various goals of everyday living rather than talk about mental handicap
as if it is some absolute condition with a fixed
meaning irrespective of social context.

The Problem of Incontinence. Coping with incontinence poses one of the most difficult care and
management problems for the majority of the mothers
in the present study. Apart from the physical
drudgery of managing an incontinent child, e.g.
lifting and carrying a heavy non-ambulant 15 year
old severely incontinent child, incontinence also
limits the mothers' social life and causes extra
financial expenses. Most study mothers had no
knowledge of what assistance was available from the

services.

NOTES

1. See for example M. Blaxter, The Meaning of
    Disability; A Sociological Study of Impairment,
    Heinemann, 1976 especially Introduction.
2. Insightful account of the uses, limitations and
    inconsistencies of IQ scores with regard to the
    mentally handicapped can be found in A.
    Kushlick and R. Blunden, 'The epidemiology of
    mental subnormality', and A.D.B. Clarke and
    A.M. Clarke, 'The changing concept of
    intelligence: a selective historical view',
    both in A.M. Clarke and A.D.B. Clarke (eds.)
    Mental Deficiency: The Changing Outlook,
    Methuen, 1974 (3rd edn.); J.R. Mercer,
    'I.Q.: the lethal label', Psychology Today,
    6, 4, 44-47 and 95-97, 1972; J. Ryan, I.Q. -
    The illusion of objectivity', in K. Richardson,
    D. Spears and M. Richards (eds.), Race,
    Culture and Intelligence, Penguin, 1972; and
    P.G. Sqibb, 'The concept of intelligence - A
    sociological perspective', Sociological Review,
    N.S., 21, 57-75, 1973.
3. J. Ryan with F. Thomas, The Politics of Mental
    Handicap, Penguin, 1980. For a more detailed
    discussion of I.Q. as primarily a rate measure,
    see also Ryan, 'I.Q. - The illusion of
    objectivity', and H. Rose and S. Rose, 'The IQ
    Myth', Race and Class, 20, 63-74, 1978.
4. J.R. Mercer, Labeling the Mentally Retarded,
    University of California Press, Berkley,
    California, 1973, p. 2. See, also, J.R.
    Mercer, 'Social system perspective and clinical
    perspective: frames of reference for under-
    standing career patterns of persons labelled as
    mentally retarded', Social Problems, 13, 18-34,
    1965.
5. H.S. Becker, Outsiders: Studies in the
    Sociology of Deviance, The Free Press, New
    York (revised ed.), 1973.
6. A. Kushlick, R. Blunden and G. Cox, 'A Method
    of rating behaviour characteristics for use in
    large scale surveys of mental handicap',
    Psychological Medicine, 3, 466-478, 1973.
7. This was a detailed interview schedule which
    included the kinds of behaviours regarded as
    particularly important for determining special
    service needs. See L.G. Wing and J. Gould,
    'Systematic recording of behaviours and skills

of Retarded and Psychotic Children', Journal of Autism and Childhood Schizophrenia, 8, 79-97, 1978.

8. We developed our classification technically. The mean score of the sample was 8.18 and there was a standard deviation of 5.05. Children with an incapacity score of more than one standard deviation below the mean (0-3) were classified as having little or no disability. Children with an incapacity score of more than one standard deviation above the mean (14-18) were classified as very severely disabled. Children with scores within one standard deviation were classified as moderately disabled if their score was below the mean (4-8) and severely disabled if it was above the mean (9-13).

9. For 51 children we cross-checked the mothers' reply with the child's school teacher assessment. There was a high degree of agreement between the two sets of answers.

10. 12 of these 67 children were under 5. Age is an important factor in the acquisition of this skill. Many children are not reliably toilet-trained till they are 5. The National Child Development Study reported that 12% of the boys in their sample were still incontinent at the age of 5. M.L. Kellmer Pringle, N.R. Butler and R. Davie, 11,000 Seven-year Olds, Longmans, 1966, p. 195.
J. Newson and E. Newson, Four Years Old in an Urban Community, Allen and Unwin, 1968, reported that only just over one half of normal 4-year olds were reliably toilet-trained.

11. No mother in the present study said she contemplated long term care for her child. D. Wilkin, Caring for the Mentally Handicapped Child, Croom Helm, 1979, p. 86, reported that incontinence in an older child was frequently a major factor in the family's decision to seek long term care. See also M. Bayley, Mental Handicap and Community Care: A Study of Mentally Handicapped People in Sheffield, Routledge and Kegan Paul, 1973, p. 143.

12. Bayley, Mental Handicap and Community Care, p. 119.

13. Wilkin's figure of 42% was based on a sample of 42 children, four of whom were below 5 years of age. Wilkin, Caring for the Mentally Handicapped Child, p. 84.

14. J. Bradshaw, <u>Incontinence: A Burden for</u>
    <u>Families with Handicapped Children</u>, Disabled
    Living Foundation, 1978, p. 6.
15. P. Dobson, <u>Management of Incontinence in the</u>
    <u>Home: A Survey</u>, Disabled Living Foundation,
    1974. The 77 adults in the survey included
    people who, though incontinent, were mentally
    alert and independent.
16. The desire to work among many study mothers is
    consistent with recent general increase in
    women's labour force participation. The in-
    creased availability of part-time work and
    temporary work in the 1970s was associated with
    a rise in the number of mothers working part-
    time from 26% in 1971 to 35% in 1978. Office
    of Population Censuses and Surveys, <u>General</u>
    <u>Household Survey</u> 1978, HMSO, 1980. The same
    study also showed that in 1978 52% of women
    aged 16 and 59 with dependent children were
    working, ibid., p. 95.
17. For example Tew and Lawrence identified incon-
    tinence as a major cause of stress amongst
    mothers with spina bifida children. B. Tew and
    K. Lawrence, 'Some sources of stress found in
    mothers of spina bifida children', <u>British</u>
    <u>Journal of Preventative and Social Medicine</u>, 29,
    27-30, 1975.
18. N. Butler et al. <u>Handicapped Children: Their</u>
    <u>homes and life styles, A Study in Avon</u>, Depart-
    ment of Child Health, University of Bristol,
    1978, pp. 49-54. For a report with similar
    conclusions about non-handicapped children and
    their mothers see Equal Opportunities
    Commission, <u>I want to work ... but what about</u>
    <u>the kids</u>? The Equal Opportunities Commission,
    Manchester, 1978.

Chapter 5

THE DISCOVERY OF MENTAL HANDICAP

INTRODUCTION

The word discovery suggests a sudden recognition. This happens in relatively few cases of
mental handicap and sudden recognition is usually
associated with clearly defined signs that point to
a defined and specific handicapping condition, i.e.
the abnormal chromosome count associated with
Down's Syndrome. The awareness of possible handicap
usually develops gradually as the child fails to
achieve expected milestones of development or manifests behaviour that is difficult to understand or
interpret. It is common for the child's parents to
notice these abnormalities first but it is often the
professionals who interpret their meaning in terms
of the child's future.
We do not believe that discovery is a
simple process of recognising 'a handicap'. Rather
we see it as a process of interpreting and understanding: interpreting what certain signs mean
and understanding what these signs mean for the
future of the child and his family. Since neither
interpretation nor understanding are easy, straightforward processes, discovery can best be seen as a
negotiation between parents who have a 'problem
child'and official agencies, who are recognised as
having special knowledge about this type of problem.
The negotiation is complete and the handicap is
'discovered' when the parents and agency agree on a
'label' for the child and some, at least, of the
implications of this label for the child. Although
in this book we are concentrating on the mother's
point of view, since discovery is a process of
negotiation it is important to consider how professionals understand and view mental handicap and
its implications for the family. In the first part

99

of this chapter we shall discuss two contrasted
views of the impact of a mentally handicapped child
on the family. In the second part we shall examine
the ways the mothers in our study 'discovered' their
children were mentally handicapped. In the concluding part we shall discuss the implications of
our study for the ways in which negotiations between
families and professionals should be handled.

TWO CONTRASTING VIEWS

Two contrasting views of the impact of mental
handicap on the family can be discerned. One we
shall refer to as the pathological model. This view
stresses the negative effects and the 'abnormality'
of the family. The second we refer to as the normal
family model. Writers using this perspective stress
the similarities between families with mentally
handicapped children and other families. The problems of families with mentally handicapped children
differ in degree rather than kind from the problems
experienced by other families.

The Pathological Model. Some writers believe that
mental handicap not only affects the child but also
damages, in some irreparable fashion, the family.
Kew in a study of the brothers and sisters of handicapped children lables the families as 'handicapped
families'.[1] Similarly Dupont, who wrote about
severely mentally handicapped children living at
home, stated that 'the development of a family life
of a near normal character, not only for the parents
but also for the other siblings, is beyond the
possibilities for most of these parents'.[2]
Writers who use this perspective devoted very
little attention to the processes by which a child's
handicap is 'discovered'. The discovery of handicap
is treated as an unproblematic and straightforward
process. If there are difficulties then they are
explained by problems the parents experience,
especially their inability to cope with reality and
their need to deceive themselves about the 'self-
evident' handicap and implications of this handicap.
Differences of interpretation between parents and
professionals are seen as a product of parents'
misunderstandings. A good example of this approach
can be found in the following extract in which
Pinkerton identifies an array of pathological processes associated with parents' inability to accept

the 'reality' of handicap:

> The most obvious of these (mechanisms of non-acceptance) is overt <u>denial</u>, or rejection by parents of the diagnosis submitted. This in turn may lead to 'doctor shopping'... that is, trundling the unfortunate child from one specialist to another in the hope of securing more palatable, or less unequivocal pronouncements, and thereby fostering false aspirations ... the diagnosis of significant handicap may leave the parent with a sense of <u>impotence</u> ... This affective state, in turn, may breed a secondary set of pathological reactions. Commonest among these perhaps is <u>over-protection</u> or emotional <u>smothering</u> of the child ... Next, there is a widespread sense of <u>stigma</u> so often experienced by parents in the face of superstitious prejudice about contamination or genetic tainting ... The term <u>ambivalence</u> might best be used to convey the sense of such negatively charged parental attitudes which militate against acceptance.[3]

<u>The Normal Family Model</u>. In contrast writers who adopt a normal family model stress the normality of the family with a handicapped child and the importance of accepting parents' statements of their situation at face value. When parents say 'We are just like any other family', this is not interpreted as an attempt to deny or conceal reality but a description of the parents' view of their situation. Families with a handicapped child are subject to strains and stresses, but so are families that do not have a handicapped child. Hewett has emphasised the 'normality' of many of the problems experienced by families with a handicapped child and has concluded that such families meet the 'day-to-day problems that handicap creates with patterns of behaviour that, in many respects, deviate little from the norms derived from studying the families of normal children. They have more similarities with ordinary families than differences from them'.[4]
    The process of defining the situation in which a family with a handicapped child finds itself extends also to the child himself. Jaehnig found that the parents he interviewed emphasised the child's normality and resemblance to non-handicapped children. He emphasised that most of the parents described their child as a 'child with a handicap'

101

rather than a 'handicapped child'.[5] The distinction
is important because the former term places the
emphasis on the child not on the handicap.

The effects of handicap on family life have
been the subject of considerable discussion over the
last 25 years. Writers have dealt with the matter
in different ways depending on their underlying
view-point. The pathological view-point has pre-
dominated and many workers have stressed the psychological damage inflicted by the handicapped person
on the rest of the family.[6] Speaking of parents of
mentally handicapped children Roith said that the
literature gave 'a completely biased and prejudiced
impression of these parents'.[7] As a consultant
psychiatrist in mental handicap he 'sat back and
waited for the horde of guilty and aggressive
parents to descend upon him' but after eight years
he was still waiting for them.

Sheridan suggested that it might be 'more
generous if, in future, we omitted the term "guilt
complex" not only from our discussions but from our
thoughts. If parents feel guilty, it may be that we
ourselves have been the cause, because we have
implied that they have every reason to be guilty'.[8]

If the psychological disruption created by the
handicapped child is as great as it is often
suggested, then the mothers of mentally handicapped
children should manifest higher levels of mental
problems than mothers of other children. Wing found
that, although 40% of mothers of severely mentally
handicapped children reported mental problems and
17% had received treatment for these problems in the
previous year, the figures were very similar to
those found for women in the general population.[9]
Most of the mothers interviewed by Wing attributed
their symptoms to the presence of the handicapped
child. Such a finding is hardly surprising, since
the handicapped child is clearly a source of considerable strain on many mothers, as we shall show
later in this book. Recognising this is, however,
completely different from assuming that all mothers
of handicapped children will automatically and
inevitably experience psychological damage.

Attitudes of Professionals to the Mothers of the
Mentally Handicapped. There is a consensus in the
professional literature that the effects of a
handicapped child are necessarily 'noxious'.[10]
Meyerowitz and Kaplan summarise this assumption in
the following way: 'The family is slowed up in its

affectional and emotion-satisfying performances'.[11]

Research based on the pathological view tends to be a self-fulfilling prophecy. Researchers who look for pathology, tend to find it. McMichael[12] studied families with physically handicapped children, and devoted a lot of attention to scoring the amount of 'rejection', 'over-anxiety' and 'over-protection' of their child shown in parents' responses. Yet, she provided no satisfactory definition of these terms. For example, rejection was assessed in terms of parents' contact with school teachers and their interest in the child's school work. Low levels of contact and a lack of interest were classed as 'rejection'. It would be difficult to devise a more culturally biased means of assessing rejection. If these behaviours signify rejection, then very large numbers of parents who display no interest in their child's progress at school, perhaps because they do not attach any great importance to educational achievement or because they expect little success, must be described as rejecting parents.

The pathological model underlies much of professional thinking about the treatment, care and support of mentally handicapped people and their families. This model underlies the widely reported tendency of professionals to advocate institutional care for the handicapped child.[13] Adams and Lovejoy in a social work text book stress the pathological model:

> Because of the great practical difficulties associated with mental defect the social worker is frequently tempted into offering help and though this may often serve a useful ancillary purpose in temporarily relieving some minor pressure, she must remember that the emotional burden is not affected, and in some cases material help inappropriately offered may be something of an irritant because it does not touch on the real issue of the emotional stress.[14]

Usually professionals view parents of the handicapped child themselves as 'ill' or 'handicapped' and are often suspicious about their motives for wanting to find out what is wrong with their child. Anything parents say or do can be interpreted as evidence of the parents' underlying problem. Jaehnig summarised the 'catch 22' situation created by professional use of a pathological model in the following way:

> If they (the parents) seek to contain his
> condition within the home they are open to
> accusations of being 'over-protective' and
> retarding the child's further development. If
> they try to maintain a 'normal' pattern of
> living inside and outside the home, they are
> failing to 'accept' the child's handicap, seen
> as another sign of emotional maladjustment. If
> they admit their child to residential care they
> encounter social disapproval for 'rejecting'
> him and feel a need to justify their actions to
> others.[15]

This view of the parents as somehow damage can
effect the way professionals share information with
parents. The comments of Evans are still relevant
today. In his research he saw 600 parents from a
few weeks to almost 15 years after the birth of
their Down's Syndrome child:

> I am struck by the extremely vivid and some-
> times quite horrifying memories they have of
> being 'told'. Many of them can relive in
> detail this traumatic experience even after
> 10 and 15 years; and it often seems to have
> decided their attitude to hospital and doctors
> - for good or ill - for all time.[16]

DISCOVERY OF MENTAL HANDICAP

In this section we shall examine, using the
mothers' own statements, how they tried to make
sense of their children's problems and how they
discovered their children's handicaps. We are
interested in the processes by which mothers interpreted, made sense of and understood the situation
they were in and the impact of professionals on
these processes.
For all parents, child-rearing has to be learnt.
As Voysey[17] has pointed out having a first baby may
be a 'crisis' but competent adults have a ready-
made stock of knowledge handed down from ancestors,
or acquired in 'anticipatory socialization', which
provides a guide to the kinds of situations likely
to occur and trustworthy 'recipes' for interpreting
the baby's behaviour and handling the baby in such
a way as to attain the desired consequences. Thus,
most children start to teeth in their first year of

life and increased crying or broken sleeping
patterns may be explained by teething. Mothers with
previous experience of babies and children are more
likely to know about specific practices for dealing
with such events, but other routinely available
sources of information are relatives, neighbours and
friends who have children of similar age. Their
opinions can be more or less trusted as those of eye
witnesses, especially given the mothers' previous
experience of their normal honesty, reliability and
so on. Of course, mothers may also seek the opinion
of others such as doctors or child-rearing manuals,
but even those who attempt to rear their child
'according to Dr. Spock' do so from choice. Since
'all children vary' mothers can choose which knowledge is relevant to their unique child. They
develop their own stock of knowledge from their own
experience and other sources and use this as a guide
in caring for their own child.

Mothers may have some vague knowledge about
mental handicap but are unlikely to have any direct
experience. Many mothers are worried that something
will go wrong in childbirth but in the absence of
specific evidence this fear is usually allayed.
Mothers know that the majority of babies are born
'normal' and if they seek out such assurances as
'is he alright?' they are likely to receive a
positive reply.

As mothers become aware that something is wrong
with their child so their existing stock of knowledge becomes unreliable as a guide. They may not
be able to understand their child's behaviour or
know how they should treat the child. New areas of
knowledge are needed and previous sources of information, relatives, friends or Dr. Spock, are no
longer adequate.

Where the 'problem' child is referred to
'experts', the knowledge of these experts, usually
medical practitioners, is relied upon to make
sense of the child's behaviour and to provide a
guide to the child's treatment.

Mothers' awareness of problems may not be the
result of their own experience of their child, but
may itself be a result of expert assessment.
However many mothers identify the problem themselves. In both situations the mother's task was
the same: to make sense of the situation so that
she knew how to treat her child and what to expect
in the future. To explore the process through which
mothers discovered that their child was handicapped,
we identified a number of themes to talk about.

These included the way mothers become aware that there was a problem; their interactions with professionals; and especially who told them their child was handicapped. In this chapter we shall emphasise the common aspects of mothers' stories.

Initial Awareness. In the majority of cases (71 mothers, 59.2%) it was the mother who suspected something was wrong. Of the 33 cases (27.5%) in which doctors identified a problem, 31 involved cases in which doctors could readily recognise conditions like Down's Syndrome, meningitis or other serious problems. Other studies of the discovery of mental handicap indicate that in the majority of cases mothers are the first people to recognise something is wrong. For example, in a study of the mothers of Down's Syndrome babies, Cunningham and Sloper found that 63% of the mothers interviewed suspected something was wrong and initiated investigations.[18] Many mentally handicapped children are discovered in the pre-school period when they fail to reach the normal 'milestones' of development. In other cases problems did not become obvious until the primary school age. In the present study as many as 108 (90%) mothers suspected something was wrong before their child was two years old.

There was considerable agreement among mothers on the nature of the signs and the clues which first occasioned their suspicion. Though there was often a wide variation in the age at which these clues were organised into a 'problem'. Mrs. G. became suspicious when Diana was a year old. She said:

> That was when I had my first suspicion because she had no self awareness. She didn't seem to realise she had hands, she couldn't eat a biscuit by herself, she wouldn't clap her own hands and she didn't speak. I had two other children who were talkative by the time they were 13 and 14 months, so by the time she was 18 months, still not saying anything I took her to my doctor.

Mrs. A. suspected something might be wrong after Tina's second birthday:

> When I couldn't get her clean and she wouldn't talk, I decided to see my doctor.

Mrs. J. said:

John was six months old. He was just like a
rag doll, he couldn't sit up or anything so I
took him to the clinic.

The mothers had developmental milestones,
although different mothers allowed their children
different amounts of time to reach these milestones.
Failure to reach a specific milestone 'in time'
made the mother aware something was wrong and often
started the process of discovering mental handicap.
But the suspicion that one's child is 'different'
in some way calls into question the normal 'recipes'
of child-rearing. As the difference between the
child's performance and mother's common sense
readings of the problem mounts, mothers become concerned about the child's well-being and uncertain
about his future. At this stage an undefined
question mark hangs over the child.
On the basis of the clues provided by common
sense timetables of child development the parents
have worked up a generalized suspicion about their
child's well being. Their interpretation of these
clues at this point amounts to nothing more specific
than the fear that there is 'something wrong'. This
verdict that all is not well with the child provokes
the decision to seek professional advice on the
causes of the trouble and marks the beginning of the
change in the status of the child.

Making Sense of the Situation. Mothers who were
worried that something was wrong usually looked to
'experts' for an explanation. In the majority of
cases mothers were referred to a hospital doctor
and 93 (77.5%) of the mothers were told their child
was mentally handicapped by the hospital doctor
(usually a paediatrician).[19] Other medical experts
were also involved. In 16 (13.3%) cases the family
doctor was the key person and in 3 (2.5%) the midwife. In six cases (5%) where the mother consulted
the child's school the child was assessed by an
educational psychologist and the mother was told by
either the psychologist, a school teacher or a
school nurse.
Only a few of the mothers who took their suspicions for professional appraisal and consulted
their family doctor or the local health clinic
received an immediate diagnosis of mental handicap.
For the remainder, the outcome amounted to a declaration of a moratorium on further change in the
child's already fragile and vulnerable status.

Parents in this group experienced greater problems later in the process of discovery.

Mothers experienced a variety of professional responses. Some mothers made repeated visits to their local clinics or family doctor to convey their suspicions but their suspicions were dismissed and they were told that they were over anxious or fussy. Matthew was one year old when Mrs. M. asked to see a specialist. She said: 'Because Matthew wasn't talking. The doctor did a blood test and said there was nothing wrong with Matthew'. Mrs. M. went on complaining. She said: 'But the doctors still thought I was being fussy until he came to school age and then I was suddenly presented with "well we'll have to decide which school he's going to go to"'. When Mrs. J. took her son to the clinic the doctor said he could see nothing wrong with John. She was advised to give it a couple of months and see what progress he made. Mrs. J. said: 'So we let it pass and he was still all floppy, so we got in touch with my own doctor and he referred me to the specialist'.

These parents were dismissed with no more than a vague reassurance and the advice not to worry. They were offered no plausible alternative explanation that would allay their fears and help them to satisfactorily account for their child's behaviour.

A doctor's knowledge of handicap is that of the expert. His or her knowledge is restricted to a limited area but inside this area it is clear and distinct. The knowledge is based on a system of 'normal cases'[20] organised by a doctor's knowledge of things that can be 'wrong' with children. Medical categories and interpretations tend to turn attention away from the child's unaffected abilities.[21]

The problem doctors have with mothers who demand reasons why their children are behind is that many descriptions given by mothers do not clearly differentiate their child's development from the development of other children. 'Young handicapped children differ from normal children mainly in potential rather than in capacity'.[22] The insecurity which characterises the mother's feelings about her child is mirrored in the uncertainty which the doctor faces. He has to devise a strategy which allows him both to cope successfully with his own clinical uncertainty and to appease the mothers who search for and demand a diagnosis and certainty. The strategy the doctor frequently adopts is to resist all demands and pressures to make a decision or diagnosis while relieving or neutralizing the suspicions which urge the mother to press for a definite judgement.

In retrospect many mothers were willing to believe that the doctors 'didn't say anything really' because 'I don't think they knew themselves'. Others were sceptical. Mrs. N. said:

> I certainly think they knew. I went for a chromosome test at the Infirmary in December, and this Infirmary is one of the major hospitals ... and they fobbed me off until the middle of April that their microscope was broken and they couldn't diagnose Joseph's blood test which was jolly strange, but I'm sure they knew.

For 7 months nurses went to Mrs. P's home and showed her how to bath Elizabeth 'because she was so small' and to make sure that the baby's tongue was down when she was feeding. On two occasions a nurse went and took a sample of blood from her daughter's heel. Neither of these nurses explained anything to her when she asked. Mrs. P. found it very distressing to be living under this mistrust. Mrs. P. said:

> We had friends who were in the medical profession who knew and had heard. I had worked in the hospital and I had friends who were reading her notes, knowing things about my baby that I hadn't been told. Whenever we went there, I saw their eyes went moist when they held her. They knew and I didn't. I felt resentful the way I was treated. I felt very angry.

Some mothers developed their own explanations for this apparent attitude of silence and mistrust. Mrs. O. got the general impression that doctors were too frightened to give mothers sufficient information.

Mrs. O.: I felt I was being fobbed off with anything other than the truth. They were too frightened to tell me the truth in case I panicked and I wouldn't have.

The decision not to tell the parents or to nurture their suspicions by suppressing information can be justified by professionals adopting a

pathological view of the family. It can be argued
that mothers will be more ready to receive and
grasp the diagnosis if they are already convinced
that something is wrong with their child and that
any effort to unmask the truth is likely to compound
the shock for the parents and provoke resentment
against the doctor and a rejection of the diagnosis.

Cowie[23] suggests the doctors' own anxiety may
subconsciously make them delay telling the parents,
rationalising their decision by arguing that the
parents are not ready or couldn't yet cope. There
is a genuine uncertainty about diagnosis but this
uncertainty can be used as a means of control.[24]

Whatever the cause of doctor's prevarication,
the effect is to maintain the child in an ambiguous
and transitional status midway between health and
sickness and between normality and abnormality. The
child is left straddling two classifications of
reality, one of which grants him a weak hold of his
personal integrity while the other threatens life-
long dependency.[25] This stage then is characterized
by a state of marginality for both mother and child
before the final phase of the process of discovery in
which the parents are told and the child acquires a
new status.

<u>Confirming Suspicions</u>. If mothers want to be told
their childs' condition as soon as possible they
also want to be told the truth. Having talked to
46 mothers of Down's Syndrome infants Carr commented,
'One firm rule might be agreed: no mother should be
told lies about her child'.[26] As Reech, himself
the father of a handicapped child said:

> The truth must be expressed. No purpose can
> possibly be served by concealing the truth and
> indeed a great deal of damage may be done in
> not stating the facts clearly and gently.[27]

Most professionals accept that parents must be
told the truth. Few professionals explicitly
advocate lying to parents. However many withhold
information until the 'appropriate' moment arrives
to disclose it and 'appropriate' is defined by the
professionals. As Lucas and Lucas[28] point out
telling parents that they have a handicapped child
is one of the less agreeable responsibilities of the
medical profession. It calls for a combination of
great tact, delicacy and firmness. For parents it
is often a traumatic experience involving shock,

reduced self confidence, bewilderment and anxiety.[29]
Many survey mothers appreciated the distressing
nature of the occasion. One mother said: 'There is
no easy way of telling; however it is told it's
going to come as a terrible shock'.

Drillien and Wilkinson[30] examined the issue of
the appropriate time to tell parents. They argued
that parents' views should be considered. Their
work arose from the disagreement amongst medical
experts about when parents of handicapped babies
should be told. Some experts, worried about maternal rejection, said it was better to wait to allow
the mother 'to get really to know the baby',[31]
other experts stressed the damaging effects of uncertainty and marginality, and argued that parents
should be told as soon as possible.[32]

Most of the work on the timing of the initial
interview and subsequent maternal reaction has been
done with parents of Down's Syndrome children as the
condition can usually be identified at birth. In
these studies,[33] as in our study, mothers were
unanimous that they would prefer to know as soon as
possible.

Mothers' experiences of how the news was broken
to them varied widely. Some mothers recalled that
they were given a full clinical diagnosis of the
origins and causes of the child's handicap.

In some cases fathers were used as an inter-
mediary between the professionals and the mother:

> The specialist told my husband, he didn't tell
> me. He said to my husband if you want me to
> tell her myself I'll come back to your house
> and I'll tell your wife. Or you can go home
> and tell her yourself. He (the husband) pre-
> ferred to come and tell me himself. But the
> specialist did offer to come home and tell me
> himself... He (the specialist) couldn't have
> done more than he did. He was very patient and
> understanding. He didn't want to hurt my feel-
> ings. That was why he didn't tell me when I
> was alone. He knew I would take it badly so
> he asked my husband to tell me. Looking back
> I think he handled my case with great concern.

A similar experience was recalled by Mrs. T:

> The specialist told my husband and then my
> husband told me. I preferred my husband to
> tell me. With being in the maternity home they
> sent for my husband and told him and they asked

him to tell me when he thought it was the most
convenient time. Really I think it was quite
good because it was really giving me a chance
to get over the shock of having the baby, and
it was good the way they put it over.

Other mothers felt professionals were careful to
pick an appropriate time. Mrs. U. said her doctor
didn't tell her sooner because:

he knew the state I was in. If the family circumstances had been different I think I would
have been told earlier. Just before I had
Jonathan my grandmother died and I was very
upset. I was happy the way he handled the
whole situation, he gave me time to recover
from that emotional upset before he told me
about Jonathan's handicap.

More often mothers were resentful as the professional who broke the news seemed to them unfeeling, abrupt or impersonal. Mrs. Y. recalled the
events in the following way:

We were just told on the spot ... We were told
in a ward full of people, nurses, doctors on
their rounds and other patients. I think he
(the doctor) should have told us privately. I
was very upset and I thought he handled it
insensitively and without any regard for my
feelings at all. When he said abruptly that
John was retarded I tended not to believe it at
first. I refused to accept it and it took me
a long time to bring myself to accept it. I
think if he had told us in a proper interview
and had endeavoured to explain it fully I would
have found it less difficult to come to terms
with it.

Mrs. A.B. was told when her daughter was 19 months
old:

I took her to my own doctor and I just said to
him 'I think her behaviour is odd, she screams
and bangs her head on the wall all the time'
and he just sat there and he said: 'Oh dear,
she's retarded', and that's how he put it to
me. I just said to him 'It can't be right' and
I just put her back in her pram and just ran
all the way home like a lunatic crying my eyes
out!

It is hardly surprising that Mrs. A.B. described the event as 'a terrible moment, the worst thing that ever happened to me. It was a moment I'll never forget'.

Mrs. A.B. 'discovered' that her daughter was handicapped and had Down's Syndrome because of the behaviour of the doctor and the nurse after the child was born:

> The baby was delivered and my doctor whom we'd known for years, he delivered my other daughter and my son, walked away shaking his head, and I saw it and I sort of raised myself a bit and said 'What's the matter'? and the nurse walked away as well ... I turned my head as I was lying on the delivery bed and there was some writing at the side of my bed and I read that writing, I remember seeing 'First Stage Labour' ... 'Second Stage' ... the time and 'Third Stage' and then underneath, which was the only thing which seemed to stand out, it said - 'Mongoloid appearance'. Well I remember screaming ... and the doctor and the nurse didn't come back ... I was very distressed.

In other cases mothers said that the doctors told them their child was handicapped by using euphemisms or everyday language such as 'He said she'll be alright until it comes to the books' or 'He just said she was backward. The doctor never gave it a name'.

At the end of this irksome, exhausting and distressing initial interview many mothers had an explanation for their child's abstruse behaviour and retarded development which had puzzled them almost since his birth: 'Through this process the past was made to fit the present, so to speak'.[34]

Summary. Many professionals make the error of thinking of the discovery of mental handicap as an event. It is often seen as an event in which a skilled practitioner who understands about the nature and implication of a child's condition and handicap explains it to a vulnerable and 'uninformed' parent.

It is clear from mothers' accounts that the discovery is a complex process. This process takes many forms from a sudden revelation in which the various stages of the process occur close together, to a slow and gradual growth of awareness. However three

distinctive phases can be identified in the process.
An initial stage in which someone becomes aware that
something is wrong with the child. The evidence
used and cited for identifying that something is
wrong may vary but it is usually associated with the
child's failure to reach a developmental milestone
at the 'right time'. The second phase is one of
uncertainty and often confusion. Both parents and
professionals try to make sense of the situation and
the child's condition and behaviour and try to establish its meaning for the future. This phase is
often characterised by negotiations between parents
and professionals over the nature of the problem
and its meaning. The length and nature of this
period depends on the nature of the child's condition, the experience and perspectives of
professionals and parents and their ability to nego-
tiate and communicate. The third and final phase is
the 'discovery' in which the professionals and
parents reach an agreement, explicit or implicit,
about the child and his or her handicap. This
agreement is usually made in terms dictated by the
professionals who play the dominant role and tell
the parents what is wrong. The agreement is often
symbolised by the use and acceptance of such terms
as 'mental handicap'. It is important not to over-
stress the importance of one single event or interview. Although parents may accept the label there
is still room for negotiation over the meaning and
implication for the child of that label.

From the child's point of view the different
phases of the process of discovery make important
changes in status and people's attitudes and behaviour. Until somebody notices something is unusual
or different, the child is a normal child with
normal prospects of growth and development and is
treated in the same way as any other child. When a
problem had been identified but its nature and
meaning are unclear, the child moves into a marginal
status. A question mark hangs over his or her
future and the child's behaviour, development, etc.
are subject to special scrutiny to reveal additional
information about the 'problem'. If and when the
agreement is reached between the parents and the
experts, the child moves into a new position as a
mentally handicapped person. The question mark
about the future is removed and replaced by a pessimistic assessment of life long dependency. The
parents learn new ways of thinking about and
relating to their child.

CONCLUSION - IMPLICATIONS FOR PRACTICE

The process of discovering mental handicap is, rightly, seen as a crucial phase in the development of family relations and there has been considerable discussion about how and when parents should be told. A MIND Report made the following recommendations: (1) that parents should be told as soon as the condition is diagnosed; (2) that the person giving the information should be sympathetic to the parents; (3) that parents should be told of the likely special needs of their child; (4) that after an initial interview parents should have a further chance to talk about the situation and proper counselling and support should be available.[35]

In this concluding section we shall discuss two issues: who should break the news and how should the news be broken.

Who Should Break the News? Much has been made of the question of who should tell the mother. Professionals often feel that mothers will feel resentful towards the one who tells them. At present it is no one person's or profession's duty to break the news to mothers.[36] The main responsibility usually falls on the hospital doctor, often a specialist in child medicine.

However, there seems little reason for the task of breaking the news to be done only by the hospital doctor.[37] There is no substitute for insightful knowledge of the family such as may be held by the family doctor, the health visitor or the midwife. For example, Mrs. U. reported that her family doctor's knowledge of her circumstances spared her further emotional trauma. Another mother preferred to have been told by her health visitor because they knew each other 'so well'. Sometimes the father is the most appropriate person to break the news to the mother, as happened in the cases of Mrs. Y. and Mrs. A.B. Fathers are by no means automatic candidates for telling their wives and they are no substitute for a discussion with experts.[38]

It is wrong for any professional to be evasive if they do not feel that they have the authority to give direct answers to the parents. Mothers interpret this as a lack of sympathy or disinterest. Above all professionals must beware of non-verbal communication to the mother as happened to Mrs. A.C.

115

when both doctor and nurse walked away from her
delivery-bed shaking their heads on the birth of
her Down's Syndrome daughter. None of the mothers
we interviewed felt resentful towards the informant.
As one mother put it: 'I think they (the doctors)
are really as upset as the parents, because they are
in a caring profession'. Mothers only resented the
informant when they felt they had been handled
badly.

How Should the News be Broken? Once mothers became
aware something was wrong, the suspicions escalated
and they were not satisfied until they had received
an acceptable explanation.[39] Mothers want to be
told of their child's condition early and they also
want to hear the truth.

Of far greater importance than who does the
telling is how it is done. Resentment arises when
the teller seems unfeeling or informs the parents
briefly or abruptly - as Reech calls it the 'get it
over with' school.[40] Mothers are often too dis-
traught to absorb and understand what is being said
to them at the first occasion. One mother said:
'I remember being very very stunned and a lot of it
didn't actually go in at the time'. Another said:
'I don't think I really took in what they were saying at the time'. As one paediatrician has
observed: On the first interview at which the news
of the defect is broken, little of what is said is
remembered but the telling makes a deep impression.[41]
Spain and Wigley have commented that:

> Whether the breaking of the news is fully
> planned or not the emotional anguish of the
> parents is such that frequently the information
> is not properly understood or remembered
> however sympathetic and skilled the teller may
> be. At least two or three sessions are usually
> required before the parents can comprehend the
> diagnosis. It may be best to follow up any
> important interview with another from a differ-
> ent person, another paediatrician or a social
> worker, who asks 'what were you told', to
> elicit the parents' perception of the situa-
> tion.[42]

Mothers' questions need to be answered fully.
However, some mothers are unable to formulate the
questions that they want to ask. Mrs. A.C. recalled:

(The Doctor said) 'I've seen baby and she's
very healthy and very strong, she'll be alright
until it comes to the books'. Those were his
very words. Now I was so shocked of course I
didn't say what did he mean. I didn't ask him
anything about the baby or what would happen to
us or anything. I remember just hearing him
say that and then he went out.

Mothers in the present study were not alone in
criticising the manner in which they had been told.
Both the Court Committee[43] and the Warnock Committee[44] received harrowing evidence from parents
testifying how badly the telling had been managed
by professionals of all disciplines.
    In this chapter we have used mothers' own
accounts of their experiences to trace the processes
by which they discovered that their child was mentally handicapped. We have argued that the
discovery of mental handicap is not an event in
which the 'informed' expert tells the 'uninformed'
mother what is wrong with her child, but a process
in which both the expert and the mother are trying
to make sense of some apparent discrepancies, between what the child 'ought' to be and what the child
'is'. It is really better thought of as a process
of negotiation between two different experts - the
mother who has an intimate knowledge of her child
and the professional who has wider experiences of
other children. They should be engaged in a common
enterprise of trying to understand what has
happened and what it means for the future.

NOTES

1.   S. Kew, Handicap and Family Crisis: A Study of the
     Siblings of Handicapped Children, Pitman, 1975.
2.   A. Dupont, 'Severely mentally retarded children
     at home', REAP 1, 107-12, 1975. Examples of
     writers who adopt the pathological model
     include: A.R. Schaffer, 'The too cohesive
     family: a form of group pathology', The
     International Journal of Social Psychiatry, 10,
     4, 1964; M.D. Sheridan, The Handicapped Child
     and his Home, National Children's Home, 1966;
     C.M. Fowle, 'The effects of the severely men-
     tally retarded child on his family', American
     Journal of Mental Deficiency, 73, 468-73,
     1968; K.S. Holt, 'The home care of the
     severely mentally retarded', Paediatrics, 22,
     744-55, 1958; J.K. McMichael, Handicap: A

Study of Physically Handicapped Children and Their Families, Staples, 1971.

3.   P. Pinkerton, 'Parental acceptance of the handicapped child', Developmental Medicine and Child Neurology, 12, 207-12, 1970, p. 207. Emphasis in the original text.

4.   S. Hewett, The Family and the Handicapped Child A Study of Cerebral Palsied Children in Their Homes, Allen and Unwin, 1970, p. 194.

5.   W.B. Jaehnig, Mentally Handicapped Children and their Families: Problems for Social Policy, unpublished Ph.D. Thesis, University of Essex, 1974.

6.   Other recent researchers have also commented on the supposed pathological effects of the handicapped child on his family. See, for example, D. Wilkin, Caring for the Mentally Handicapped Child, Croom Helm, 1979 and Jaehnig, Mentally Handicapped Children and Their Families.

7.   A.I. Roith, 'Chairman's address: The Myth of parental attitudes', The Journal of Mental Subnormality, 9, 51-4, 1963.

8.   Sheridan, The Handicapped Child and his Home, p. 56.

9.   L. Wing, 'Problems experienced by parents of children with severe mental retardation' in B. Spain and G. Wigley (eds.), Right from the Start: A Service for Families with a Young Handicapped Child, National Society for Mentally Handicapped Children, 1975.

10. H.R. Kelman, 'The effect of a brain-damaged child on the family', in H.G. Birch (ed.), Brain Damage in Children: The Biological and Social Aspects, Williams and Wilkins, 1964.

11. J.H. Meyerowitz and H.B. Kaplan, 'Familial responses to stress: the case of cystic fibrosis', Social Science and Medicine, 1, 3, 249-66, 1967.

12. McMichael, Handicap: A Study of Physically Handicapped Children and Their Families.

13. K. Jones, A History of the Mental Health Services, Routledge and Kegan Paul, 1972; Hewett, The Family and the Handicapped Child; Jaehnig, Mentally Handicapped Children and Their Families; Wilkin, Caring for the Mentally Handicapped Child.

14. M. Adams and H. Lovejoy, The Mentally Subnormal: Social Work Approaches, Heinemann, 1972, p. 80.

15. Jaehnig, Mentally Handicapped Children and Their Families, p. 179.

16. K.A. Evans, 'Letter, Mentally Handicapped Children', 974, 5/5/1962.
17. M. Voysey, A Constant Burden: The Reconstitution of Family Life, Routledge and Kegan Paul, 1975, pp. 98-9.
18. C.C. Cunningham and P. Sloper, 'Parents of Down's Syndrome babies: their early needs', Child: Care, Health and Development, 3, 325-47, 1977.
19. Lucas and Lucas also reported that a majority of the mothers they interviewed (62.3%) said they were told by the hospital doctor. P.J. Lucas and A.M. Lucas, 'Down's Syndrome: telling the parents', The British Journal of Mental Subnormality, 26, 21-31, 1980.
20. T.J. Scheff, Being Mentally Ill: A Sociological Theory, Aldine, Chicago, 1966, p. 180.
21. S.A. Richardson, 'The effects of physical disability on the socialization of a child,' in D.A. Goslin (ed.), Handbook of Socialization Theory and Research, Rand McNally, Chicago, 1969.
22. A.G. Davies and P.M. Strong, 'Aren't children wonderful: a study in the allocation of identity in development assessment' in M. Stacey (ed.), The Sociology of the NHS, Sociological Review Monograph, 22, 1976.
23. V. Cowie, 'Parental counselling and spina bifida', Developmental Medicine and Child Neurology, 9, 110-2, 1967. Survey mothers' experience is part of the general struggle over information in medical encounters between doctors and patients. See, for example, E. Freidson, Profession of Medicine: A Study of the Sociology of Applied Knowledge, Harper and Row, New York, 1970, especially chapter 14.
24. F. Davis, 'Uncertainty in medical prognosis: clinical and functional', American Journal of Sociology, 66, 1, 41-47, 1960.
25. T.A. Booth, 'From normal baby to handicapped child: unravelling the idea of subnormality in families of mentally handicapped children', Sociology, 12, 2, 203-221, 1978.
26. As Carr points out the case for telling the parents as early as possible is a strong one. See, for example: J. Carr, 'Mongolism: telling the parents', Developmental Medicine and Child Neurology, 12, 213-221, 1970.
27. H. Reech, 'A parent discusses initial counselling', Mental Retardation, 2, 25-6, 1966.
28. Lucas and Lucas, 'Down's Syndrome: telling the parents', p. 21.

29. R. Brinkworth, The Reactions of Parents to The Diagnosis of Mental Subnormality, D.C.A., Birmingham, 1970.

30. C.M. Drillien and E.M. Wilkinson, 'Mongolism: when should parents be told?', British Medical Journal, 2, 1306-7, 21/11/1964.

31. A.W. Franklin, 'Care of the Mongol baby: the first phase', The Lancet, 256-258, 1/2/1958, p. 257.

32. A.H. Parmalee, 'Management of Mongolism in Childhood', International Research in Medicine, 169, 358-61, 1956.

33. For example, J. Tizard and J.C. Grad, The Mentally Handicapped and their Families: A Social Survey, Oxford University Press, 1961; Carr, 'Mongolism: telling the parents'; J. Carr, Young Children with Down's Syndrome: Their Development, Upbringing and Effects on Their Families, Butterworth, 1975; B. Spain and G. Wigley (eds.) Right from the Start: A Service for Families with a Young Handicapped Child, National Society for Mentally Handicapped Children, 1975; Cunningham and Sloper, 'Parents of Down's Syndrome babies; Lucas and Lucas, 'Down's Syndrome: telling the parents'.

34. F. Davis, Passage Through Crisis: Polio Victims and Their Families, Bobbs-Merrill, Indianapolis, 1963, p. 11.

35. For a detailed report of the MIND working party see E.F. Carr and T.E. Oppé, 'The birth of an abnormal child: telling the parents', The Lancet, 1075-7, 13/11/1971. For the MENCAP report see Spain and Wigley, Right from the Start.

36. W. Yule, 'Handicap', P. Feldman and J. Orford (eds.), Psychological Problems: The Social Context, Wiley, Chichester, 1980, p. 235.

37. J. Carr, Mongolism: 'telling the parents', p. 218.

38. R. Wrigglesworth, 'Stating the Problem', in Spain and Wigley Right from the Start, states: 'The father is more detached and less intimately involved emotionally with the child at this crisis stage, but nevertheless, when first told the news it is the fathers who faint and not the mothers; so much so that I have learned always to see that the father is seated in a secure chair, with sides before I impart the news', p. 17.

39. L. Burton, The Family Life of Sick Children, Routledge and Kegan Paul, 1975, found

in cases of cystic fibrosis 'diagnosis ...
required parental efforts to effect', p. 27.
40. Reech, 'A parent discusses initial counselling'
    p. 25.
41. R.W. Smithells, 'The management of congenital
    abnormalities', British Journal of Hospital
    Medicine, 2, 432, 1969.
42. Spain and Wigley, Right from the Start, p. 62.
43. Fit for the Future, Report of the Committee on
    Child Health Services (Chairman, Professor
    S.D.M. Court) Cmnd. 6684-I, H.M.S.O., 1976,
    especially pp. 7-11.
44. Special Educational Needs, Report of the
    Committee of Enquiry into the Education of
    Handicapped Children and Young People (Chairman
    Mrs. H.M. Warnock), Cmnd. 7212, H.M.S.O., 1978.

Chapter 6

CARE IN THE FAMILY

INTRODUCTION

      Families in our society provide the bulk of
the care for dependent individuals. To understand
the nature of this care it is important to assess
the extra problems these families face and the
resources they can mobilise to deal with these
problems. In this chapter we shall focus on the
problems of day-to-day caring and the way families
mobilise and utilise their own resources, especially
the division of labour in the family. In Chapter 7
we shall examine the availability and utility of
informal support from relatives, neighbours and
friends. In Chapter 8 we shall examine the nature
of formal support available from government-funded
organisations and charities.
      This chapter is divided into three sections.
In the first section we discuss the nature of the
family in Great Britain and the extent to which traditional roles and division of labour in the household have become blurred. In the second section we
shall look at the work associated with caring for
severely mentally handicapped children and discuss
the allocation of caring factors within the family.
In the final section we shall discuss in more
detail the division of labour in the family.

THE EGALITARIAN FAMILY?

      The modern nuclear family in Britain emerged at
the time of the industrial revolution. A normal
household became an adult man, the husband, an
adult female, the wife, and their dependent children.
Occasionally a dependent relative would be added to
this household. Inside the household a specific

122

division of labour developed. The adult male was defined as economically active, as the breadwinner. He went out to work and earned the money. The adult female was defined as the main carer who provided the bulk of the domestic labour in the household and was responsible for caring for all dependents in the house. The mother's place was in the home. The children were defined as economically inactive. Their primary task was to acquire the skills necessary for competent adulthood. This, of course, is an ideal-type model and actual families and households in the 19th century undoubtedly varied considerably from it.

Researchers studying the family in the 20th century have been especially interested in the division of labour in the household and have examined the extent to which a more egalitarian division of labour is developing.

Researchers investigating the family in the 1950s and 60s identified a blurring of roles between men and women. They argued that as more women were going out to work and becoming economically active so more men were becoming involved in household jobs. Young and Willmott described the situation in the following way: 'In the interests of symmetry it was only fair, as far as husbands and wives saw it, for the men to do more so that their wives could do less'.[1] In Bott's terminology there was a tendency towards joint conjugal roles and away from segregated roles in the family.[2] Researchers suggested that equalisation between men and women roles in the family was most developed in middle class families, but they also identified similar trends in working class families.[3]

More recently researchers have questioned earlier studies and the trends they identified. Platt has argued that within a single household there are often a variety of different patterns of interaction related to different activities. A general classification of a household as either 'joint' or 'segregated' in terms of its internal organisation and division of labour will usually conceal more than it reveals.[4] Oakley has argued that in many studies an asymmetrical division of labour is used as a starting point and baseline and any variation from this asymmetrical division of labour is cited as evidence that families are becoming more symmetrical and egalitarian. Some studies have concentrated on domestic tasks in which men have traditionally had higher rates of participation, i.e. gardening, domestic repairs and car

maintenance.[5] She cited a study by Toomey in which
households are classified as 'joint' in which the
husband did the laundry either 'very often', 'often',
'sometimes' or even 'rarely'. There was in Toomey's
study a systematic tendency to overstate the degree
of jointness in households.[6]

Oakley has argued that 'only a minority of
husbands give the kind of help that assertions of
equality in modern marriage imply'.[7] Oakley examined the participation of husbands in various areas of
household activities and concentrated on the ex-
tremes of involvement which she classified as 'high'
and 'low'. She interpreted low levels of participation in domestic work and child care as evidence
of conjugal role segregation. She found that conjugal role separation was the predominant pattern in
her sample of families. 60% of men had low levels
of participation in domestic tasks, 45% in child-
care activities and 43% in decision-making and
leisure activities. Only 15% of husbands had high
levels of participation in housework and 25% had
high levels of participation in child care. Oakley
concluded that contemporary marriages might 'be
characterized by an equality of status and
"mutuality" between husband and wife, but inequality
on the domestic task level is not automatically
banished'.[8] Even in marriages that are egalitarian
in respect to some activities such as leisure and
decision-making, there may be areas of inequality.[9]

Oakley also examined attitudes to appropriate
male and female activities. Most of her respon-
dents, both men and women, held the view that women
ought to take primary responsibility for the home
and the children. She found that 'even in joint
role marriages where a man's level of participation
in domestic affairs is high a dimension of one-
sided responsibility persists'.[10] Oakley was
extremely sceptical of arguments that marriage was
becoming more joint or more of an equal partnership.[11]

Outside the household a similar asymmetrical
relationship between men and women persists.
Despite recent legislation, taxation and social
security practice are based on the assumption that
men are the head of the household and are primarily
responsible for the household income.[12] For example
social security regulations require that fathers in
single parent families 'register for work and take
any available job which is suitable' whereas mothers
in single parent families can decide for themselves
'whether the family will benefit more from her

presence at home or from the earnings she could get from full-time work'.[13] According to the Finer Report, 'this policy is based partly on the view that the (Supplementary Benefits) Commission believe still to be generally held, that it is usually better for children to look to a father who conforms to the normal role of bread winner'.[14]

In English society husbands tend to be identi- fied as breadwinners and wives as homemakers. When women are economically active outside the family as in dual-career marriages or men cease to be econom- ically active as in situations of high unemployment, women still tend to retain the primary responsi- bility for the home and the children.[15] In the majority of households women still carry the main burden of child-care and housework with only limited support from their husbands.

Discussion. Researchers have tended to neglect the topic of the allocation of activities in the house- hold and in so far as the topic has been investiga- ted the starting point has usually been the conventional division of labour in the house. This is hardly surprising as the whole welfare state is based on the assumption that unpaid female labour will be available to care for the sick and infirm in the family.[16] Welfare agencies such as the health services generally only take on the full caring responsibilities in exceptional circumstances and then usually for short periods.

Individuals, who experience chronic disability such as mental handicap, need care for much longer periods than the acutely sick. Yet it is taken for granted that a women will be available to provide the necessary care. Wilkin has suggested that 'the policy of encouraging care in the community for the chronically sick person is based on assumptions about the ability of families to meet the demands placed upon them, which, in practice, usually means the willingness of mothers to carry the burden of care'.[17] We shall argue in this chapter that we could find in our sample of mothers little evidence in families with severely mentally handicapped children of a major redefinition of roles and relationships in the household. Mothers carried not only major responsibility for organising and main- taining the household but also took the main res- ponsibility for the extra work created by their child's disability.

CARING FOR A SEVERELY HANDICAPPED CHILD IN THE
FAMILY

In this section we shall concentrate on caring
for severely mentally handicapped children at home
or in the words of one mother 'my daily grind'. We
will focus on the work involved in performing or
supervising the activities involved in everyday
living. As it is difficult if not impossible to
focus on all the activities we shall examine in
detail three specific aspects of care - bedtime and
sleeping, meal-times and eating and bathtime.
    Most children up to the age of two are heavily
dependent on their parents for the performance of
these activities. However after the age of two
children normally become increasingly independent in
these spheres and by the time they go to school
they usually require minimal assistance. However
severely disabled children do not follow the same
pattern of development. It is important to examine
the extent to which mothers were involved in performing these basic activities of living.

Bedtime and Sleeping

    Most parents experience problems with bedtime
and sleeping in the first two years of their children's lives but generally these problems disappear
after the age of two. The majority of the mothers
in our sample (87, 73%) did not experience problems
with putting their child to bed or with their
child's sleeping. However a group of mothers
experienced either minor problems (11 mothers) or
major problems (22 mothers).
    To examine the nature of these problems and
their impact on family life we asked 9 mothers who
experienced major problems with bedtime and sleeping
to keep a diary for a short period of their children's sleeping patterns. We shall in the following
discussion concentrate on the experiences of one
mother, Mrs. R.A. who kept a diary for 2 months.
    Mrs. R.A. had three children: Wendy, aged 12,
George, aged 6 and Diana, aged 10, the subject of
her diary. Diana had frequent fits, sometimes during the night. We classified Diana as 'severely
disabled' with a score of 11 on our scale. Diana
shared a room with her brother but 'she often sleeps
where her mood takes her'.
Mrs. R.A. said:

Bedtime is terrible. We all suffer nights
without sleep. This is one of my biggest
problems. Diana has sleeping tablets but they
have no effect on her.

Eight days of Mrs. R.A.'s diary illustrates many of
the problems she faced and Diana created at night.

Sunday: Diana came home again in a bit of a
temper, a little restless but not so
much that it got me down. She wouldn't
go to bed ... put her in with me. She
slept until 2.20 a.m. She was screaming
for no apparent reason. I locked the
bedroom door so that she wouldn't disturb my other children. The screaming
went on till 6.00 a.m.

Monday: A bad night again. I don't think I can
stand much more again, the screaming
drives me crazy. Diana pulled the
drapes down, stripped the bed and herself and awoke George by sitting on his
head. I put George in with Wendy and
locked the door. I kept vigil all
night to make sure she didn't disturb
the other children's sleep.

Tuesday: Not too bad tonight, a little naughty
but dropped off to sleep at 10.20 p.m.
She woke up at 7.10 a.m. My other
children slept all night. I slept well.

Wednesday: Diana came home from school full of
mischief, wouldn't eat at all, screaming
all the time. I knew I was in for a bad
night. Bedtime came, she didn't want to
know. All the bedding came off, she
emptied the drawers, pulled wallpaper
off. We went to bed at 12 o'clock but
didn't get any sleep. My other children
didn't sleep well but put up with it as
always. I was really glad to see her
go to school.

Thursday: Very restless, screaming and stripping
bed. George didn't get to sleep until
I got Diana settled which was 12.30 a.m.
Diana was awake at 3.45 a.m. I put her
in bed with me and locked the bedroom
door. The screaming went on till 6.30
a.m.

Friday: Very restless again. She didn't go to
bed until 10.35 p.m., sat stroking her
hair until she went to sleep. Wendy

woke me up at 4.10 a.m. Diana had crept
into her bed ... she was in a fit. It
didn't last long, three minutes, then
she fell into a deep sleep until she
woke up at 7.20 a.m.

Saturday: Still very restless. Reluctant to go to
bed again ... I was up and down the
stairs most of the night. She pulled
the drapes down which is one of her
usual antics. She finally went to sleep
at 11.30 p.m. and woke up at 6.00 a.m.
My other children slept well.

Sunday: Diana was very tired. I put her in bed
and she went to sleep at 9.15 p.m. She
was no bother until 5.10 a.m. when I
woke up to find her in Wendy's room.
Diana had painted her face and eyes with
blue nail varnish. Wendy's sleep was
disturbed. I put Diana in my bed and
locked the bedroom. Both stayed awake
for the rest of the night. George
slept all night.

When we talked to her, Mrs. R.A. said the bedtime disturbance remained an unsolved problem. She
said: 'The only time Wendy and George get any peace
is when Diana goes in the hostel for a rest, or
shall I say a rest for us all'. Even the hostel did
not provide the temporary solution Mrs. R.A. hoped
for. She had decided not to send Diana to the
hostel because she had found out that 'they lock her
up all night in the hostel'.

Some mothers dealt with bedtime problems by
sleeping in the same room as their child, occasionally in the same bed. Mrs. M's strategy was to let
Joan come into her bed, so that her other daughter's
sleep was not disturbed. This problem had been
solved but at a price. Joan was 8 years old. She
was severely disabled and on our scale scored 10.
Joan's sister was 6 years old. Mrs. M. said:

They had a bedroom each, and Ann settled alright but Joan didn't. We couldn't even get
her to stay in her bed. She was in and out of
the bedroom all night so we put them together.
It does work out well but Ann does get annoyed
sometimes when Joan doesn't let her go to
sleep. I put them to bed between 7.30 and
8.00 p.m. on school days. Without fail just
after midnight Joan wakes up. She comes
straight into our room and she gets into our

bed, and she goes to sleep when she comes into
our bed. She seems quite insecure. We think
that's probably why she does it. She doesn't
like to be on her own.

Interviewer: Does this cause any inconvenience for
both you and your husband?
Mrs. M.: Yes, because my husgand gets out.
I've tried getting out myself but
she'll just follow me. I do feel
guilty about it. In fact he's started
having a sleeping bag on an airbed so
he just rolls out of bed and into the
sleeping bag.
Interviewer: How does your husband take this?
Mrs. M.: Very good, we've got a very strong
marriage.

Like Mrs. M., Mrs. R.B. also had problems at
bedtimes. Mrs. R.B.'s only child Sara was over 8
years old. She was very severely disabled and on
our scale scored 15. Sara would not sleep in her
own bed. Mr. R.B. had to take a night job.

Mrs. R.B.: My husband has to work nights because he
just couldn't get up in the morning
after a bad night with her ... and we
were both getting argumentative because
when you're both tired, you get a bit
edgy. She goes to bed with me. She
won't go in her own bedroom. We try and
she just screams and makes herself sick
until we have to give in to her. She's
in our bed when she goes to sleep but
she's very restless, sometimes terrible.
I feel like throwing her out of the
window. Now he's working nights I can
cope better with her on my own.

Mrs. C.R. had in the past experienced problems
with her son Rob who was nearly 8 years old and
moderately disabled. She had adopted a different
coping strategy to Mrs. R.B. She had sought advice
from a psychologist at the local assessment centre:

Mrs. C.R.: Rob just wouldn't go, and that was all
there was to it. He would kick and
scream, and we'd put him up to bed and
he would come down... We went to see
the psychologist about him and he told
us that Rob was ruling us, and we'd

brought a lot of it on ourselves because we'd been too soft with him, and
we just had to put him to bed and let
him scream, and every time he got out
put him back and just continue like this
until he got the message. It worked in
the end, once he found out he couldn't
get his own way. It was true the
psychologist said we were too soft with
him.

Interviewer: How do you manage in the morning?
Mrs. C.R.:   I shout a lot. I usually have as
              much organised the night before as I
              can. I have all their clothes ready
              the night before and get the break-
              fast done as much as I can the night
              before ... He has a chain on his
              door to keep him in, because he used
              to wander about the house during the
              night, and he fell down on the stairs
              one night and cut his mouth open.

Discussion. Difficulties with bedtime and sleeping
can affect the whole family. Only a minority of
mothers said they currently experienced problems but
other mothers had adopted strategies that 'solved'
the 'main problem' at a price, e.g. Mrs. M.'s husband had to sleep in a sleeping bag and Mrs. R.B.'s
husband changed his job. In these cases the mother
now defined bedtimes and sleeping as a minor
problem. In only 3 cases was a major problem resolved to the mothers' satisfaction. In all three
cases, as in Mrs. C.R.'s, the mothers had sought
professional advice and guidance.
      Most of the parents, who had problems at bed-
times, seemed to have adjusted to these problems, to
have accepted them as part of everyday life and to
have organised their lives around them. These
mothers tended to summarise the situation in terms
of 'we've learnt to live with it after so many
years'. Our interviews indicated that it was the
mothers themselves that made the major adjustment
and they sought to protect the sleep of their husbands and other children through taking the main
burden on themselves.
      We asked mothers about the division of labour
in putting the child to bed, attending to the child
at night and getting the child up in the morning
and the same pattern emerged (see Table 6.1). In

only 5 families did the father or other member of
the family play a dominant part in any of these
activities. The mother either did it alone or with
help.

Table 6.1 Division of labour in the family in
relation to bedtime and sleeping
activities

Activity	Mother always did it	Mother received help from another member of the house- hold	Another member of household always did it	Total number of children requiring assistance
Putting child to bed	39 (45%)	45 (52%)	3 (3%)	87
Attending to child at night	45 (60%)	25 (33%)	5 (7%)	75
Getting child up in the morning	71 (63%)	36 (32%)	5 (5%)	112

Bathing
        For many mothers bathing was a regular part of
the daily routine that created serious difficulties.
If the mother had limited help and her child was
heavy and frequently incontinent, then bathing was
frequently difficult, especially in the mornings
when the handicapped child and his or her siblings
had to be prepared for school.
        Mrs. R.D.'s bathing routine illustrated many
of the problems. John was a heavy boy, always
covered in faeces in the morning and needing a bath
before going to school. He was a very disabled
child who scored 18 on our scale and who was totally
dependent on his mother for all his basic needs.

Mrs. R.D.: Bathing is a big problem. He is heavy
            and needs a bath every morning because

131

Interviewer: | he is always dirty. I have to get his sister ready for school and then I have John to get ready. I have such a short time between getting him ready and the school bus coming. You're just trying to do everything at once.

Interviewer: How do you manage?

Mrs. R.D.: He's very heavy and I get a lot of pains in my back. Now I find it a lot easier to put a big towel on the floor and wash all his front and turn him over and wash his back down. It is terrible ... he screams when you put him in the bath. It's hectic in the morning. It's not so bad in the evening because my husband helps with the lifting.

In the case of Mrs. R.A. her back had been affected by lifting her daughter and she had to wear a surgical corset.

Mrs. R.A.: Diana likes to get bathed, but she is such a weight having to lift her in and out of the bath. I'm only 8 stones and she's 7½. She's such a big girl ... My back went first. I lifted her up and strained my spine for which I had treatment for six months - traction and a corset, but having this corset on, it was so strong I couldn't bend down to see to her so the corset had to go. I then developed lumps under my arms which were caused through stress and strain, which I had out in hospital.

Discussion. Bathing is a good example of an activity which most parents of young children have to perform but which has become a special problem with older, heavier and more disabled children.

Mothers again played the dominant role in the bathing and the activities associated with it such as dressing and lifting and carrying (see Table 6.2).

Table 6.2 Division of labour in the family in relation to bathing and associated activities

Activity	Mother always did it	Mother received help from another member of the household	Another member of household always did it	Total number of children requiring assistance
Bathing and Washing child	77 (72%)	20 (19%)	10 (9%)	107
Dressing child	81 (74%)	28 (25%)	1 (1%)	110
Lifting and Carrying child	21 (40%)	25 (48%)	6 (12%)	52

Fathers generally helped with children who were heavy. In all the cases in which mothers relied on their husbands' help, bathing involved a lot of heavy lifting or the child was resistive or awkward to deal with. Mrs. E.R. was one of the mothers who relied on her husband's help.

Mrs. E.R.: Bathing Janine is a two-person job. I find it difficult to manage on my own. I can bed-bath her but it is not the same as giving her a proper bath ... She needs a proper bath in the mornings because she dirties herself so much. But to sit her in a bath requires two of us. I usually do it with my husband. He works on night shifts so we both bath her as soon as he comes from work. One of us goes in the bath with Janine and the other takes her out and dries her. It is a lot easier that way. She is not heavy but she's long and she's awkward to do on my own ... she can't

133

sit up or support herself.

However, in some cases, husbands were not available to help. For example Mrs. R.A.'s husband was a
seaman and he could only help when he was on leave.
In cases like this some sort of adaptation to the
bathroom, such as a hoist or lift, would have been
useful. However Mrs. R.A., like many other mothers,
had never been offered any advice on the help that
might be available. Only 9 mothers in our study
had had adaptations made to their bathrooms.

Mealtimes and eating
58 mothers had to feed their children and 29
mothers said that mealtimes were very difficult. In
12 cases mothers had difficulty with the process of
feeding whereas in the other 17 cases the children
were disruptive at mealtimes.
Mrs. F.R. had difficulty feeding her 13 year
old daughter, Judith and described the experience in
the following way:

Mrs. F.R.: You have to sit and spoon-feed her like
a baby ... In actual fact she's worse
than a baby. She chokes frequently.
She finds it very difficult to chew and
swallow. It comes back and then she
starts again. So you have to be pre-
prepared to sit for anything from an
hour to an hour and a half to feed her.
You've got to forget everything else.
That's it Judith has to be fed and everything else has to wait.

In contrast Mrs. R.A. had problems with her daughter
Diana's behaviour.

Mrs. R.A.: She's messy. She's forever pinching off
everybody's plate. It puts Wendy (the
eldest daughter) off her food. Wendy is
very particular, a speck of dust on her
knife or fork and it has to be washed ..
and Diana has a habit of poking the
potatoes and pinching a sausage or something like that, and Wendy then won't
eat it. We have this trouble all the
time but I insist on the family eating
together.

Difficult mealtime behaviour could seriously

restrict the families social relations and
activities outside the house. Mothers could be
embarrassed in public places by behaviour that they
could tolerate in the privacy of their own home.
Mrs. G.R. described the problems in the following
way:

> She won't sit still, she's shooting from table
> to table and shooting into the other corner,
> and she's like that all the time. She'll be
> pinching off the other people's plates. I
> could never take her into a restaurant.

Eight year old Lillian's eating behaviour also
caused Mrs. R.H. a lot of inconvenience and embarrassment in public.

Mrs. R.H.:   Mealtimes is a messy job. Her table
             manners are shocking ... embarrassing if
             there are other people around in a
             restaurant or some place like that. She
             spits and generally makes a hell of a
             mess. She'll lift her hand up and push
             you away and if you've got soup or rice
             pudding you've got it all down you
             before you know where you are.

Discussion. Meals are a social activity that form
the focus of most households and families. Indeed
in some ways a family may be defined as not only a
group of people who live together but also a group
of people who eat together. Eating, food and
mealtimes can both express and symbolise social
relations.[18] Disruption at mealtimes can, therefore, be especially disruptive of family life.
Again it was mothers who took the brunt of the
responsibility for the work. 69 children had to be
fed. 31 (45%) were always fed by their mothers, in
36 (52%) cases mothers sometimes got help and only
2 (3%) children were always fed by another member of
the family.

Occupying and supervising the children
    In discussing the work involved in caring for a
mentally handicapped child at home, we have concentrated on the caring activities. These activities
do not occupy all the time during which the children
are at home. The rest of the time can be classified
as leisure-time or play-time for the child. The

amount of work involved depends on how much the
child can occupy himself or herself and how much
supervision the child needs.

81 (67.5%) mothers said they had no problems in
supervising and occupying their child. Although
they would not leave their child alone in a
dangerous environment such as the kitchen or garden
they could safely leave them to play for half an
hour in a suitably prepared room. Mothers' confidence was closely related to their child's ability.
26 (96%) mothers of children with little or no
disability believed their child could play unattended for at least half an hour compared to 34 (89%)
mothers with moderately disabled children; 17 (47%)
mothers with severely disabled children and 4 (21%)
mothers with very severely disabled children. The
age of the child did not seem to be an important
factor in mothers' assessments.

Mrs. J.R. did not experience any problem in
keeping her seven year old daughter Helen occupied:

> She loves music. She colours a lot, and if we
> put toys out she'll come down and play with
> them. She likes playing in sand and in water.
> She can be left to play by herself for at least
> an hour sometimes.

Similarly Mrs. K.R. did not find much trouble
occupying her 16 year old son, Stanley, even though
she had reservations about the usefulness of his
leisure activities.

> He likes television, he likes playing cards but
> he can't read or write so there are lots of
> things he can't do. He just messes around the
> house half the time. This is very heart-
> breaking if I consider that he is now 16 but
> can't do anything constructive. He can't con-
> centrate at all ... but won't misbehave or
> endanger himself or anything.

In contrast Mrs. F.R. experienced difficulties
with her daughter Judith and the 24 hour a day
supervision Judith required placed considerable
restrictions on the whole family:

Mrs. F.R.: At these times you have all members of
the family around, but we can't do anything because we've got Judith with us
all the time. It's not so bad when my
husband is at work or her brother is at

at school ... a lot of frustration
builds up at these times because of
the restrictions on the whole family.
It's too tiring and difficult to take
her anywhere so we just don't bother.

11 mothers found the problems of supervision
extremely difficult. They believed their child was
in constant danger of injury or of damaging the
environment and needed continual supervision. Mrs.
K.K.'s son David was overactive and tended to
destroy his surroundings.

Interviewer: What might happen if you left David in
a room by himself?
Mrs. K.K.: Well, everything will go up in flames
for a start. TV will be switched off
(TV switches had been detached, the
gas fire was in a cage to prevent
David tampering with them). All
drawers will be left open with their
contents scattered about, lights will
be switched on and off. Oh no, you
daren't. You have to be there. You
can't leave him by himself. I learnt
that long ago!
Interviewer: What did he do?
Mrs. K.K.: He turned the hot tap on and scalded
himself ... he's always on the go.
He has no sense of danger whatsoever.
He needs constant attention.

Mrs. O.'s experience with her overactive and
demanding son seemed to sum up the plight of many
mothers.

Mrs. O.: You can't trust him not to touch the
things you've told him he mustn't
touch. He's always on the go ... so
can never trust him not to go anywhere near the things that could harm
him. I belt to the loo and belt
back down again because he'll have
done something naughty in the space of
time it takes me to get up and come
down again. It is the constant attention ... you have to be there. During
the holidays and weekends he sends me
up the wall ... you're sort of on edge
all the time. This is the biggest
drawback with a mentally handicapped

                    child, you can't leave him alone.

Discussion. The need to keep a child occupied was
related to the extent mothers felt they could leave
the child. By the time most children reach their
third year at school, mothers need to provide only
limited supervision. For mentally handicapped
children the amount of supervision required tends
to relate more to the child's disability than to his
or her age. Many mothers were tied to the care of
a highly dependent child for many hours each day
with no break apart from the time that their child
attended school.
     Again it was the mother that provided the bulk
of the support, although in this case, as Table
6.3 indicates, she tended to receive rather more
support with this range of activities compared to
the support they received with caring activities.

Table 6.3   Division of labour in the family in
            relation to supervision

Supervision	Mother always does it	Mother receives help from another member of household	Another member* of household always does it	Total number of children requiring supervision
After school	50 (43%)	64 (56%)	1 (1%)	115
Weekends	29 (25%)	84 (73%)	2 (2%)	115
School holidays	44 (37%)	73 (62%)	1 (1%)	118
Baby-sitting	18 (18%)	58 (59%)	22 (22%)	98

* For baby-sitting the figure in this column
  includes 7 families who regularly used an outside
  babysitter.

THE DIVISION OF LABOUR IN THE FAMILY

     In the first section of this chapter we examin-
ed the type of care families have to provide for
their mentally handicapped children and suggested
that the bulk of the work is carried out by mothers.
The mothers did the majority of the physical care

jobs, such as dressing and feeding the children. In this section we shall extend this discussion by looking in more detail at the division of labour in the household.

Father's participation in different types of activity

The study of housework and child-care is a relatively neglected area in spite of the fact that a large proportion of the population spend most of their time engaged in rearing children and looking after the home. Researchers have recently devoted more attention to this topic and it casts some light on the division of labour inside the family. As in other studies of other aspects of the family, the perspective adopted by the researcher has affected the type of questions asked and answers received.

Two studies illustrate the problem. Young and Willmott in their study of families reported that 72% of the fathers performed tasks other than washing dishes at least once a week. They used this evidence to conclude that there is increasing symmetry in role relationships in the nuclear family. Young and Willmott commented on the men in their London sample:

> Husbands also do a lot of work in the home, including many jobs which are not at all traditional men's ones ... There is now no sort of work in the home strictly reserved for 'the wives', even clothes-washing and bed-making still ordinarily thought of as women's jobs were frequently mentioned by husbands as things they did as well. The extent of the sharing is probably still increasing.[19]

Oakley in contrast found that 60% of fathers in her sample had low levels of participation in housework and 45% had low levels of participation in child care.[20]

The difference between responses and classifications in these two studies is related to the type of questions asked and the way different responses were classified. Young and Willmott asked 113 questions in their interviews but only one question related to the domestic division of labour. Furthermore they did not differentiate between husbands who gave an occasional helping hand and husbands who helped regularly. In contrast Oakley asked for information about a whole range of child-care and household tasks and asked how frequently husbands had performed these tasks in a specified period.

In our study most of the women were married and lived with their husbands. We asked women how frequently their husbands participated in child care, child-minding and household jobs and our results tended to support Oakley's rather than Young and Willmott's view of the domestic division of labour. In all the main areas investigated fathers rarely took on major responsibilities. The main difference between specific tasks were ones in which the majority of fathers sometimes helped (Table 6.4) and tasks in which only a minority of fathers sometimes helped (Table 6.5). All the child-minding tasks appear in Table 6.4 and therefore in all these activities the majority of fathers always or sometimes helped. In contrast all the household chores appear on Table 6.5 and therefore in all these activities the majority of fathers never helped.

Table 6.4 Domestic Division of Labour: Activities in which the majority of fathers sometimes or always help

	Children needing help	Father helps: Always	Sometimes	Never
Child Minding				
At Weekends	105	2 (2%)	76 (72%)	27 (26%)
During School Holidays	108	1 (1%)	66 (61%)	41 (38&)
Babysitting	91	1 (1%)	50 (55%)	40 (44%)
After School	105	1 (1%)	51 (49%)	53 (50%)
Child Care				
Taking Child out for Play	107	4 (4%)	87 (81%)	16 (15%)
Keeping Child Occupied	105	1 (1%)	83 (79%)	21 (20%)
Putting Child to Bed	77	3 (9%)	36 (47%)	88 (44%)
Lifting Child	45	6 (13%)	17 (38%)	22 (49%)

The child care tasks were split between the two
tables. The main group of child care tasks appear
on Table 6.5 and the majority of fathers never helped in the basic caring tasks such as feeding and
toileting the child. In contrast fathers were more
willing to help with child care tasks that had a
child-minding component such as taking the child out
to play or keeping the child occupied (see Table
6.4).

Table 6.5   Domestic Division of Labour: Activities
            in which the majority of fathers never
            helped

	Children needing help	Father helps:		
		Always	Sometimes	Never
Child Care				
Attending to child in the night	73	5 (7%)	25 (34%)	43 (59%)
Feeding child	56	1 (2%)	23 (41%)	32 (57%)
Toileting child	74	1 (1%)	21 (28%)	52 (71%)
Getting child up in the morning	97	3 (3%)	23 (24%)	71 (73%)
Bathing child	92	3 (3%)	21 (23%)	68 (74%)
Washing child	96	1 (1%)	20 (21%)	75 (78%)
Dressing child	97	1 (1%)	17 (18%)	79 (81%)
Taking child to school	103	4 (4%)	14 (14%)	85 (82%)
Collecting child from school	102	4 (4%)	14 (14%)	84 (82%)
Getting child ready for school	101	2 (2%)	12 (12%)	87 (86%)
Household Tasks				
Shopping	–	2 (2%)	32 (27%)	86 (72%)
Washing dishes	–	2 (2%)	29 (24%)	89 (74%)
Cleaning house	–	2 (2%)	24 (20%)	94 (78%)
Cooking meals	–	1 (1%)	15 (13%)	104 (87%)
Washing/ironing	–	1 (1%)	6 (5%)	113 (94%)

Our interviews revealed a relatively low level
of participation of fathers in the household
activities. In general fathers' participation reflected the traditional concepts of divisions of
activities in the family. Studies of families without handicapped children indicate that fathers see
it as part of their role to play with their

children and keep them occupied whereas they see the
more physical aspects of care and housework as
female work.[21] This traditional division of labour
was transferred to families with a dependent or
handicapped member even though the amount of work
traditionally defined as female had increased greatly and mothers had to cope with a disproportionate
amount of the extra work.[22] Fathers had the power
to legitimately avoid, if they so wished, those
tasks they found less interesting and rewarding.[23]
For example many of the children in our study
generated large amounts of extra washing yet 94% of
the fathers in the study never provided any help
with the washing or ironing.

The women we interviewed generally accepted
this low level of participation as natural and
normal. For example Mrs. R.H.'s husband provided no
help with housework and she described the situation
in the following way:

Mrs. R.H.: He doesn't do any housework, unfor-
tunately.
Interviewer: Would you like him to?
Mrs. R.H.: Oh yes, anyone can do it, as far as
I'm concerned. Well, I suppose I
wouldn't expect him to put on an apron
and wash up and hoover unless I was
ill or something. A wife's work is to
look after one's family, feeding,
clothing, keeping clean and tidy ...
I would like him to help with the
children but I wouldn't expect him to
stay in and do the housework while I
went out to work ... somehow this
would be the wrong way round. He
works very hard (as a police officer)
and I wouldn't expect him to come
home and do anything in the house.

Differences between fathers in overall participation

To assess the overall contribution of fathers
to household activities we devised a scoring system
based on fathers' contribution to specific child-
care and household activities. For each item
individual fathers were given a score of one if they
always undertook the activity, half if they sometimes undertook them and zero if they never undertook them. A score of 18 for child care activities
indicated maximum participation in these activities
by an individual father and a score of 5 for house-

hold activities indicated maximum participation in household activities.

The overall scores of individual fathers was low. Only one father obtained a maximum score of 23 for both child-care and household activities. Only 2 other fathers scored over 11½. In view of the general low level of participation we focused on the relative participation of fathers in household activities and divided fathers into three groups: 'high participators', 'medium participators' and 'low participators'. High participators did more than other fathers in our sample but this doesn't mean they did a lot. Tables 6.6 and 6.7 indicate that even in relative terms the majority of fathers in our sample had low levels of participation in child care and especially in housework.

Table 6.6   Fathers' Participation in Child-Care
            (maximum score is 18)

Level of participation	Score	No.
Low	1½ and under	72 (60%)
Medium	2 - 4½	36 (30%)
High	over 4½	12 (10%)
TOTAL		120

Table 6.7   Fathers' Participation in Housework
            (maximum score is 5)

Level of participation	Score	No.
Low	1½ and under	108 (90%)
Medium	2 - 3	11 (9%)
High	3 and over	1 (1%)
TOTAL		120

There was some evidence to indicate that fathers did adjust to their activities to some extent, especially when their child was severely handicapped. 80% of fathers whose children we classified as very severely disabled had medium to high levels of participation in child-care activities. However when all child-care and household tasks were taken together no great difference emerged between the levels of participation of fathers with children of different types of disability. The child's severity of disability tended to be related more to the type of activities fathers participated in, e.g. lifting and feeding, rather than their overall level of participation.

As the severity of the child's disability had little effect on the fathers' level of participation we decided to explore other factors that might explain variations, especially social class, employment, status and age.

Fathers' participation and social class. Researchers have found that middle-class fathers tend to be more involved in child-care and household activities than working class fathers.[24] Although the numbers in our study were fairly small, the same pattern emerged in child-care activities but not in the housework (see Tables 6.8 and 6.9).

Table 6.8   Participation in Child-Care by Fathers: Social Class
(maximum score is 18)

Level of participation	Score	Middle class	Working class	Total
		Fathers' social class:		
Low	1½ and under	22 (49%)	34 (62%)	56
Medium	2 - 4	17 (38%)	17 (31%)	34
High	over 4½	6 (13%)	3 (6%)	9
TOTAL		45	54	99

Table 6.9   Participation in Housework by Fathers: Social Class
(maximum score is 5)

Level of participation	Score	Middle class	Working class	Total
		Fathers' social class:		
Low	1½ and under	41 (91%)	46 (85%)	87
Medium	2 - 3	3 (7%)	8 (15%)	11
High	3 and over	1 (2%)	0	1
TOTAL (100%)		45	54	99

However it is important to stress that both middle class and working class fathers had

144

relatively low levels of participation in domestic
activities. For both groups high levels of participation, even defined in relative terms, was the
exception not the rule. To suggest, as some
researchers have done, that the middle class families have joint conjugal roles whereas working class
families have segregated conjugal roles,[25] would be
seriously misleading. In only one of our families
was there anything approaching an even division of
labour between husband and wife.

Fathers' participation and employment status. The
low levels of fathers' participation we identified
in our study could have been the result of tension
experienced by many fathers between their family
and their job. There was no evidence in our study
to support this view. Unemployed fathers provided
the least support in either child-care or in housework. Furthermore the involvement of unemployed
fathers in child-care tended to take the form of
'keeping an eye' on the child (see Tables 6.10 and
6.11).

Table 6.10   Participation in Child-Care by Fathers:
              Employment
              (maximum score is 18)

		Fathers' Employment		
Level of participation	Score	Employed	Not Employed	Total
Low	1½ and under	56 (58%)	16 (71%)	72
Medium	2 - 4½	31 (32%)	5 (17%)	36
High	over 4½	9 (9%)	3 (13%)	12
TOTAL		96	24	120

Table 6.11   Participation in Housework by Fathers:
              Employment
              (maximum score is 5)

		Fathers' Employment		
Level of participation	Score	Employed	Not Employed	Total
Low	1½ and under	88 (88%)	24 (100%)	108
Medium	2 - 3	11 (11%)	0	11
High	3 and over	1 (1%)	0	1
Total		96	24	120

Fathers' participation and age. We felt there might be some relationship between fathers' age and their participation in domestic activities. This was indeed the case. Younger fathers tended to participate more in child care activities and in housework. The variations were fairly small and the disability of the child was an important factor. The younger fathers, in our study, tended to have the more severely disabled children. (See Table 6.12 and 6.13)

Table 6.12   Participation in Child-Care by Fathers: Age   (overall score is 18)

Fathers' Age

Level of participation	Score	Under 35	35 - 44	45 and over	Total
Low	1½ and under	11 (46%)	28 (50%)	33 (83%)	72
Medium	2 - 4½	10 (42%)	20 (36%)	6 (15%)	36
High	over 4½	3 (13%)	8 (14%)	1 (3%)	12
TOTAL		24	56	40	120

Table 6.13   Participation in Housework by Fathers: Age   (overall score is 5)

Fathers' Age

Level of participation	Score	Under 35	35 - 44	45 and over	Total
Low	1½ and under	20 (83%)	51 (91%)	37 (93%)	107
Medium	2 - 3	4 (17%)	5 (9%)	2 (5%)	11
High	3 and over	0	0	1 (2%)	1
TOTAL		24	56	40	120

Discussion. The fathers of the mentally handicapped children in our study provided their wives with minimal support in domestic activities. If fathers provided more help it tended to be help with child care activities rather than housework. Oakley's studies have identified similar trends.[26] She has suggested that increased involvement of fathers with children can in some cases have a detrimental effect on the woman's work load as the fathers' involvement

is often confined to the more enjoyable tasks such
as play and outings and the women are usually left
with the bulk of the hard, time-consuming tedious
domestic jobs.

The impact on mothers

The division of labour between mothers and
other members of the household varied according to
the type of job involved. Those jobs which required
a lot of physical contact with the child tended to
be done by the mother on her own. Conventionally
close physical contact is associated with 'mothering'
and the maternal role. Most fathers play little
part in the physical care of babies and young
children.[27] Our study indicated that this conventional division of responsibilities is to be found
in families with severely mentally handicapped
children even though these children are much older
and the burden of care is much greater.

Mothers generally found the supervision of
their children difficult. Although some of the
children had achieved a fair degree of independence
in areas such as dressing and eating, they still
frequently required constant supervision. The extent to which mothers received help with supervision
depended on the availability of other members of the
household. Although mothers received more support
with these activities a large minority still took
major responsibility for supervision. When mothers
received help with these child-minding responsibilities it often meant that both they and their
husband stayed at home. They were still closely
tied to the child even though another adult shared
the caring.

Mothers found the school holidays particularly
difficult. Mrs. L.M.'s comments summarised many
mothers' feelings about school holidays:

> During school terms I can always arrange my
> times in such a way that I'll do my shopping
> whilst he is at school. It is very difficult
> during school holiday time ... of course he
> doesn't go to school and he's at home all the
> time. I'm just tied at home all the time. I
> just cannot go out at all, and if I do attempt
> to go out, I'm a bag of nerves before I start
> because I don't know what I'm going to get when
> I eventually take him out. If I'm visiting
> relatives on the estate ... it's alright, but
> to go out and do shopping, this is the time

> when I just can't cope with him, because he
> just doesn't like the shopping, he doesn't like
> going into shops, he doesn't like waiting in
> queues and that's it.

Mothers took the brunt of both the physical
care and supervision. Conventionally supervision
and leisure activities are not identified as women's
work in the same way as physical care, and women
tend to receive far more assistance with these
activities. As Wilkin has observed, 'it is difficult
for most people who have not experienced such
problems to comprehend what life for these mothers
was like'.[28] It is a life of hard work and social
restrictions.

<u>Mothers and Care</u>. The mothers took and accepted the
main burden of care. All mothers reaffirmed their
determination to keep their child at home and out of
long-term residential care. None of the mothers we
talked to seemed to be 'cracking up' under the
strain or to find the burden intolerable. Indeed
some mothers did not find the caring all difficult.
For example a mother of a 4 year old Down's Syndrome
girl said she had been waiting for the terrible
problems to emerge but so far they had not and she
was actually enjoying looking after her child.
Where, she wondered, had she gone wrong?
    However many mothers resented the fact that
fathers took much less responsibility, emotionally
and practically, for the child. This resentment
exists in other families. McCormack, a mother of a
teenage multiply handicapped boy, has argued that it
can be much harder for a father with work commit-
ments to get to know a mentally handicapped child.[29]
Often, fathers do not have the time to get close to
their child. Some mothers we talked to felt their
husbands never understood or genuinely cared about
their handicapped child. The majority of mothers
(64%) we talked to felt that having a handicapped
child had improved their relationship with their
husband by giving them a common interest and a
common set of problems to deal with.[30]
    Most mothers found it difficult with the con-
stant burden of care to get a regular break. The
disabilities and behaviour of many of the children
imposed serious restrictions on the social activities of the family. Over half the mothers had not
gone out without their child in the six months
preceding our interview. Some mothers made a virtue

out of necessity and said they no longer wanted to
go out. 25 mothers who had not been out socially
in the previous 6 months said that nobody else could
look after their child while they were out. Typical
comments included:

> 'If I don't go with all the children, don't go
> at all'.
> 'I couldn't be bothered'.
> 'I'm not a going out person'.
> 'I don't like to leave her because she'd play
> up'.
> 'There's no suitable baby-sitter'.

Many mothers were worried about the future. 94
(78%) mothers said they were very worried about
their child's future. The greatest anxieties
existed amongst the mothers who felt they could not
leave their child unattended even for short periods.
Mothers were asked what they thought would
happen to their child when they became too old to
care or if they died.
4 (3%) mothers envisaged an independent future
for their child. In each case the child had little
or no disability. However even in these cases
mothers were worried about their child's ability to
function as a competent adult, especially in a
period of high unemployment. One mother was looking for a guardian to protect her child's financial
interests.
32 (27%) said their child would move to a
substitute family provided either by relatives or by
fostering. Most of the children were between 4 or
5 years old and these younger mothers had not yet
had time to worry about the future. They tended
to make comments such as 'It's not possible to
assess the future' and 'difficult to say as he's
young at the moment'.
46 (38%) expected their child to move to residential facilities. Most of these mothers had
children who were severely disabled. These mothers
were worried about the nature and quality of available facilities. Most were very hostile to the
idea of the traditional mental handicap hospital and
some talked about the scandals in these hospitals.
They were prepared to consider hostel facilities but
even for these facilities they were worried about
the lack of individual care and attention. All the
mothers stressed their children were unique, with
unique personalities, interests and preferences.
38 (32%) of the mothers did not want to talk

about the future and found the question threatening
and disturbing. Their comments illustrate their
serious worries about the future and includes such
remarks as, 'We couldn't bear to think about the
future', 'We never look ahead' and 'I live from day
to day'.

Comments. As in other families, the mothers in our
study provided the bulk of the care. The extra
burden of care did not result in greater support or
involvement from other members of the house.
Mothers were prepared to accept this care and did not
look for relief from within or outside the family.
The tension did manifest itself in their concerns
about the future.

CONCLUSION

The mothers we talked to were caring for children who required far more care and supervision than
other children of the same age. Moreover these
mothers could not look forward towards a decline in
their responsibilities and workload. In some cases
caring would become more difficult as both the
mother and child aged. Caring for the child tended
to dominate the mother's and the family life and in
spite of the increased workload there was little
evidence of a more equitable distribution of responsibilities between family members. There was little
evidence in our study to support Schaffer's view
that in families with mentally handicapped children
the workload is more evenly spread.[31]
All the mothers we interviewed wanted to keep
their severely mentally handicapped children at
home. These mothers were devoting their lives and
emotional and physical energy to the care of their
child. However, they cannot be on duty 24 hours a
day, 365 days a year and remain efficient. Many
mothers have reached breaking point because they
have never been given a break in caring for the
child.[32] The concept of community care, we have at
present, tends to stress the interests and needs of
the child but fails to give equal prominence to the
interests and needs of the family and especially the
mother. The family is a remarkably cheap and continuous treatment resource but it can be over
exploited.
There was little evidence of imminent collapse
of either mothers or the family in our study but a

lot of evidence of stress, especially concerns about
getting a break and worries about the future. The
school holidays seemed to create a special problem.
The special school provides both child-minding and
therapy services. It seems logical that the
facilities they possess should be accessible outside
the official school day. McCormack has identified
the long school holiday as the single biggest cause
of exhausted families who, dealing with difficult
children, were asking for residential care.[33]
There is a need for a flexible and acceptable baby-
sitting service and for 'neighbourhood units' where
mothers can leave a child for a few hours or over-
night. The short-term fostering schemes in Leeds,
Somerset and Northumberland demonstrate the practical and emotional support which can be given by
substitute families.[34]

Many mothers were extremely worried and concerned about the future, especially they were
worried about the nature and quality of existing
residential facilities. Most mothers were unaware
of the developments of alternatives to traditional
facilities such as projects involving mentally
handicapped people living in ordinary houses and
flats, small group homes or substitute family care.

NOTES

1. M. Young and P. Willmott, The Symmetrical
    Family, Penguin, 1975, p. 114.
2. E. Bott, Family and Social Network, Tavistock,
    (2nd ed.), 1971.
3. See for example, R. Fletcher, The Family and
    Marriage in Britain, Penguin, (2nd ed.), 1966;
    R.O. Blood and D.M. Wolfe, Husbands and Wives,
    Free Press,Glencoe, 1960.
4. J. Platt, 'Some problems in measuring the
    jointness of conjugal role-relationships',
    Sociology, 3, 3, 287-97, 1969. See also C.
    Turner, 'Conjugal roles and social networks: a
    re-examination of an hypothesis', Human
    Relations, 20, 2, 121-30, 1967; B.E. Harrell-
    Bond, 'Conjugal role behaviour', Human
    Relations, 22, 1, 77-91; R. Rapoport and
    R.N. Rapoport, Dual-Career Families, Penguin,
    1971.
5. A. Oakley, The Sociology of Housework, Robert-
    son, 1974, pp. 161-5.
6. D.M. Toomey, 'Conjugal roles and social net-
    works in an urban working class sample', Human
    Relations, 24, 5, 417-31, 1971.

7.   A. Oakley, The Sociology of Housework, p. 138.
8.   Ibid., p. 146.
9.   Ibid., p. 149.
10. Ibid., p. 159.
11. Ibid., p. 160.
12. H. Land, 'Women: supporters or supported' in
     D.L. Barker and S. Allen (eds.), Sexual
     Divisions and Society: Process and Change,
     Tavistock, 1976; H. Wainwright, 'Women and the
     Division of Labour', in P. Abrams (ed.), Work,
     Urbanism and Inequality, Weidenfeld and
     Nicholson, 1978, pp. 160-205.
13. Report of the Committee, One-Parent Families,
     Vol. 1 (Chairman: Sir Morris Finer, Cmnd.
     5629, H.M.S.O., 1974, p. 338.
14. Ibid., p. 338.
15. See for example, Rapoport and Rapoport, Dual-
     Career Families; and D. Marsden, Workless:
     Some Unemployed Men and Their Families,
     Penguin, 1975.
16. Patrick Jenkin, Secretary of State for the
     Social Services, recently reaffirmed this point
     in a speech to the Association of Directors of
     Social Services when he said: 'Family, not
     state, should be the first port of call'. See
     excerpts of his address in DHSS Press Release
     No. 80/233, 19 September. See also DHSS, A
     Happier Old Age: A Discussion Document on
     Elderly People in Our Society,
     H.M.S.O., 1978; H. Land and R. Parker, 'United
     Kingdom' in S.B. Kamerman and A.J. Kahn (eds.),
     Family Policy: Government and Family in
     Fourteen Countries, Columbia University Press,
     New York, 1978.
17. D. Wilkin, Caring for the Mentally Handicapped
     Child, Croom Helm, 1979, p. 63.
18. M. Douglas, 'Deciphering a Meal' in M. Douglas,
     Implicit Meanings, Routledge and Kegan Paul,
     1975.
19. See Young and Willmott, The Symmetrical Family,
     p. 94.
20. Oakley, The Sociology of Housework, p. 137.
21. Ibid., p. 139 and J. Newson and E. Newson,
     Infant Care in an Urban Community, Allen and
     Unwin, 1963, p. 135.
22. See also Wilkin, Caring for the Mentally
     Handicapped Child, p. 127.
23. See also S. Edgell, Conjugal Role Relation-
     ships among Professional Workers and Their
     Wives at the Child-Rearing Stage of the Family
     Cycle,

unpublished Ph.D. Thesis, University of
Salford, 1975, esp. Chapter 4.

24. See Oakley, The Sociology of Housework; Edgell,
Conjugal Role Relationships; Newson and
Newson, Infant Care in an Urban Community.

25. See especially Bott, Family and Social
Network.

26. A. Oakley, Sex, Gender and Society, Temple
Smith, 1972.

27. Newson and Newson, Infant Care in an Urban
Community.

28. Wilkin, Caring for the Mentally Handicapped
Child, p. 116.

29. M. McCormack, A Mentally Handicapped Child in
the Family, Constable, 1978.

30. See for example ibid.

31. H.R. Schaffer, 'The Too-cohesive family: a
form of group pathology', The International
Journal of Social Psychiatry, 10, 4, 1964.

32. See for example, Wilkin, Caring for the Handi-
capped Child; McCormack, A Mentally Handi
capped Child in the Family; G. Pugh and P.
Russell, Shared Care: Support Services for
Families with Handicapped Children; National
Children's Bureau, 1977.

33. M. McCormack, 'The handicapped child in the
family', in British Institute of Mental Handi-
cap, Family Placements for Mentally Handicapped
Children: Report of a Residential Workshop,
British Institute of Mental Handicap,
Kidderminster, 1980.

34. J.D. Cooper, Patterns of Family Placements:
Current Issues in Fostering and Adoption,
National Children's Bureau, 1978.

Chapter 7

CARE BY THE COMMUNITY

INTRODUCTION

In Chapter 6 we examined the care problems
created by the mentally handicapped children in our
study. We found that these children generated extra
work, especially extra household work, and they
needed more care and supervision. We, then,
examined the extent to which the structure of the
family adjusted to deal with this additional burden
of work and we found that there was little evidence
of a radical change in the division of activities in
the family. Mothers provided the majority of the
labour and tended to take on the extra work involved in caring for a mentally handicapped child. In
this chapter we shall develop the discussion by
examining the availability and use of informal
support outside the family, especially the help
provided by relatives, neighbours and friends.

THE SOCIAL NETWORK IN THE COMMUNITY

It is generally agreed that the industrialization and urbanization of society has radically
changed the nature and role of the family and its
relationship to its social environment. In pre-
industrial society the family is part of a web of
kinship and an individual's identity and social
status is closely identified with his or her
position in this web of kinship. The family and
associated kinsmen form the basic economic, social
and political units of society. A person without
kin is virtually a non-person.[1] Industrialization
reduces the importance of the family and kinship.
Many of the functions of the kin network are taken
over by specialist institutions. For example the

socialization of children is increasingly undertaken by an education system and the care of the
sick by a health care system.

The reductions in the scope and significance of
kinship is associated with the increased importance
of the nuclear family, a unit of husband, wife and
dependent children residing in a single household.
Some researchers have suggested that the nuclear
family is a product of and fits ideally with
industrial society. Parsons has described the
'isolated conjugal family' as the normal household
unit in American society. He has argued that the
modern economic system demands individual social
and economic mobility and therefore weakens kinship
that ties an individual to a specific geographic
location. If the mobile nuclear family is, indeed,
characteristic of industrial society then the
capacity of the community to care for disabled and
dependent individuals is seriously reduced when
compared to the caring capacity of pre-industrial
societies.[2]

Research work conducted in the 1950s and 60s
had indicated that the nuclear family may not be so
isolated as initial research in the USA indicated it
was. Litwak, Sussman and Burchenall[3] have argued
that kinship ties outside the nuclear family remain
important for most individuals in industrial
society. Litwak has suggested that modern society
is characterized by modified extended families
rather than isolated families. Nuclear families
linked by kinship ties tend to cluster together for
mutual support. Each family unit acts autonomous
but there is mutual exchange between families at
times of crisis or to symbolise continuing relations
at annual festivities such as Christmas.[4]

These networks or clusters of linked nuclear
families have been identified in both middle class
and working class communities in England. For
example studies by Young and Willmott and Townsend
identified working class communities with patterns
of inter-family aid and support.[5] Similarly Bell,
in his study of middle class families during the
early years of marriage, identified patterns of
support and aid even though these families were
mobile and were often geographically separated from
relatives.[6] The interrelationship between families
remains important even though the precise pattern
of relationship and support is dependent on the
circumstances and needs of the family.

The families we studied experienced additional
problems with the care and support of a mentally

handicapped child and we were interested to examine the extent to which these families could mobilise the assistance of support of relatives.

As well as relations with kin, the nuclear family can utilise and exploit non-kin relations. Litwak and Szelenyi have identified primary groups as important units in the social fabric of industrial society. These primary groups include kinship groupings, neighbours and friends.[7] Litwak and Szelenyi suggest that primary groups play an important part in industrial society by providing a rapid and flexible response to problems and crises that agencies with their formalised and bureaucratic structure cannot provide. For instance neighbours can look after children for five minutes, can take messages or even provide a cup of sugar needed for a meal. Bott has argued nuclear families are not isolated. They possess social networks of varying densities and can usually mobilise support in a crisis.[8]

The concept of community care implies that the family with a mentally handicapped child can and will draw on a variety of support systems. Studies have indicated that this tends to be official wishful thinking. For example Moncrieff's study of 150 families with adult mentally handicapped members indicated that 'although informal community support in this study did exist it was slight in content and sporadic in application'.[9] In the rest of this chapter we shall examine what support was available to our mothers from relatives and other informal sources.

SUPPORT FROM RELATIVES

The concept of a relative contains some ambiguities between relations by marriage and relation by blood. For the purposes of this study we disregarded these ambiguities and asked mothers who they recognised as relatives. With surprising consistency mothers described a well-defined group of people as relatives. These included her own and her husband's parents, brothers and sisters and nephews and nieces. In a few the circle was widened to include her own and her husband's aunts and uncles. In three cases mothers mentioned grown-up adopted sons.

The importance attached to the relations with these kinfolk varied considerably. Some mothers described relatives as if they were part of the

family, i.e. although living in separate houses they
interacted frequently and were important in the life
and organisation of the family. In five cases a
relative lived in the same house and was part of the
household. Three families had moved house to be
closer to their relatives. In contrast some mothers
classified relatives in a more distant and formal
way and treated them as secondary in importance to
real friends who lived closer and with whom they had
more in common. In a few cases relatives had not
been seen for years and contact consisted of an exchange of Christmas cards and infrequent letters.
In one case a family had changed houses to move
away from relatives 'because it was so embarrassing
for them'. The main difference between relatives
seemed to be between those that lived close and
those who were more distant and we shall consider
interactions with these two groups of relatives in
turn.

Support from relatives who lived close

We defined relatives who lived close as relatives who lived within 30 minutes travelling time.
87 (73%) of the families had relatives who lived
close. In the majority of cases these relatives
provided regular (65 cases) or infrequent (6 cases)
support. Only 16 mothers with close relatives said
they never received support from their close
relatives and in 10 cases they themselves had to
provide support for an aged relative. Mrs. R.A.
described her situation in the following way: 'I
couldn't ask my mother because she's over eighty and
she's the one we have to look after'.

The 6 mothers who did not receive help from
relatives were rather evasive about the reasons:

Interviewer: Do you feel you could ask them for
help if you need it, for instance, if
you were ill?

Mrs. L.R.:   I'm not sure. We never ask. You
always feel if people volunteer they
want to do it, and if they don't volunteer they don't so you don't ask.
None of our relatives have ever
offered to have him for a weekend to
give us a break. They never offer to
help in any way.

An important factor in the type and extent of
support appeared to be the precise relation of close

157

kinsfolk to the mother. Mothers were more likely to
receive support from their own blood relatives than
from their husband's blood relatives. For example
of the 65 mothers who received support from close
relatives 52 received it from mothers' blood relatives and 45 mothers received regular help from their
own mother. In contrast only 5 mothers received
help from her husband's mother. As Jaehnig has
noted, most mothers preferred assistance from their
blood relatives.[10] Relatives on the husband's side
of the family tended to act as a secondary source of
support, supplementing aid from the mothers side or
giving primary support only when the mothers'
relatives could not. Mothers did receive a significant amount of support from their relatives. The
support was rather similar to the sort provided by
their husbands. Relatives helped mainly with the
supervision and baby-sitting. The mother had to do
the bulk of housework and child-care herself. (See
Table 7.1).

Table 7.1   Areas in which relatives provided support

	Number of mothers receiving help
Baby-sitting	67 (56%)
Moral support	55 (46%)
Caring for another child	46 (38%)
Caring for handicapped child	41 (34%)
Housework	11 (9%)
Finance	7 (6%)

41 mothers said that relatives sometimes cared
for their handicapped child but this help was
usually restricted to emergencies and restricted.

Mrs. F.R.:   They'll look after her for the odd
hour provided there's no feeding or
changing or anything of that nature
involved. I could take her in while
I went to the shop for five minutes,
when it is raining, but not long-term
help.

4 mothers said that their parents frequently took
their handicapped child for weekends. In all 4
cases the child concerned had little disability. In
10 cases relatives were willing to take non-handicapped children for weekends and in 6 families the
non-handicapped children spent their summer holidays

with their grandparents so that their mothers could
devote more attention to the handicapped child.
Over half the families in the study had received help with baby-sitting in the previous month.
This help was greatly appreciated but some mothers
felt that even this type of help was not available
when it was most needed.

Mrs. F.R.:   They (relatives) are too busy looking
after their own, so, of course, their
own needs come before yours. My oldest sister is more one for her own
little family, but she's very good and
in an emergency I could rely on her.

Many mothers (55) referred to the moral support
they received from relatives. This support did not
take the same tangible support as baby-sitting or
help with child care but was intangible emotional
and psychological support. Often it took the form
of regular visits and contacts which actually
increased the workload. Nevertheless mothers
derived considerable comfort from these visits. One
mother commented 'My sister's sons and three neices,
they come every other Saturday. I always have a
houseful on Saturday'. The ability to engage in
normal reciprocal social activities was highly
prized even if it increased the workload.
There were five mothers who received regular
daily help with housework and child care but in all
cases the relative who provided the help was living
with the family and could therefore be seen as a
member of the nuclear family.

Support from distant relatives
Mothers generally did receive limited support
and help from close relatives. But a sizeable
minority of mothers (33) had no close relatives.
Litwak and Szelenyi have argued that the mobility of
families in industrial society means that help from
close kin must be supplemented by help from more
distant kin. For kin network to function as viable
support system kin must learn to communicate and
exchange help in other ways than the traditional
face-to-face exchanges, especially through loans or
gifts.[11]
25 of the mothers who did not have close kin
to provide support also did not receive any support
from more distant relatives. Many of these mothers
said they would not have expected these relatives to

help them even if they had lived closer. The other
8 mothers all received help in one way or another.
Two families received regular help with financing
their holidays and two families had received help
with buying a car. In four cases the relative who
provided help lived abroad. Again the help provided
was mainly financial. However one mother said her
parents lived in Sweden and her mother regularly
visited England to help her. Another mother said
her mother lived in Canada and during the summer
holidays 'the other children go to stay with their
grandparents so I could be free to devote my attention to the handicapped boy'.

Discussion. Many survey mothers obtained help and
support from their kinfolk. The amount of help
varied according to the precise relationship and the
physical distance. The mothers tended to receive
the maximum amount of help from their own mother,
especially if she was physically able and actually
formed part of the household. Mothers tended to
receive less help from their husbands' relatives
and more distant relatives.
    The type of help and assistance these relatives
were able and willing to provide varied considerably
but it tended to be similar to the support provided
by husbands. The mothers maintained major responsibilities for housework and child care and the
relatives were willing to help with baby-sitting and
moral support. It is important not to undervalue
the help of activities such as moral support. They
may be essential in helping the mother maintain
social relations outside the house and a sense of
normality.

SUPPORT FROM FRIENDS AND NEIGHBOURS

    Sometimes relatives were both neighbours and
friends but generally the mothers we interviewed
clearly differentiated four separate groups: close
relatives, distant relatives, friends and neighbours
and they had different expectations of each group.

Support from friends
    Friendship is a difficult relationship to
define and different individuals define it in
different ways and have different expectations of
their friends. However a key characteristic is

choice. Individuals choose their friends and can
change their friends. As Allan suggests 'a friend's
"real self" is appreciated and enjoyed for its own
sake'.[12]

Survey mothers chose and developed their
friendship in a variety of manners and from a
variety of sources including neighbours, workmates,
childhood acquaintances, people met on holiday and
members of their church. Mothers seemed to select
friends with whom they had common interests and
backgrounds and with whom they could share activities and friendships.

Mothers indicated that changes in their life
style such as a move to a new neighbourhood resulted
in the neglect of some friendships and the development of new ones. The birth of a handicapped child
created a change in their life styles and led to a
changed pattern of friendship. The birth of the
handicapped child generally disrupted the basis of
friendship patterns. It created a new range of
experiences and problems that these friends could
not share. For example the handicapped child did
not grow up and develop in the same way as the
children of friends. There were often practical
difficulties in visiting. Friends unfamiliar with
mentally handicapped children often did not know
how to react to the child or were embarrassed by the
child's behaviour.

23 (19%) mothers said they had lost friends
after the birth of their handicapped child. Mrs.
N.S. who, in addition to her mentally handicapped
children, had two other grown-up mentally handicapped children, described the effect of having
mentally handicapped children on her friends in the
following way:

Mrs. N.S.: Yes definitely. I had a lot of
friends before the mentally handicapped children were born ... but
they (friends) just seemed to drift
away.

Interviewer: Why did they drift away?

Mrs. N.S.: With close friends we found that the
children and their parents began to
be self-eliminating. Their children
grew and left yours behind. They
didn't know how to react to you and
the children and they easily became
embarrassed by your child's behaviour.

161

For mothers the selection and maintenance of
friendship was influenced by the problems of their
mentally handicapped child. For example some
mothers felt that they should warn all potential
friends of their situation to avoid embarrassment or
disappointment at a later stage in the development
of the friendship.

Mrs. N.T.:   We sort of made friends with people and
              having brought into the conversation
              that we have a handicapped child, or
              when children have come into the
              conversation and we've said straight
              out that we have a handicapped child,
              you don't see those people any more
              because they don't know how to talk to
              you after that.

Some mothers chose friends who could be useful
and understanding. 46 (38%) mothers had friends who
had a handicapped child at school and 38 mothers
said that they had found new friends at organisations
associated with mental handicap such as the special
school, the local branch of MENCAP or the Down's
Syndrome Association.

15 mothers said they had nobody they could
classify as a friend and saw their mentally handicapped child as the main cause of their social
isolation. Many housewives who are mothers of non-
handicapped children experience similar isolation
and it was difficult to disentangle from mothers'
accounts their precise cause of their isolation.[13]

Mothers, if they had a friend, did not see them
as a major source of practical assistance and, as
Table 7.2 shows, the majority did not receive any
practical help from friends.

Table 7.2   The practical help received from friends

Type of help	No. of mothers	
Baby-sitting/child minding	16	(13%)
Playing with child	8	(7%)
Taking child for a day or two	7	(6%)
Taking child for a walk	4	(3%)
Watching child play in the street	4	(3%)
Shopping for mother	4	(3%)
Feeding child	2	(2%)

The type of support which friends provided was
similar to the support provided by fathers and close

relatives. There was some evidence of help with
child supervision but the basic work of housekeeping
and child care was very much the mothers responsibility. Only in exceptional cases did the actual
quality of support significantly ease the mothers'
work load. Three families had developed relationships with students. These students had no children
of their own and provided help with baby-sitting and
occupying the child. Six families established
relationships involving payments for services.
These payments were for baby-sitting but in two
cases the baby-sitter also fed and played with the
child and was willing to shop.

   Some families had developed reciprocal exchange
relationships mainly concerned with baby-sitting
and mainly with other parents of mentally handicapped children. Mrs. N.U. described one of these
arrangements in the following way:

Mrs. N.U.:   My friend has a Down's Syndrome girl.
              Anne would go there and sleep the
              night. My friend's girl is coming for
              the weekend after next because her
              parents would be away.

   As with relatives many mothers valued friends
more for the emotional than the practical support
they provided, especially if these friends shared
the same experiences.

Mrs. R.:   We all cry together. One of my
              friend's little girl has just come off
              a life support machine and I got a
              phone call last night that the other
              friend, her little girl, has gone in
              and she's in the next bed to Lucy who
              has just come off the life support
              machine. Then I'll be in there next
              week with my Diana. The three of us
              always go to the coffee mornings
              together, and quite frankly, I think
              mothers of handicapped children are
              the best friends.

Support from neighbours and the neighbourhood

   Families do not choose their neighbours.
Families may choose to live in specific neighbourhoods but they have little control of the other
people who live in the same neighbourhood. Neighbours share certain services and facilities such as

shops, bus routes, school and pubs. Neighbours
have social organisations such as tenants' associations, churches, school parent-teacher associations
that may form an important focus of local social
interaction.[14]
   Families of mentally handicapped children face
a dilemma in relationship to their neighbours. The
relationship with a friend is voluntary but their
interaction with neighbours is a result of having
chosen accommodation in the same neighbourhood. The
families in our study all had neighbours yet their
experience of the neighbourhood and use of neighbourhood facilities was very different to their
neighbours. For example, most children go to local
neighbourhood schools, whereas mentally handicapped
children attend special schools that are usually
outside the neighbourhood and go in a special bus.
Thus the social activities and interactions associated with taking a young child to school are not
available for the mothers of mentally handicapped
children.
   Mothers identified three different types of
neighbour. In the first group were neighbours they
referred to as friends because they shared confi-
dences with these neighbours and exchanged help. 35
mothers said they had this type of neighbour and 7
of the 16 friends who baby-sat for mothers (see
Table 7.2) were neighbours. These neighbours provided a variety of the assistance identified in
Table 7.2 as help from friends. One particular
mother (Mrs. N.U.) had established a network of
supportive neighbours to help her care for her
handicapped child. One of these neighbours also had
a handicapped child and the relationship of these
two families was so close that Mrs. N.U.'s daughter
Anne referred to Mrs. N.U.'s friend as 'Auntie
Barb' even though the two families were not related.[15]
The other four neighbours Mrs. N.U. described as
her friends did not have mentally handicapped
children and Mrs. N.U. described her relationship
with them in the following way:

Mrs. N.U.:   We help each other with the children,
               we go out socially and we go on
               holidays together. There are four of
               us around here ... we all help and
               rely on each other. We've known our-
               selves for so long.

   The development of close relationships with
neighbours was related to the families' length of

residence in the neighbourhood. The longer a mother
had lived in a neighbourhood, the better was her
relationship with her neighbours. All 7 mothers who
received neighbours' help with baby-sitting and
child-minding and all 4 mothers whose neighbours
watched the child play in the street were well-
established in the neighbourhood and had lived in the
same house since the birth of their handicapped
child.

In the second group were neighbours described
by mothers as understanding, sympathetic and
congenial but detached. They were acquaintances
rather than friends. 76 (63%) said they received no
practical help from their neighbours but they saw
and communicated with them quite frequently. The
following comments were typical:

Mrs. N.W.: They understand, but we don't have a
            great deal to do with them ... they
            don't ignore him. They have a chat to
            him, but they don't get really
            involved.

Mrs. N.X.: They don't complain about the noise
            ... they're not nasty, but they just
            don't want to know.

A small minority (10, 8%) of mothers found
their neighbours unfriendly or hostile. Neighbours
in this group were unsympathetic to the mother and
her handicapped child.

Mrs. N.Z.:   My neighbours don't bother with us ...
               there's one women down the terrace who
               had a lot off about Mark, but I put
               her wise about him and since then
               she's been alright to him.
Interviewer: What happened?
Mrs. N.Z.:   Her son went by and tapped Mark on the
               nose. I was looking out of the win-
               dow and I saw him walking up to Mark
               and saying to the other children
               things about Mark and I shouted to him
               to leave my Mark alone ... His mother
               came out and there was a bit of a row
               ...

Although mothers received very little and
limited help from neighbours, such support as they
received was greatly appreciated because it established their identify as good and normal neighbours.

CONCLUSION: SUPPORT FOR MOTHERS

In this conclusion we shall discuss the support that mothers received both inside and outside the family. We found it difficult to use the findings of other researchers as a basis for comparison with our findings because most other studies have used a different approach. For example Bott and Gavron concentrated on families assessment of what fathers would and should do rather than on what fathers actually did.[16] As Wilkin points out, finding out what people believe fathers should do may be useful in examining attitudes to the domestic division of labour but it may not tell us much about what fathers actually do.[17] There are other studies that have used similar techniques to the ones we employed and asked questions about the type of activities fathers and others performed and the ways in which they helped and supported mothers.

In the main these studies indicated rather higher levels of support than we were able to find in our study. For example Hewett described half of the fathers in her study as high participants in domestic work; Bayley reported that 39% of the fathers contributed a lot and Wilkin found a quarter of the fathers contributed a high level of support.[18] Even with fairly low criteria of support we could only classify 10% of the husbands in our study as providing a high level of support. With contributions from outside the family the discrepancies between our findings and those of other studies were somewhat similar. Carr reported that 50% of the families she studies received help from relatives and we identified 59% of the families as receiving help from relatives.[19] Jaehnig found that 37% of the families in his study received some help from neighbours and Bayley identified 26% of the families in his study as receiving a lot of support from neighbours.[20] In our study we identified 29% of mothers as receiving help from neighbours of a fairly limited kind.

There was no evidence that the discrepancies between our studies and these other studies was a result of looking at different families. As far as we could judge there was little difference in the families examined in terms of composition, social class or area of residence. The reasons for the discrepancies related to the ways the studies were conducted, especially in the type of activities studied and the ways in which different levels of support were defined. We specifically excluded

activities that we felt were peripheral to the basic
job of running the house and caring for the child,
such as gardening or decorating. We collected
specific information about what individuals did in
relationship to specific domestic jobs and did not
ask vague generalised questions such as 'do you get
any help from the neighbours'. We also defined
levels of participation in specific quantitative
ways. In other studies terms such as 'highly
participant', 'much', 'considerable support' and 'a
good deal' tend to remain as vague undefined
generalisations. Our findings are closer to the
finding of other studies that examined specific
activities and quantify the results. For example,
Oakley in her study of housework found that 60% of
fathers had low levels of participation.[21] In our
study we identified 60% of fathers as having low
levels of participation.

In examining the support received by mothers we
have identified a fairly consistent pattern.
Mothers have to take the main burden of housework,
they receive limited help with child care and most
of the help they receive is with child supervision.
The difference between the help provided by members
of the nuclear family, relatives and friends or
neighbours is not in terms of type of help provided
but in amount, i.e. neighbours could be relied on
to keep the occasional eye on the child whereas
fathers could usually be relied on to consistently
supervise the child. This pattern of help meant
that mothers with the most disabled children often
received the least help and support. The most
disabled children needed a lot of physical care,
which the mothers tended to provide and had little
need for supervised play, an area in which mothers
would have received more help and support. Thus the
general problem of the low levels of support and
help identified in our study is exacerbated by the
fact that the mothers of most disabled children tend
to receive the least help.

The burden of caring for a severely mentally
handicapped school child at home falls mainly on the
mother. Conventionally women are seen as primarily
responsible for the home, housework and child-care.
Despite the increased workload associated with a
mentally handicapped child, the mother maintains
primary responsibility and takes on the majority of
the extra work. Indeed the more disabled the child
the more responsibility she takes on. Father,
relatives, friends and neighbours do provide support
and help of a limited specific type. Mothers

valued this help and support as it often established
and maintained their status as a normal person, a
normal mother, a good friend and neighbour.

NOTES

1. A dominant theme in the study of other cultures
    is the study of kinship. See for example, J.A.
    Barnes, <u>Three Styles in the Study of Kinship</u>,
    Tavistock, 1971, p. xxi.
2. T. Parsons, 'The kinship system of the contem-
    porary United States', reprinted in T. Parsons,
    <u>Essays in Sociological Theory</u>, (revised ed.),
    Free Press, New York, 1964.
3. E. Litwak, 'Extended kin in an industrial
    society' in E. Shanas and G.F. Streib (eds.),
    <u>Social Structure and the Family: Generational</u>
    <u>Relations</u>, Prentice-Hall, Englewood Cliffs,
    1965; M.B. Sussman and L. Burchenall, 'Kin
    family network: unherald structure in current
    conceptualisations of family functioning',
    <u>Marriage and Family Living</u>, 24, 231-40, 1962.
4. See for example, E. Litwak, 'Occupational
    mobility and extended family cohesion', <u>American</u>
    <u>Sociological Review</u>, 25, 1, 9-21, 1960.
5. M.D. Young and P. Willmott, <u>Family and Kinship</u>
    <u>in East London</u>, Routledge and Kegan Paul, 1957;
    P. Townsend, <u>The Family Life of Old People:</u>
    <u>An Inquiry in East London</u>, Routledge and Kegan
    Paul, 1957.
6. C. Bell, <u>Middle Class Families: Social and</u>
    <u>Geographic Mobility</u>, Routledge and Kegan Paul,
    1968, p. 89.
7. E. Litwak and I. Szelenyi, 'Primary group
    structures and their functions: kin, neigh-
    bors and friends', <u>American Sociological Review</u>
    34, 4, 465-81, 1969.
8. E. Bott, 'Family and crisis' in J.D. Sutherland
    (ed.), <u>Towards Community Mental Health</u>,
    Tavistock, 1971.
9. J. Moncrieff, <u>Mental Subnormality in London</u>:
    <u>A Survey of Community Care</u>, Political and
    Economic Planning, 1966, p. 79.
10. W.B. Jaehnig, The Mentally Handicapped and
    Their Families, unpublished Ph.D. Thesis,
    University of Essex, 1974, p. 249.
11. Litwak and Szelenyi, 'Primary group structures
    and their functions'.
12. G.A. Allan, <u>A Sociology of Friendship and Kin-</u>
    <u>ship</u>, Allen and Unwin, 1979, p. 41.

13. H. Gavron, The Captive Wife: Conflicts of
     Household Mothers, Routledge and Kegan Paul,
     1966, Chapter 15; A. Oakley, The Sociology of
     Housework, Robertson, 1974, and A. Oakley,
     Housewife: High Value, Low Cost, Penguin,
     1976, Chapter 5.
14. E. Litwak, 'Voluntary associations and neigh-
     borhood cohesion', American Sociological Review,
     26, 2, 258-71, 1961; A.C. Emlen and J.B. Perry,
     'Child care arrangements', in L.W. Hoffman and
     F.I. Nye (eds.), Working Mothers, Jossey-Bass,
     San Francisco, 1974.
15. The use of kinship terms to identify close
     friends is a widespread phenomena that Firth
     et al. suggest emphasises the idealised
     qualities of both categories. See R. Firth,
     J. Hurbert and A. Forge, Families and their
     Relatives: Kinship in a Middle-Class Section
     of London, Routledge and Kegan Paul, 1969,
     Chapter 4.
16. E. Bott, Family and Social Network, Tavistock,
     (2nd ed.) 1971; Gavron, The Captive Wife.
17. D. Wilkin, Caring for the Mentally Handicapped
     Child, Croom Helm, 1979, p. 129
18. S. Hewett, The Family and the Handicapped Child:
     A Study of Cerebral Palsied Children in Their
     Homes, Allen and Unwin, 1970, p. 107; M.
     Bayley, Mental Handicap and Community Care: A
     Study of Mentally Handicapped People in
     Sheffield, Routledge and Kegan Paul, 1973,
     p. 265; Wilkin, Caring for the Mentally Handi-
     capped Child, p. 145.
19. J. Carr, 'Effects on the family of a child with
     Down's Syndrome', Physiotherapy, 62, 20-4,
     1976.
20. Jaehnig, The Mentally Handicapped and Their
     Families, p. 252; Bayley, Mental Handicap and
     Community Care, p. 281.
21. Oakley, The Sociology of Housework, p. 137.

Chapter 8

CARE IN THE COMMUNITY: THE ROLE OF WELFARE AGENCIES

INTRODUCTION

     In Chapters 6 and 7 we discussed the care
severely mentally handicapped school children need
and the sources of support available for mothers
from informal social network. We argued that the
children in our study created a great deal of extra
work and it was mainly the mothers that took on the
burden of this extra care. In this chapter we shall
examine how and in what ways formal agencies such as
the health services supplement the caring capacity
of mothers and the family and the extent to which
mothers found these services useful and helpful.
     It is difficult to assess the overall contri-
bution of different welfare agencies to the care and
well-being of the mentally handicapped. Therefore
in this chapter we examine the mothers' assessment
of the role of specific services. In the first
section we shall look at the role and relationship
of specific professionals. For the health service
we shall look at the relationship mothers have with
general practitioners and health visitors, for
personal social services their relationship with
field social workers and for the education service
their relationship with school teachers. In the
second section we shall contrast the contribution of
these professionals with the role and utility of
voluntary organisations. In the final section of
the chapter we shall examine in more detail the
provision of two types of support services - short
term care and financial assistance.

THE CONTRIBUTION OF WELFARE AGENCIES

     The mothers in our study had all, as a result

of their child's handicap, come into con
range of welfare agencies. The birth of
handicapped child resulted in changes in
and quality of support they received fro
agencies. In some cases they had to es
develop relationships with agencies or specialists
with whom they would not otherwise have had
relationships, e.g. teachers at special schools or
the Rowntree Family Fund and in other cases it
meant changes in an established relationship, e.g.
with a family medical practitioner. We have already
considered in Chapter 4 some aspects of the interactions mothers had with specialists during their
discovery of their child's mental handicap. In this
section we shall consider their current relationship
with various types of practitioner starting with the
family doctor.

The Family Doctor

The family doctor is a general medical
practitioner who provides his patients with advice
and medical services and acts as a point of entry to
a variety of more specialist services. An official
report has defined the family doctor as the co-
ordinator of 'services and especially as the link
point between the resources of the hospital and
those ... of the community services'.[1]
The family doctor should be a central figure in
the provision of welfare support for mothers and
families. The family doctor should have a wealth of
experience and knowledge that enables him or her to
counsel, advise and guide mothers in the care and
management of their handicapped child or to steer
them to the appropriate adviser or specialist. As
Wilkin, in his study of handicapped children in
Salford, reported 'parents wanted advice and information about the nature of the child's condition and
prospects for the future, particularly during the
early years and they wanted treatment for the usual
range of childhood illnesses which took account of
the special circumstances of a family with a mentally handicapped child'.[2]
The reality was very different. Mothers in our
survey had developed very low expectations of their
family doctor and their main contact with them was
in relationship to the treatment and management of
minor physical ailments. Many mothers said their
family doctors appeared to be unwilling to spare
the time to offer advice and information. Only 51
(42%) mothers found their GP helpful in caring for

ir child. For example the GP is in a position to
request home help services from the local authority
social service departments. These services include
cleaning, laundry, shopping and cooking and 59 (49%)
mothers said they would welcome such help. Only 5
(4%) received this help.[3] Mrs. A.D. summarised the
attitude of many mothers to their GP in the following way:

> He hasn't been of any particular help since he
> told me that Edward (now 4½ years old) was
> handicapped. He's never asked how I'm coping
> with Edward.

GPs are generalist and many have had little or
no training in mental handicap and its implications.
Compared to hospital specialists general practitioners undergo fairly limited post-registration training and their experience of both child care and
care of the handicapped can be limited. Holt and
Huntley's survey of medical school training highlighted the virtual absence of training at pre-
registration level in mental handicap.[4] The Court
Committee, which was appointed by the DHSS to review
child health services, recommended that the pre-
registration course for medical students should be
altered to include more information on child
development and handicap and called for more post-
registration training in this area.[5] Many mothers
felt that their general practitioners lacked
knowledge, understanding and experience of the
problems of families with mentally handicapped
children and therefore they did not expect practical
help from their GP.

Mrs. L.R.: They (family doctors) are there to
treat people and cure them, and I
think that's as far as they go. They
don't have a hand at all in the
handicapped child. I don't think they
really know what to do. They don't
know anything about it. They didn't
know about the Family Trust (Family
Fund) or who to get in touch with to
help me.

Some mothers felt that the GPs and the way they
organised their work created difficulties for the
parents of mentally handicapped children. Mrs. N.T.
described the special problems she experienced in
consulting her GP in the following way:

Mrs. N.T.:   It's not only tedious if you have to
                wait all morning with a handicapped
                child at the doctors; it's also dis-
                tressing and embarrassing. People
                stare. She looks normal until she
                starts to talk or dance about like
                she does, then people stare and pull
                faces because they don't realise that
                she's handicapped, and trying to keep
                her quiet is out of the question. It
                would be far better if you didn't
                have to sit and wait.

     Mothers in the present study were not alone in
experiencing problems in obtaining satisfactory
support from their family doctors. The Warnock
Committee, which enquired into the educational need
of handicapped children, commissioned research into
services for the under fives and this showed that
very few general practitioners visited families with
handicapped children when the problems were first
identified or subsequently.[6]

Health Visitors
     General practitioners are generalist who are
responsible for the general medical care of large
lists of patients and therefore tend to respond to
problems that patients bring to their surgery. In
contrast health visitors generally visit their
clients at home and they have traditionally concen-
traded on providing health advice to mothers with
babies and young children. The health visitor
ought to be able to overcome many of the problems
and limitations of the general practitioner. Indeed
the Warnock Committee identified health visitors as
potential 'named people' to whom parents of mentally
handicapped children under 5 could turn for advice
and counselling.[7]
     Only 17 (14%) mothers had been visited by a
health visitor in the previous year and 8 in the
previous six months. These visits had started when
the child was born and the mothers had had about 3
or 4 visits a year until the child reached school
age. From then on visits were related to specific
requests for services such as disposable nappies for
an incontinent child and the health visitor visited
to assess the need. Only one mother with a child
over 8 continued to receive regular visits and in
this case a special relationship had developed
between the mother and her health visitor. Mrs. R.J.

described her relationship with her health visitor
in the following way:

Mrs. R.J.: She will come occasionally of her own
accord, but I have her number and she
just says to me 'How's Frank, how are
you, do you need anything?', and
usually everything is alright so she'd
say, 'You've got my number, if you
want me, I'm there'.
Interviewer: How often does she come?
Mrs. R.J.: About two or three times a year, sometimes more, it depends.
Interviewer: Do you find this contact helpful?
Mrs. R.J.: Yes, she knows Frank and she knows me
and I really feel that I can talk to
her and let her know everything and
she's very interested. I have complete confidence in her, she's very
good.

The relationship between Mrs. R.J. and her
health visitor was atypical. Most mothers (90, 75%)
found their contact with their health visitor unhelpful. As with general practitioners mothers felt
health visitors lacked knowledge and understanding
of families with handicapped children. In addition
the rapid turnover of staff prevented the development of a long-term relationship. One mother with
7 children, three of whom were mentally handicapped,
commented:

I never bothered with the health visitor. I
didn't have a lot of patience with them because
half of them didn't have kids of their own, and
they tried to tell me how to bring mine up and
it just didn't work.

Another with a four-year old Down's Syndrome daughter said:

One used to come but she was totally useless.
She wasn't married, she had no children of her
own. She didn't know anything if I asked her.
I just dreaded the woman arriving. She was
positively unhelpful and on occasions quite
unpleasant. She used to think it was me spoil-
ing her.

As with general practitioners, the problems can
be related to inadequate preparation of health

visitors for work with families with handicapped
children. Health visitors do a three year nursing
course, followed by experience in midwifery and
finally a one year basic training course. In the
basic nursing course for state registration as a
nurse there is a component related to mental handicap. However this component is hospital based, as
is the bulk of the course, and there is little contact with families of mentally handicapped people.
The health visitor course includes a period of 12
weeks supervised practice in which the skills of
counselling and teaching are practiced with families
and in settings such as clinics and schools. However there are no specific requirements that the
families should have mentally handicapped children.
The training of health visitors does not include
detailed study of mental handicap and opportunities
for in-service training are limited.

Although health visitors traditionally have
concentrated on visiting mothers with young children
and 60% of their time is spent working with
families of children under 5 years old,[8] increasingly health visitors are under pressure to visit and
devote time to other client groups such as the
elderly. Health visitors carry heavy case loads and
must work out their own priorities for visiting.
Few health visitors place the mentally handicapped
and their families top of their priority list.

The Social Worker

The creation of social service departments in
1971 was seen as heralding a new phase in the
development of community care for the mentally
handicapped. The Seebohm Committee recommended that
new social service departments should be responsible
for the community care of the mentally handicapped,
and that these departments should form an important
part of the network of services in the community.[9]
Despite opposition from the medical profession, the
Secretary of State for Social Services, Richard
Crossman, accepted these recommendations and under
Section 2 of the Chronically Sick and Disabled Act
of 1970 local authority social service departments
are required to provide a comprehensive range of
services for the mentally handicapped in the community.

The field social worker has been identified as
the key service provider and as the person best
placed to assess the needs of the family, to
mobilise necessary resources, to ensure that the

175

efforts of different agencies are properly co-
ordinated and to maintain a family focus. The 1971
White Paper saw the social worker as the basis of
community care. 'The person best placed to act as
co-ordinator is likely to be the social worker, who
should take her part in the multi-disciplinary team
as soon as the handicap is suspected and thereafter
maintaining a continuing relationship with the
handicapped child and his family'.10

Again actual practice is very different from
the hopes and aspirations of official reports. Only
19 (16%) mothers had seen a social worker in the
previous year and only 9 (8%) had been visited by
one in the previous 6 months. Only 2 of these
mothers had found the contact or visit useful and in
both cases the social worker has arranged a specific
service, short term care so that these mothers could
have a holiday. In one case this was the first
holiday the mother had had with her family in 14
years. She said:

> I don't think you can do without the social
> worker, because if I hadn't rung him up I
> wouldn't have been able to get her away while
> we had a holiday together.

Very few of the other mothers reported positive
feelings about their social workers. 89 (74%)
mothers said their contact with social workers was
not helpful. More typical of mothers' attitudes
were the following criticisms made by a mother with
a 4½ year old son:

> I rung up the social services and asked if
> there was anywhere or any society where there
> was just another mother with a child like mine
> that I could talk to, because we seemed to be
> very much on our own. All I got was that they
> were mostly elderly people in Bridlington, but
> they would see what they could do and if there
> was anything they would send someone round to
> see me, and I've never had anybody and that's
> two years ago.

Again many mothers were critical of the expertise and knowledge of many social workers as in
the following comments:

> My social worker is one of those who brags
> about how well her kids are coming on at school,
> how she goes swimming at dinner time - that's

not helping me is it? We've been trying to get
out of this house for seven years and get a
bigger house so that we could have Michael (20
year old mentally handicapped son who lives in
hospital) home, at least for a holiday, and all
I asked was if she'd write me a letter which
helps a lot when it's corporation. She said:
'You'll have to wait until I come back because
I've got this other girl to see in court first'.
And this was a normal child. I reported her.
I rang the social services and I said: 'I
want a social worker who understands the needs
of the mentally handicapped - she doesn't.
She's not a caring person'. The social service
wouldn't change her so I've never bothered them
since.

Social workers encountered special difficulties
in providing services for families with mentally
handicapped children. Whereas GPs and health
visitors are usually involved in the discovery of
mental handicap, social workers usually are not and
rely on self-referals or referals from health
workers. Generally social workers are only informed
when a crisis develops in the family or an aid or
adaptation to the house is required. As Hanvey
pointed out: 'Doctors are reluctant to pass on
information, believing either that it would contra-
vene confidentiality or that social service departments have nothing to offer anyway'.[11]
    Like health visitors, social workers carry
heavy case loads and must prioritize their time.
Social workers tend to allocate priorities to crisis
cases or cases in which they have a statutory duty
to visit. Most of the families in the present study
were not in crisis, rather they were ordinary
families that experienced the special difficulties
associated with the long-term care of very dependent
children. The help they required was mundane - so
often social workers did not see them as the interesting cases to which they should devote their scarce
resources. Rees has argued that 'the social workers'
ideology of casework (has) influenced them into
identifying certain tasks as prestigious and ones
which they would enjoy spending time on'.[12] Owens
and Birchenall suggest that 'mental handicap is
often near the bottom of the list of priorities
requiring social intervention'.[13]
    Social workers are generically trained and
their basic training often lacks input on the
problem and needs of the handicap. There is a

general concern felt about the nature of training and
practice and some discussion of the need to return
to more specialist training and practice. A discussion document by the central training council
discussed the situation in the following way:
'There is in particular much questioning of the
generic ideal and many people feel there must be more
specialisation, though not necessarily as there was
pre-Seebohm'.[14] The difficulties mothers experienced in relating to generic workers such as general
medical practitioners, health visitors and social
workers may be related to the difficulties these
workers have in developing experience and understanding of the problems that mothers have in caring
for their mentally handicapped children. These
problems are compounded in the case of health
visitors and social workers by the rapid turnover of
practitioners. One mother summarised the position
in the following way:

> I find that with health visitors and social
> workers they change so frequently and you've
> got to go back to square one every time. In-
> stead of you gaining from them, they're bene-
> fitting from your experience. I feel it would
> be helpful if one person did have Julie's case
> and knew about our circumstances so that if
> problems arose I would be speaking to someone
> who knew a bit about her and about our circum-
> stances. As it is there isn't anyone like
> that.

In the next section we shall contrast mothers'
experiences of generic workers with their experiences of specialists who concentrate exclusively on
the severely mentally handicapped - teachers at
special schools for the severely educationally subnormal.

Teachers
        Until 1971 most severely mentally handicapped
children were officially classified as ineducable
and excluded from the education system. They were
'trained' in Junior Training Centres provided by
the local health authority. On 1 April 1971 local
education authority took on responsibility for the
education of all children of school age and a major
programme of school construction was started to
provide places for the severely and profoundly
mentally handicapped.

Some local authorities experimented with the integration of mentally handicapped children in ordinary schools, for example in Bromley, South Derbyshire and South Oxfordshire.[15] Most local education authorities have built special schools for the severely mentally handicapped on separate sites. These schools are classified as ESN (S) schools and teachers in them teach only mentally handicapped children.

All the children in our study attended one of three ESN (S) schools in North Humberside. All three schools were purpose built and opened between 1972 and 1974. The schools were all well equipped and had special care units for profoundly handicapped children, but some mothers were concerned about the relative absence of specialist services such as physiotherapy and speech therapy.

Mothers generally had a very positive attitude to the special schools and their teachers: 108 (80%) of the mothers said the schools were very helpful. Mothers generally found their interactions with teachers useful and they frequently used teachers as a source of information. The following statement was characteristic:

> They'll (teachers) tell you the truth if you ask them for anything. I trust them. Whatever I ask they'll give me a truthful answer. They'll go out of their way to find out and give you the necessary information. Her teacher mentioned the Family Fund, the attendance allowance, the mobility allowance and disposable nappies to me the first week she was in school. Then I asked my doctor before he said I was entitled to them. They're always very helpful.

Mothers valued the schools in two ways. The teachers helped develop the social skills of their children which reduced their dependency and the associated burden of care. 63% of study mothers said that teachers were mainly responsible for training their children to dress and getting them toilet trained.

The teachers, also, acted as child minders who took care of the children during the day, kept them clean, fed and occupied and allowed mothers to devote their time to other activities, such as the housework. Almost all the mothers talked about the teachers' child-minding functions. Mothers, especially if their child was severely disabled,

tended to stress the child-minding functions rather
than the educational function of school teachers.
This contrasts strongly with the emphasis in official reports where the stress is almost entirely on
the training or educational role and very little
emphasis is placed on the wider social support role.
For example the Central Health Services Council
described the main aims of junior training centres
in the following way:

> To develop as fully as possible their (i.e.
> mentally handicapped children's) physical,
> intellectual, social and practical skills and
> powers of expression; to help them, too, to
> understand more clearly the world around them
> and to enable them to live in it as happily and
> as competently as possible.[16]

The Warnock Committee on special educational needs
described the main objectives of education in very
similar terms:

> The (long-term goals of education) are, first
> to enlarge a child's knowledge, experience and
> imaginative understanding, and thus his aware-
> ness of moral values and capacity for enjoy-
> ment; and secondly, to enable him to enter the
> world after formal education is over as an
> active participant in society and a responsible
> contributor to it, capable of achieving as much
> independence as possible.[17]

Some of the critical comments mothers made of
the schools reflected the high value they placed on
the child-minding and social support role of the
teachers. 51% of the mothers said they were worried
by the school holiday, especially the 6 weeks long
summer holidays. Similar problems have been reported in other studies. For example McCormack in her
study of 50 families with a mentally handicapped
child, was convinced 'that school holidays often
prove the final straw that makes parents give up
their good intentions and ask for hospital care'.[18]
Other difficulties related to the travelling
and the distance between the child's home and
school. As the educational facilities for severely
mentally handicapped children in North Humberside
were separated from other educational facilities
and concentrated in special schools most of the
children had to travel, in some cases over 10 miles
by school bus, taxi or in their parents' car. In

particular 6 mothers complained that their children
had to travel over 40 miles a day by taxi. These
mothers were the only ones that classified teachers
and schools as unhelpful in caring for their
children.

Many mothers experienced problems with school
transport. In some cases mothers said it stopped
them going out to work. One mother described the
problems in the following way:

> You've always got to put her on the bus, and
> you've got to be there dead on time for her
> coming home from school. Sometimes you're
> waiting up to an hour for the bus, as it some-
> times breaks down or there isn't a bus for
> them. You can't keep a proper time and you
> can't get a job when you're not reliable.

Many mothers were critical of the supervision their
children received on their long bus journey to
school. The local education authority did provide
special escorts on these buses but they were largely
untrained. Some mothers felt the escorts were unsympathetic and intolerant of the children and failed to take into account the problems they experienced in getting their children ready on time.

In some cases the distance between home and
the school severely restricted interaction between
the parents and school teachers. For example the 6
mothers who lived more than 20 miles from the
school, all said that the distance prevented them
from going to the school, meeting their children's
teachers and discussing their children's progress.

As the mothers found both advantages and disadvantages to the segregated system of education we
asked mothers how they felt about the education of
their children in special schools. The subject was
of great interest to mothers and most talked at
length about the pros and cons of separating their
children from other children for educational purposes. 73% of mothers wanted their children to be
educated in special schools. For these mothers the
special facilities of special schools, the concentration of equipment, resources and expertise, and
the availability of specialist support services such
as physiotherapy and speech therapy, outweighed the
problems of travelling and the separation from other
children.

24% of the mothers would have preferred their
children to attend the local schools. These mothers
acknowledged the advantages of the special school.

However they stressed the disadvantages of segregation especially the travelling time and the loss
of educational and social experiences when a child
was cut off from the local community and the children who lived in it. These mothers stressed the
stigma associated with segregated education. 6
mothers argued that the inclusion of mentally handicapped children in ordinary schools would help other
children learn about and accept children with disabilities.

Discussion. We have in this section examined
mothers' attitudes to four groups of care professionals: the family doctor, the health visitor, the
social worker and the school teacher. Between them
these professionals constitute mothers main point of
contact with the caring services of the welfare
state. We were surprised at how unhelpful most
mothers found these professionals in caring for their
handicapped children (see Table 8.1).

Table 8.1   Mothers' attitudes to the utility of
family doctors, health visitors, social
workers and teachers

	Family Doctor	Health Visitor	Social Worker	Teachers
Very helpful	16 (13%)	7 (6%)	4 (3%)	108 (90%)
Helpful	35 (29%)	10 (8%)	13 (11%)	5 (4%)
Somewhat helpful	23 (19%)	13 (11%)	14 (12%)	1 (1%)
Not helpful	46 (38%)	90 (75%)	89 (74%)	6 (5%)

Mothers wanted informed professionals who could
give them practical advice and help. The majority
of mothers did not see social workers or health
visitors as either helpful or well-informed. The
exceptions were generally cases in which a special
relationship had developed between an individual
mother and an individual worker. Although family
doctors are also generalists mothers found them more
useful than health visitors or social workers. We
found it difficult to identify the reasons for this
but it seemed to be related to the control mothers
exerted over different practitioners. Mothers
generally initiated contact with their family doctor
and went to see him when they thought they had a
problem. In the cases of health visitors and social
workers the contact was frequently initiated by the

practitioner and therefore in terms dictated by the
practitioner.

Our findings are confirmed by a recent DHSS
review of services for the mentally handicapped.

> There is little information available about the
> extent to which mentally handicapped people
> benefit from 'generic services' or the degree
> of priority given to them. When studies of
> community care are reported they have been dis-
> quieting and suggest that many families are not
> receiving the help they need. Social work and
> primary health care agencies are fully stretch-
> ed and have to decide priorities amongst many
> competing claims and 'at risk' cases, according
> to an assessment of local and individual needs.
> Most professionals working in the community
> will individually come across relatively few
> mentally handicapped people. In these circum-
> stances it can be difficult for a person who
> has little experience of mentally handicapped
> people or training on this subject to apprec-
> iate the kind of development which might be
> possible, or the sort of help which would be
> most effective.[19]

In contrast mothers expressed very positive
attitudes to help they received from school teachers.
However some mothers were concerned about the
problems created within a segregated system of
education. Although their children received the
help of experts and specialists there were costs in
terms of travelling, of being cut off from the
local community and of being deprived of the experiences of normal schools. Mothers wanted the best
of both worlds. They wanted to have the provision
of expertise and practical help within the framework of generalist services. Although there are
tentative movements in health and social services
towards a degree of specialisation amongst generic
practitioners[20] and within the education service
towards the integration of special education,[21]
these are as yet very tentative moves.

VOLUNTARY ASSOCIATIONS

The current Conservative administration has
placed great emphasis on encouraging a partnership
between statutory agencies, voluntary agencies, and
families. For example the Secretary of State for

Social Services, Patrick Jenkin, described the
approach of the government in the following way:

> My colleagues and I ... have stressed the key
> role of the family, of friends and of neigh-
> bours. We have sought to persuade local social
> service departments to try to build partner-
> ships with voluntary agencies and with informal
> caring networks.[22]

Thus voluntary agencies can be seen as a supplement
to both statutory agencies and informal networks of
support. In this section we shall examine the extent to which the voluntary agencies fulfilled this
function.
    The term voluntary agency refers to a wide
variety of organisations ranging from organisations
set up by service providers such as Stroke Clubs set
up by hospital consultants, through long established
charities such as Dr. Barnado's to self-help or
mutual aid groups. Self-help groups are organised
and run by the disadvantaged and disabled themselves.
For example alcoholics and former alcoholics run
local groups of Alcoholics Anonymous and parents of
mentally handicapped children run Kith and Kids.
Self-help groups have an important role to play in
helping parents care for their severely handicapped
children. However as there were no such groups
amongst the families we studied we shall defer our
discussion of these groups to the last chapter.
    Voluntary agencies played an important role in
pioneering social services. With the development of
the welfare state their function in providing basic
routine services has largely been taken over by
statutory agencies. However voluntary agencies
remain an important part of the social services and
a recent review by the Wolfenden Committee reported
that 'what is known as the "voluntary movement" is
a living thing'.[23] Broadly the voluntary agencies
have adjusted to the development of the large scale
public provision of social services by maintaining
their traditional role of pioneering service development but also developing new roles in terms of
advocacy for specific client groups and as critics
of the nature and level of current provisions.[24]
    It is, of course, difficult to differentiate
between the service development and pressure group
functions of voluntary agencies. Most service
departments are intended to influence the development of routine services. For example in 1975 in
South Wales the National Society for Mentally

Handicapped Children (now referred to as MENCAP)
developed a training scheme for adults known as
Pathway. The Society has used the Pathway scheme as
an example and as a way of advocating improvements
within adult training centres.[25]
   While the national associations and national
organisations act as pressure groups and focus
primarily on the policy-makers, local associations,
which in MENCAP have considerable autonomy, have
acted far more as self-help groups attempting to
provide direct practical help. The activities of
the local MENCAP associations include advice and
counselling for parents in the process of 'discovering' their child's mental handicap, the provision of
information about services, the provision of play
groups, toy libraries, aids and equipment, the
organisation of holiday schemes and in some cases
even the provision of financial help.
   Most of the mothers in our study belonged to
one or more voluntary groups. These included
MENCAP, The Down's Children's Association, The
Association for Spina Bifida and Hydrocephalus, the
Spastics Society and various Parent-Teacher
Associations. MENCAP seemed to be the most active
local association and 47.5% of the mothers belonged
to the local branch. The proportion of mothers in
this study belonging to a voluntary association
(excluding PTAs) were similar to those identified
in other studies. The Wolfenden Committee commissioned a national postal survey of parents of
handicapped children. 47.8% said they belonged to
a voluntary association.[26] Hewett, in her study of
children under 9 with cerebral palsy, found that
50.5% of the families considered themselves to be
members of the Spastics Society.[27]
   Some mothers contributed to the activities of
their association in an active way. 10 parents were
officers or committee members. 6 mothers had
helped to organise and run play schemes during the
school summer holidays. However the majority of
mothers made fairly minimal contributions to the
organisation and work of the association. Mothers
gave a variety of reasons for their low involvement.
One mother said

   Rather a non-participating member (of MENCAP).
   I do get the quarterly magazine (Parents Voice)
   and the newsletter but I don't attend meetings
   as I should.

Another said:

> I joined MENCAP but I haven't been to meetings
> as I couldn't bring myself to admit that my son
> was handicapped.

One mother regularly attended the monthly MENCAP
meeting 'but all issues seemed to be financial and
these are not the most important points'.
Mothers used the voluntary associations in a
variety of ways. Generally the associations seemed
to function more as a source of mutual support and
advice than as a source of practical help (see
Table 8.2). For example the majority of mothers
found their association enabled them to share
problems with other parents, and was an important
source of support, advice and help, whereas few
mothers looked to their association for practical
help with baby-sitting or for equipment. The only
exception to this pattern was the provision of
leisure facilities. Most mothers found their
association provided opportunities for outings. In
this case the social support function combined with
a measure of practical help. Many mothers said they
had found great comfort and reassurance by talking
to other parents with mentally handicapped children.
A recurrent phrase was 'It makes you realise you're
not the only one'. However the association did
provide some mothers with extremely useful help.
One mother said her society raised money to pay for
flights to America for her daughter's treatment.
Another said

> The society's (MENCAP) holiday scheme is help-
> ful. I take Victoria to the holiday accommo-
> dation in Blackpool and I know that the man is
> not going to say 'Oh my God, another Mongol'.

We asked non-members why they did not belong
to a voluntary association. 30, of the 63 non-
members, said they did not know about the local
associations or did not know how to contact them.
Professionals involved in the discovery of mental
handicap and subsequent support did not routinely
provide parents with information about the voluntary
associations nor did they provide information to the
associations so they contact parents. The other 33
mothers gave a variety of reasons including 'I'm
not a mixer, I just can't mix with people' and 'I
haven't bothered, I don't think they can help me'.
One mother had been told about MENCAP by her

daughter's school teacher but she wanted to keep the child's social life separate from the social life of other mentally handicapped children. 'I didn't want her to mix with children having similar problems'.

Table 8.2 The ways in which mothers who belonged to voluntary associations made use of these associations

Type of help	Great help	Some help	No help
Enabling parents to share their experiences and problems	66%	24%	10%
Providing leisure facilities including outings and social events	62%	27%	11%
Campaigning for improvement in services	60%	32%	8%
Counselling and support for families	50%	15%	35%
A source of advice and information about where to get help	49%	30%	21%
Providing facilities, e.g. toys, equipment for the children	12%	19%	69%
Giving practical help for parents, e.g. baby-sitting	8%	11%	81%

Discussion. Voluntary associations played a part in reinforcing mothers' abilities to care for their children by providing psychological support and information about resources. They did not act as self-help groups but rather as middle-man between the families and other service providers. Their ability to perform this role depended on the co-operation both of the statutory services, especially in providing information to mothers about the existence of the voluntary associations, and of mothers in their willingness to use and contribute to the voluntary organisations.

TWO SERVICES

In the first two sections of this chapter we have examined the general role of four different

types of service providers and of voluntary
associations. In this section we shall develop our
discussion by examining the availability and utility
of two specific services that can be provided by a
variety of agencies: short term care and financial
support.

Short Term Care

The mothers in our study took the main responsibility for caring for disabled children. They
received some help from their family, informal networks and schools but this still left a continual
burden of caring. Agencies, with residential
facilities, can help mothers by taking the child into
care for short periods. This is commonly known as
short term care.

It is now generally recognised that short term
care is a key part of community care. Younghusband
et al., in their review of services for the handicapped, said that the 'relief from the care of a
handicapped child at home was the most pressing of
all personal and social needs'.[28] Similarly Vaughan
in an evaluation of short term care found that it
was an important factor in enabling families to
keep their child at home.[29] Numerous official
publications have identified both the importance and
shortage of short term care facilities.[30]

In North Humberside a variety of agencies
provided short term care facilities for mentally
handicapped children. The local health authority
provided facilities in mental handicap hospitals,
in children's wards at the general hospital and in
an assessment centre. The local authority social
services department provided facilities in children's
hostels. The local education authority had
facilities in hostels attached to special schools.
Two voluntary agencies, Dr. Barnado's and the Church
of England Children's Society, had facilities in
children's homes.

The majority of mothers (65, 54%) in the study
had made use of this facility in the previous year.
The extent to which mothers used the facility
varied considerably. 38 mothers used less than 2
weeks of short term care, 15 mothers used between
2 and 4 weeks and 12 mothers used over 4 weeks in
the preceding year. Generally mothers found the
service a considerable help. One mother, with four
children, describes the service in the following way:

I find it extremely helpful because it gives us
a break and it lets us do things with the other
children that we wouldn't do when Wendy was at
home.

Mothers valued the service because it provided
them with relief from the burdens of care but short
term care facilities could be used as an opportunity
for observation, assessment and review of the
child's progress, so that specific programmes of
training could be designed. There was little
evidence in our study of short term care being used
for more than relief of the mothers.

Mothers had experienced problems with access to
and the suitability of short term care facilities.
The variety of agencies providing short term care
was confusing to many mothers. They did not know
who to approach to obtain access to the facilities.
Mothers who had regular and easy access to short
term care facilities had generally developed close
relationships with the staff inside the residential
facilities. Other mothers had to make requests
through their family doctor or social worker and
most mothers felt that it was very difficult to obtain a place in a local authority social services
hostel. As one mother said 'The social worker will
almost certainly say "all the places are full"'.
Many mothers felt the procedure for the allocation
of places was both difficult to understand and unfair. Some parents seemed to be specially favoured
and could obtain facilities at weekends and during
the summer holidays.

Some mothers were worried about the quality of
the facilities, especially in the mental handicap
hospital. 9 mothers had been offered places at a
mental handicap hospital and had refused to take
them up. 5 of these mothers said they turned down
the offers because they disliked the hospital and
they did not want their child to be cared for with
long stay residents. Some mothers had had unsatis-
factory experiences both with hospital and with
hostel facilities and were reluctant to use them
again. One mother, with an over-active son, said of
hospital facilities, 'He was heavily drugged while
he was there'; another commented about hostels,
'I'm not taking her to the hostel again because they
lock her up at night'. Most mothers preferred
hostel facilities but found hostels would not take
children with difficult behaviour or who needed
continuous nursing care. Some families found the
difficulties of obtaining suitable facilities so

great that they used private residential homes.

Comment. Short term care is a highly valued service
that can provide invaluable help for mothers.   It
can also be important as an opportunity for evalua-
ting and assessing the child and his progress.
Although mothers in North Humberside valued the
service they received it had problems.   The mothers
were confused about the variety of agencies involved,
about the problems of obtaining the service, about
the quality and suitability of the service and the
equity of its allocation.   Mothers wanted a flexible,
easily arranged, immediately available and local
service.   They generally did not feel they were
getting this type of service.   Bayley has made an
obvious comment that is frequently over-looked that
'unless short term care is acceptable to parents
they will not use it'.[31]

Financial Support
     The families of mentally handicapped children
are entitled to the same financial benefits as other
citizens of the United Kingdom.   Recently the concept of community care has been extended to include
special financial provision for families with a
disabled member.   Caring for a handicapped child
imposes an emotional, physical and financial burden
on the family.   In recognition of this a special set
of payments have been introduced including the
attendance allowance, the mobility allowance and the
family fund.
     We did not talk to the mothers about their
family incomes rather we talked to them about their
awareness of three specific sources of benefit or
financial help specifically designed to help disabled people and their families: the attendance
allowance, the mobility allowance and the family
fund.   We shall discuss each allowance in turn and
then the common problems families experienced in
claiming them.

The Attendance Allowance. The attendance allowance
is a state benefit payable to individuals who have
to provide constant attention and care for a disabled relative.   The 1969 White Paper on National
Insurance described the situation in the following
way:

> Where they (the disabled) are being care for
> at home, the strain on their families can be
> considerable. Many of them prefer to remain in
> their own surroundings rather than go into a
> hospital or home and many families are prepared
> to take on the burden of caring for a severely
> disabled relative. A new attendance allowance
> will therefore be introduced for very severely
> disabled people.[32]

For these new allowances, eligibility is determined
by type and nature of disability rather than financial circumstances. Parents cannot claim the allowance for a child under two years old. The allowance
is a weekly tax free benefit and since 1972 there
have been two rates: a lower rate for individuals
who provide attention only during the day or the
night and a higher rate for individuals who provide
attention both during the day and the night.[33]
     Most mothers (118) knew about the allowance and
110 were receiving an allowance. 8 mothers had
applied for an allowance and been refused. These
figures are similar to those of a recent study by
Jones-Davies in Surrey Area Health Authority. Jones-
Davies found that 95% of her sample had heard of the
attendance allowance and 85% were receiving an
allowance.[34]
     Many mothers were critical of the administra-
tion of the attendance allowance, especially the
delay in deciding eligibility and making payments.
Some mothers had had to wait nearly 2 years for
their first payments.

> It was a good year and a half after I applied
> for it before I finally received it. They did
> back-date it for that year and a half but not
> the other two years, not from the day they
> told me she was handicapped which I thought was
> wrong.

Mobility Allowance. The mobility allowance was
introduced in the mid-seventies by the DHSS to replace the former provision of vehicles for the
disabled. The mobility allowance is payable to any
individual who cannot walk because of severe
physical or mental disability; who is likely to
remain unable to walk for at least twelve months;
who will benefit from the enhanced facilities for
mobility provided by the allowance and who is at
least 5 years old.[35]

29 mothers had applied for a mobility allowance
for their child. Only 14 mothers had been successful in their application. Nationally about 46% of
applicants are successful.[36] The 15 unsuccessful
mothers could not understand why their application
had been rejected and were all critical of the
operation of the scheme. One mother said:

> I didn't get it. I was so angry about it. I
> talked to other parents and they said it had
> been their experience that if you were lucky
> enough to get the doctor in West Hull you were
> given it, and if you got the doctor in East
> Hull you weren't. We got the doctor in East
> Hull and we didn't receive it. I don't know
> why there is difference, because I know of one
> child who can walk much further than my Paul
> and she went to see the doctor in West Hull and
> she was given it. Paul can't walk as far as
> her and we didn't get it.

These inconsistencies in the administration of
the mobility allowance scheme have been reported in
other studies. Cook surveyed 489 child recipients
of the mobility allowance and found that 100 (20.4%)
could walk at least 40 years unaided and 67 (13.7%)
could walk at least 100 yards unaided. When adjust-
ments were made for factors such as pain, exertion
and difficulty in walking which are all considered
in assessing eligibility 51 (10.4%) children could
still walk at least 40 yards without help.[37]

The Family Fund. Attendance and mobility allowances
are routine payments made by the DHSS to help the
disabled and their relatives deal with some of the
financial consequences of disability. Once eligibility has been established the payments are made
regularly and routinely by the DHSS. The Family
Fund makes ad hoc payments to meet the special needs
of families with severely handicapped children and
'to relieve stress in the family which is due to
caring for the handicapped child'.[38] The Family
Fund is a trust fund financed by the DHSS but administered by a voluntary organisation, the Joseph
Rowntree Memorial Trust.
The fund is administered very informally. The
administrators are willing to consider written
requests from the family, the family doctor, the
social worker, the health visitor or from a voluntary worker. Requests are considered for

192

exceptional equipment and activities that would
normally not be funded by another agency.   Most
frequently requests are rejected with a suggestion
that the family should approach another agency for
help.   There is no appeal but the fund is willing
to reconsider requests if more or different information has been provided.   For example we talked to
5 mothers, whose requests for help had been rejected
and we helped them draft a fresh letter to the fund.
In each case the reapplication was successful.

31 mothers had not heard of the fund and 49 had
heard but were not aware that they were eligible for
benefits.   40 families had applied to the fund and
of these 40, 21 (53%) had received help.   Bradshaw's
study in Leeds found a success rate of 58.6%.[39]
Families had received help with a wide variety of
things including carpets;   bedding;   washing machines
and tumble driers;   special aids and adaptations the
local authority was unable to provide;   family
holidays and even driving lessons.

Comment: Awareness and Eligibility.   The payment of
special allowances to the families of handicapped
children is undoubtedly a welcomed innovation and
has been a great help to many families with handicapped children.   However the system still leaves a
lot to be desired and many mothers were critical of
the operation of the scheme.

A major problem related to mothers' awareness
of the different schemes.   Many mothers had either
delayed or completely failed to claim benefits
because they lacked information.   The benefits came
from a number of different agencies, in a number of
different ways and no single agency is responsible
for informing mothers about the nature of the
different schemes and benefits.   Bradshaw commented
about the Family Fund that 'the main reason why
families do not claim is ignorance - ignorance that
the Fund exists, that it applies to them or that
they can get help with the particular item that they
need'.[40]

To examine the problem of information we asked
mothers who knew about the three schemes how they
had found out about them.   Table 8.3 shows that the
process of finding out was fairly haphazard with
mothers using a variety of sources of information.

Table 8.3   Mothers sources of information about
            attendance allowance, mobility allowance
            and the Family Fund

Source of information	Attendance allowance	Mobility allowance	Family Fund
Other parents	45 (51%)	49 (41.5%)	15 (32%)
Voluntary association	11 (12%)	10 (8%)	13 (28%)
Other sources	13 (15%)	23 (19.5%)	8 (17%)
School teacher	7 (8%)	14 (12%)	6 (13%)
Family doctor	3 (3%)	2 (2%)	1 (2%)
Social worker	7 (8%)	5 (4%)	2 (4%)
Health visitor	3 (3%)	4 (3%)	2 (4%)

Mothers tended to use other parents and voluntary
associations as their major source of information
and received relatively little information about
these schemes from the professionals. Indeed they
received less information from professionals than
they did from other sources which included relatives
neighbours and the mass media. As Marks had argued
'professional helpers tend to tell parents only
about their own services, so that the parent-to-
parent contact may be the major link in the information chain'.[41]
     Some of the mothers were confused about the
nature and purpose of the different schemes. For
example mothers found it difficult to differentiate
between the purpose of the attendance allowance,
i.e. to provide assistance to families with a disabled member, and the basis on which the allowance
is assessed, i.e. the amount of attention the disabled individual requires. A number of mothers, who
experienced financial problems but whose child did
not require continual supervision, had had their
claims rejected. This problem became apparent in
the early stages of the scheme when Jimmy Martin, a
young boy with no legs and one arm, was rejected for
the allowance on the grounds that he did not need
continual attention or supervision. Dr. Higgings, a
Board member, stated 'no matter how sympathetic the
Board might be, this is an attendance and not a
disability allowance'.[42]
     There have been uncertainties over the meaning
of key words, e.g. 'day and night' and 'continual
supervision'. General practitioners assess the
children and interpret these key words and the
involvement of general practitioners has led to
inconsistencies in the operation of the scheme.

Several commentators have criticised the role of
doctors in assessing children and interpreting the
regulations. Bradshaw and Lawton have commented
'that doctors are not best equipped to make such
decisions'[43] and Carson has stated that 'it cannot
be said that this is an allowance for which doctors
shall be exclusively responsible because the
majority of issues are factual not medical'.[44]

To sum up, the provision of financial benefits
through schemes such as attendance allowances has
undoubtedly helped many families, but it has also
created problems. Some families do not apply for
benefits for which they are entitled because they
are not fully informed and the administration and
operation of some of the schemes seems to be
confusing and inequitable.

CONCLUSION

Recent policy developments, especially the
development of community care, have undoubtedly
improved the quality of services available to the
mentally handicapped. 25 years ago as the policy
was in its infancy Tizard and Grad reviewed the
community services. Generally families were critical of the support and help they received from
doctors, health visitors, social workers and educational services.[45] There have been important
improvements. Tizard and Grad reported that 12% of
the school aged children did not attend any training
or educational establishment; very few families
could use short term care facilities and none of
the families received home-help services.[46] In all
these respects improvements have been made and the
provision of special financial benefits have also
helped.

However in one important respect services may
have deteriorated. Many families had a statutory
supervision order for their handicapped child and
were regularly visited by a specialist social
worker. Tizard and Grad saw this as 'perhaps the
most valuable social service available to the
families'.[47] Families no longer have regular visits
from an interested specialist and most studies of
community care have identified this as a major
problem.

In a period of economic stringency, the Social
Services in general come under considerable pressure
from rising demands and falling resources. Welfare

provisions tended to be oriented towards dealing
with short term crises and emergencies rather than
coping with the long term needs of mothers who care
for their severely handicapped children.

For these mothers community care can seem an
abstract and meaningless concept. They do not want
the traditional segregated services of the large
scale institution nor do they want piecemeal, haphazard contact with a constantly changing group of
generic workers. Like the professionals they want
to prevent the development of a crisis and therefore
they want co-ordinated specialist services that
operate within the framework of generic services and
which provide them with sensitive and appropriate
practical help.

NOTES

1. Central Health Services Council, Standing
    Medical Advisory Committee, The Field of Work
    of the Family Doctor: Report of the Sub-
    Committee, H.M.S.O., 1963, para. 206.
2. D. Wilkin, Caring for the Mentally Handicapped
    Child, Croom Helm, 1979, p. 154.
3. The majority of home help is provided by local
    authority social service departments, although
    voluntary agencies such as the Red Cross do
    provide some. Various specialists such as the
    GP, the health visitor and the social worker
    can apply for the service on behalf of the
    family. Usually the needs of individual
    families are assessed by a home help organiser,
    who also administers the service. See A.
    Brechin and P. Liddiard, Look At It This Way:
    New Perspectives in Rehabilitation, Hodder and
    Stoughton, 1981, p. 160.
4. K.S. Holt and R.M.C. Huntley, 'Mental sub-
    normality: medical training in the United
    Kingdom', British Journal of Medical Education,
    7, 3, 197-203, 1973. Among the survey sample
    were two mothers whose husbands were medical
    practitioners. Their husbands said before
    their handicapped child was born they knew very
    little about Down's Syndrome.
5. Fit for the Future: Report of the Committee on
    Child Health Services (Chairman: Professor
    S.D.M. Court) Cmnd. 6684-I. H.M.S.O., 1976,
    pp. 428-39.
6. Special Educational Needs, Report of the Commi-
    ttee of Enquiry into the Education of

Handicapped Children and Young People, (Chairman Mrs. H.M. Warnock) Cmnd. 7212, H.M.S.O., 1978.

7.   Ibid., p. 301.

8.   Fit for the Future, p. 295.

9.   Report of The Committee on Local Authority and Allied Personal Social Services, (Chairman, Sir G. Seebohm), Cmnd. 3703, H.M.S.O., 1968, paras. 363 and 478.

10.   D.H.S.S., Better Services for the Mentally Handicapped, Cmnd. 4683, H.M.S.O., 1971, para. 141. The Jay Committee also envisaged an important co-ordinating role for social work. See Report of the Committee of Enquiry into Mental Handicap Nursing and Care, Vol. I, (Chairman, Peggy Jay), Cmnd. 7468-I, H.M.S.O., 1979, esp. Chapter 5.

11.   C.P. Hanvey, Social Work with Mentally Handicapped People, Heinemann, 1981, p. 85.

12.   S. Rees, Social Work Face to Face, Arnold, 1978, p. 140.

13.   S.G. Owen and P. Birchenall, Mental Handicap: The Social Dimensions, Pitman, 1979, p. 36.

14.   Central Council for the Education and Training of Social Workers, People with Handicaps Need Better Trained Workers, C.C.E.T.S.W., Paper 5, 1974, para. 38.

15.   T. Booth and P. Potts (eds.), Integrating Special Education, Blackwell, Oxford, 1983.

16.   Central Health Services Council, Standing Medical Advisory Committee, The Training of Staff of Training Centres for the Mentally Subnormal: Report of a Sub-Committee, H.M.S.O., 1962, p. 34.

17.   Special Educational Needs, para 1.4.

18.   M. McCormack, A Mentally Handicapped Child in the Family, Constable, 1978, p. 63.

19.   D.H.S.S., Mental Handicap: Progress, Problems and Priorities, D.H.S.S., 1980, para 2.9.

20.   National Institute for Social Work, Social Workers: Their Roles and Tasks: Report of a Working Party, (Chairman, P.M. Barclay), Bedford Square Press, 1982.

21.   D.E.S., Special Needs in Education, H.M.S.O., 1980 and Education Act, 1981, Elizabeth 2, 1981, C. 60.

22.   D.H.S.S. Press Release, 15 September 1980.

23.   J.F. Wolfenden, The Future of Voluntary Organisations: Report of the Wolfenden Committee, Croom Helm, 1978.

24. For a historical perspective on the role of voluntary organisations and their ability and freedom to pioneer new services and methods, see N. Johnson, Voluntary Social Services, Blackwell and Robertson, Oxford, 1981, especially Chapter 3.

25. National Society for Mentally Handicapped Children, Pathway Training Scheme, N.S.M.H.C., 1978.

26. See J. Bradshaw, C. Glendinning and S. Hatch, 'Voluntary organisations for handicapped children and their families: the meaning of membership', Child: Care, Health and Development, 3, 247-60, 1977.

27. S. Hewett, The Family and the Handicapped Child A Study of Cerebral Palsied Children in Their Homes, Allen and Unwin, 1970.

28. E. Younghusband, D. Birchall, R. Davie and M.L. Kellmer Pringle (eds.), Living with Handicap: The Report of a Working Party on Children with Special Needs, National Bureau for Cooperation in Child Care, 1970, p. 44.

29. See P.J. Vaughan, 'An evaluation of short-term care', Apex, 7, 3, 76-7, 1979.

30. See for example D.H.S.S., Better Services for the Mentally Handicapped; D.H.S.S., Mental Handicap: Progress, Problems and Priorities; National Development Group for the Mentally Handicapped, Residential Short-Term Care for Mentally Handicapped People: Suggestions for Action, Pamphlet No. 4, The Group, 1977.

31. M. Bayley, Mental Handicap and Community Care: A Study of Mentally Handicapped People in Sheffield, Routledge and Kegan Paul, 1973, p. 321.

32. National Superannuation and Social Insurance, Cmnd. 3883, H.M.S.O., 1969, p. 28.

33. The allowance was introduced by the National Insurance (Old Persons' and widows' pensions and attendance allowance) Act, 1970, Elizabeth 2, 1970, C. 51 and first paid on December 6th 1971. Detailed regulations are contained in Social Security Act, 1975, Elizabeth 2, C. 14, 1975, Section 35; and Social Security (Attendance Allowance) (No. 2) Regulations 1975, S.I. 1975, No. 598, See also MENCAP, Information Bulletin, A-Z: Your Questions Answered, New Edition, No. 16, MENCAP, 1981, pp. 8-10, and R. Lister, Welfare Benefits, Sweet and Maxwell 1981, pp. 194-196.

34. G.N. Jones-Davies, 'Awareness of the attendance

allowance', Apex, 9, 2, 62-3, 1981.

35. Mobility Allowance Regulations 1975, S.I. 1975, No. 1573, MENCAP, A-Z: Your Questions Answered, pp. 25-27 and Lister, Welfare Benefits, pp. 196-197.

36. Parliamentary Debates (Hansard), 5th Series - Vol. 928, House of Commons Official Report, H.M.S.O., 1977, Vol. 1041.

37. K. Cook, A Study of Child Beneficiaries of the Mobility Allowance, Social Policy Research Unit, Working Paper, University of York, 1979.

38. D.H.S.S. Circular, LAPSS 8/73, 1973.

39. J. Bradshaw, The Family Fund: An Initiative in Social Policy, Routledge and Kegan Paul, 1980, pp. 83-90.

40. Ibid., pp. 89-90.

41. L. Marks, 'Parents' needs and how to meet them' in G.B. Simon (ed.), The Modern Management of Mental Handicap, A Manual of Practice, Lancaster: M.T.P. Press, 1980, p. 209.

42. The Times, 8th December 1973, p. 3.

43. J. Bradshaw and D. Lawton, 'An examination of equity in the administration of the attendance allowance', Policy and Politics, 8, 1, 39-54, 1980, p. 42.

44. D. Carson, 'Attendance allowances for the severely disabled', New Law Journal, 973-4, 2/11/1972, p. 974.

45. J. Tizard and J.C. Grad, The Mentally Handicapped and Their Families: A Social Survey, Oxford University Press, 1961, pp. 94-113.

46. Ibid., p. 108.

47. Ibid., p. 109.

Chapter 9

TWO MOTHERS

INTRODUCTION

     This book is based on mothers' experiences and
accounts of their mentally handicapped children. In
Chapters 4 to 8 we have broken up individual stories
to create a composite picture and to generalise
about the experiences of the 120 mothers as a group.
This generalisation is important as it emphasises
the mothers' common problems, experiences and resources. However it makes it difficult to identify
with any particular mother. By definition we have
taken bits of mothers' accounts out of the context
of their whole story. In this chapter we focus on
two mothers and as far as possible allow them to
describe their own problems and experiences and the
resources they use to cope with these problems. The
material presented in this chapter also includes
some of our questions and the mothers' replies so
that readers can see the way and extent to which we
directed the talk.
     We selected two mothers, Mrs. Hatch and Mrs.
Jones who had severely mentally handicapped children
but in other ways were very different. Mrs. Hatch
was middle class and had the resources associated
with this e.g. a university education, good income
and good housing. Mrs. Jones was working class and
had few of the resources Mrs. Hatch could draw on.
Furthermore Mrs. Jones had more than one mentally
handicapped child.
     Our account of the two mothers follows the
same layout as Chapters 5 to 8. Following a brief
background to each case we shall examine the process of discovering mental handicap that each
mother went through; the care within the family;
informal support in the community and the role of

formal services.

MRS. HATCH

Background
Mrs. Hatch had two children; Simon who was 17
years old at the time of the interview and Krystyna,
her mentally handicapped daughter who was 14. Her
third child, Paul, was born mentally handicapped,
but he died when he was five years old.

Mrs. Hatch was a trained teacher and at the
time of the interview had a part-time job. Mr.
Hatch was a technical expert employed by a large
national company.

The Hatchs' owned and lived in a large semi-
detached house on the outskirts of Hull. They had
moved to their present house because of the children
and the problems of caring for Krystyna.

Discovering the Handicap
Mrs. Hatch became aware that something was
wrong soon after the delivery of Krystyna. Mrs.
Hatch wanted a home confinement and expected to give
birth at home. Instead she was admitted to hospital
after her waters broke and 'put on some sort of a
drip and then produced this little scarecrow who
sort of shocked everybody'. Krystyna was a full
term baby but she only weighed 4 lb 4 ozs and for
the first 6 weeks of her life she was nursed in a
premature baby unit.

Health professionals at first said that
Krystyna's low birth weight was the result of an
inadequate placenta and nutrition in the womb. 'At
that time and for 11½ years the doctors put the
reason for her handicap down to the placenta malfunction'. Mrs. Hatch was later offered another
explanation. The paediatrician who had seen
Krystyna soon after her birth decided that she was
suffering from a special syndrome associated with
mental handicap. He suggested that Krystyna's
various abnormalities could be explained by this
syndrome.

Despite the explanations of Krystyna's low
birth weight and the fancy labels, Mrs. Hatch found
it difficult to obtain useful information that would
enable her to assess the future.

The hosptial doctors obviously knew there was
something the matter with Krystyna. They sat

> back on the proverbial fence and waited until
> we said 'What's wrong'?

Mrs. Hatch felt that the medical staff had passed
the responsibility for identifying the problem to
her and her husband and thereby eased their own
job. Mrs. Hatch had the same experience when her
second mentally handicapped child, Paul, was born.
She described it in the following way:

> I mean they just sit on a fence and wait until
> you say 'Why is the baby not sitting up now'
> or 'Why is the baby not focusing'. It's this
> great glorious thing that they think it's
> better coming from you. I think you should be
> treated as adult and told right from the word
> go!

Mrs. Hatch felt that she had been left to cope
with and make sense of Krystyna by herself. She
described her early encounters with professionals in
the following way:

> Question: Did anyone get in touch with you
> about Krystyna's care?
> Answer: Until Krystyna was three nobody from
> either the health or from the social services
> seemed to be really interested in us. The
> health visitor called once every week or so and
> then once every six weeks, but that was when
> Paul was born. She didn't offer any construc-
> tive advice about how to bring Krystyna up.
> She didn't try to help this way. The care of
> the baby was uppermost, which of course was her
> job. She gave me various bits of advice about
> caring for Paul in the early weeks, as regards
> feeding and this sort of thing. I presume her
> idea was if you're coping, that's it, well you
> don't.

Comment. In the early and formative stages of
Krystyna's life Mrs. Hatch, like many mothers, felt
that she had been starved of vital information and
relatively neglected by professionals. She had no
previous experience to draw on and did not even
know the right questions to ask. She had no real
idea how Krystyna would develop and how she could
help her.

Care in the Family

Although Krystyna developed, her skills were still extremely limited and she needed a lot of assistance with the basic activities of everyday life. We asked Mrs. Hatch about Krystyna's abilities in relation to dressing, bathing, eating, toiletting and walking.

> Dressing. She needs a lot of help, she is able to dress herself but unable to tie shoe laces.
> Bathing. She needs help, because left to herself she takes unreasonable time to bathe, even then she lacks the manual dexterity for a thorough bath.
> Eating. She has to be fed, left to herself Krystyna will cause undue disturbance by messy eating. She is likely to choke with her food.
> Toiletting. She needs help with undoing her clothes and has to be cleaned after she has been to the toilet. She soils herself both night and day and wets herself frequently during the day.
> Walking. Walks alone with difficulty, she is prone to falling down and injuring herself if she is not supervised.

Krystyna obviously required a lot of care and attention and on our disability scale we gave her a score of 11 and classified her as severely disabled.

The majority of Mrs. Hatch's time was spent either caring for Krystyna or preparing the house for Krystyna and the rest of the family. All the basic activities of everyday life presented additional problems. For example Mrs. Hatch described mealtimes in the following way:

> Question: What about meal-times, can Krystyna manage like children of the same age or does she need help?
> Answer: She needs help.
> Question: In what ways does this create difficulties?
> Answer: At meal times there has to be somebody with her the entire time. It can be difficult if the telephone rings or somebody comes to the front door. You either have to drag her with you. Or if you leave her, when you go back no doubt the orange juice is in the middle of the whatever or thrown or spilt or something. Just, everything is time consuming, the fact that you have to give up

that amount of time and be with her or someone
has to, just to watch really, see that she
doesn't choke as well.

In the day Krystyna required constant care and
attention and caring for her dominated Mrs. Hatch's
life.

Question: When Krystyna is at home is there
any particular time of the day that is likely to
be difficult to cope with?
Answer: Caring for Krystyna after school.
Preparing meals when she's around is difficult.
I try to cook and do the preparing of vege-
tables and potatoes at a time when she's still
at school. Then I have more or less the free
time to be with her until I've got to dish up
the meal. She requires constant attention all
the time she's at home. Otherwise lights, gas
fires and television sets - everything will be
switched on at the same time. Or she'll put in
plugs or put her hand through a china cabinet
if she wants to. She might be a danger to herself. She's a real handful when she's around.
It's very frustrating for me because I can't
get my housework done. I just do as little as
possible, and it's niggling at you all the
time. You can't do too much because she wants
constant attention. It varies. Some days
she's marvellous. She can be persuaded to go
out and play in the garden with me keeping a
distant watch. More often you get days when
you're at screaming point with her.

Krystyna's behaviour during the day was generally good at home but her lack of awareness of
appropriate behaviour in public could cause embarrassment.

If you take her to the shops, she'd know all
what you want and she'd put them in the basket,
but she couldn't be bothered to wait at the
till to pay. There's often one big scene, very
embarrassing in public. She doesn't realise
that you have to wait your turn to pay.

At night Krystyna could also be difficult.

Question: Do you have any problems at bedtime
or night?

<u>Answer</u>   She won't go to bed. You've got to
tell her about an hour before you want her to
go to bed. Bedtime is terrible. She has
sleeping medicine but that doesn't work very
often. She usually falls asleep at about
11.30. Then she gets up to go to the toilet.
This is one of the disadvantages, only a few
disadvantages of her being in a hostel (during
the week). She gets up in the middle of the
night to go to the toilet. Now in the hostels
the night nurse, on duty sitting out in the
corridor, says 'Krystyna', and has a little
chat. Now, over the years Krystyna has grown
to like this little bit of communication with
people in the middle of the night. So, when
she's at home she believes in putting every
light in the house on and making sure that she
wakes somebody up to speak with her and play
with her before she goes back to bed. She does
the same when she's in hospital but again in
hospital there's always a night nurse on duty
who'll probably give her a biscuit or sit and
talk with her for five minutes. But when
you're in the middle of your night's sleep it's
not awfully pleasant. Unless I can get her to
sleep in my own bed, then if I stroke her head
she'll, maybe, drop off again. I usually catch
up with my sleep during the day when she's at
school. In the morning she doesn't like
getting up. She's bad tempered every morning.

Like most mothers Mrs. Hatch found the school
holidays especially difficult.

The long summer holidays is a nightmare. She
gets restless and easily bored. It is difficult to have her all day. She does need someone to encourage her to think of what she can
do. Children like Krystyna don't have an
awful lot provided for them to meet their needs
within the community. Parents are left to
cope with the long breaks from school.

In the Hatch household as in nearly all the
households in our study Krystyna's mother was the
main carer. Mrs. Hatch said that her husband
played very little part in Krystyna's daily care and
in the household and other domestic chores. Mrs.
Hatch saw her husband as an authority figure for the
children, as a provider of occasional fun and games
and as a source of help when she couldn't cope. The

only exceptions were an occasional weekend he would look after Krystyna while Mrs. Hatch went shopping.

Mr. Hatch's limited involvement in caring for Krystyna was related to his job commitment. As a technical expert employed by a national company he had to travel round the country. He was usually not available to help either with Krystyna or with the household chores. Mrs. Hatch seemed to accept the low level of involvement of her husband in running the house. Like many of the mothers we talked to she saw the care of the children and the running of the house as her responsibility. She had given up full-time work to do this and did not expect her husband to help her much. For Mrs. Hatch her husband's job took precedence. She described his contribution in the following way:

> My husband will help if I'm in desperation. The difficulty will be his work. Otherwise he is quite able to handle all Krystyna's problems. But, of course, he'll have to give up his work because he can't go out to work and look after her. He minds her and looks after her in the garden at weekends when both are at home.

As with most families in our study Krystyna had a considerable impact on family life and the Hatch household had adjusted to and was virtually built around the needs of caring for Krystyna.

Many mothers we talked to had experienced serious health problems as a result of the long-term strain of caring for a handicapped child. In the Hatch household it was Mr. Hatch rather than Mrs. Hatch who appeared to suffer from the main consequences.

> Question: Has there been any effect on your health because of caring for Krystyna at home?
> Answer: All these grey hairs. No, not really, I blow hot and cold so much that when I get exasperated I blow a gasket and that's it. Apart from my legs and that's not only Krystyna but having Paul and Krystyna to carry. My legs had to be operated on and are still not very good. Apart from that my husband, yes, he has suffered. He has a back injury which was caused by carrying the other children for so many years and which he will now have to live with for the rest of his life. Also he worries inside, while I make a song and

dance about it. Three years ago he had a heart
attack which the doctors said was caused by
tension. The sister told me I should remove
all his worries and all his tensions and he
would be alright. A little impossible with our
situation. And, of course, he worries even
more now with his back holding him up and
putting extra strain on to me in the way of his
job.

A major problem experienced by most mothers was
the cost of caring for their handicapped child.
Some of the costs were relatively obvious and Mrs.
Hatch discussed them in the following way:

Question: Do you think there is a need for
financial help for families caring for children
who are mentally handicapped?
Answer: Yes, definitely, because they're a
financial drain ... You have to cover yourself
at any time with babysitters or some sort of
minding service which costs money. Clothing
for handicapped children, not thinking only
specifically of my daughter, but physically
handicapped children as well, is expensive.
They have to have front openings and all sorts
of special features. We find shoes for example,
you can't just buy these ordinary cheap casual
summer sandals. You probably would if the
child was normal and running around. Theirs
must be the best, a certain make, built up
inside.

Some of the expenses were lost opportunities
that were sometimes difficult to identify and cost.
Mrs. Hatch identified two different types of lost
opportunity: those relating to Krystyna and those
relating to employment for herself.

Yes, they're definitely an expense. They can't
do jobs around the place. They can't run
messages. They can't take jobs as paper boys
or do things which a lot of normal children can
do to earn their own pocket money or do jobs
around the house. You know, 'if you clean the
car today that's your pocket money for the
week'. No way can they do anything for themselves that is going to make them the slightest
bit independent.
Question: Do you think Krystyna restricts you

in getting a job more than a normal child??
<u>Answer</u>:   Yes, definitely. Had Krystyna been
a normal 13½ year old I should have been a full
time teacher now. But obviously I can't be
because I must be available if she's ill. Also
she takes so much time and so much energy at
the weekends that I do need a little bit of
breathing space in the week. Monday to clean
up after her (she sometimes stays at the
school hostel week days). Friday to prepare
for her coming home and the work ahead for the
weekend.

Krystyna created restrictions on family life.
Some of these restrictions related to specific
activities, especially leisure activities. Others
related to plans or activities that could not even
be considered.

<u>Question</u>: Has Krystyna's condition affected
any family plans?
<u>Answer</u>:   Restrictions on family holidays.
Holidays, yes definitely. I personally will
not travel abroad at all. In the past year I
have been wanting to leave her either at
school or in hospital while we have a holiday.
I feel I want to be in Britain so that I can
be got at, not hundreds of flying miles away.
So I personally will not go out of the country.
Prior to that I was always insistent that we
took the children on holiday with us. However,
we'd had too many bad experiences with medical
care when we'd been away and people doing
nothing to help us and having to dash home in
a car with Krystyna when she was ill that, as
I say, the last couple of years we have left
her and gone on holiday locally. Also, you
can't emigrate. I'm not saying that we're
thinking of emigrating but had you felt that if
politics in this country were getting to such
a state that you wanted to get out, well you'll
be restricted because of her. Some countries
will not welcome a family with handicapped
children.

Krystyna was a major factor in family life and
in making decisions and had an important influence
on the development of her brother.

<u>Question</u>: Do you feel that Simon's development
or activities are restricted in any way?

Answer: The main problem is when we go away
on a holiday. If she goes into a hostel then
I don't worry at all. But if she comes with us,
which we're always determined to do because as
a family we want to be together as often as
possible on our holidays, then the problem is
finding a holiday place where we can be
accepted as a family including Krystyna.
Places like that are few and far between. We
try to look for the ordinary holiday place
which will accommodate us all. What we end up
doing is to spend a week at one of those rather
special holiday places where the handicapped
and their families are made welcome. For the
rest of our holidays Krystyna goes to the
hostel when we and Simon go abroad together.

Although Krystyna restricted family life, Mrs.
Hatch did not believe this had adversely affected
Simon. Indeed she argued that there had been some
important benefits for Simon.

Simon's activities have been restricted. As a
very small child, things like having swimming
lessons were out for him because I had two
handicapped children by then, so definitely he
lost out on certain things. As a small boy he
was made to stand on his own two feet obviously
much younger. He's always been a very independent and helpful soul. I really think he's a
better person than he might have been. He's
more thoughtful than a lot of children, or lads
of his age because he's jolly well had to think
of somebody else before himself. We all have
had to, it becomes a habit.

A major problem and concern for Mrs. Hatch was
the future. Krystyna was nearly 14 and was only
guaranteed a place at the ESN(S) school until she
was 16. The Local Education Authority did provide
facilities for children between 16 and 19 and the
social services department provided facilities in
adult training centres but Krystyna was not guaranteed a place in either.

Question: Do you think any difficulties may
arise in connection with Krystyna's education?
Answer: Yes, definitely. When she's 16
she'll have to leave school as the law stands,
although we hope that it will be extended to
19. However, what do you do when she's at 16

or 19? The answer at the moment is for them to go in to the Adult Training Centres where the age range is so vast from 16 to retiring. I really feel it's too big an age range to cope. My great fear is that she'll be at home 365 days of the year whereas now at least one has Monday to Friday to draw breath, shop, do various things.

Mrs. Hatch was also worried about the long-term.

Question: What do you think will happen to her in the future if you are too old to care for her?
Answer: Well, she won't be able to look after herself. We have no relatives apart from Simon. I am adamant that Simon will not have her to look after. He has his own life to lead. The alternative is that she'll have to go into an institution.
Question: Is this issue a problem?
Answer: Definitely yes, but there's no other answer.
Question: What is the problem?
Answer: We have looked at many many institutions, schools, settlements, whatever you'd like to call them. There are places like Botton Village on the North Yorkshire Moors. On paper, the village and what it is trying to do sound ideal. But in fact you nearly have to have a GCE in mental handicap before you're admitted. If you're too low grade as Krystyna is you're not admitted because you have to be more or less able to look after yourself. Also financially, I don't know what their terms are now but we must have looked at it about three years ago and they were looking for something in the region of £3,500 a year at that time. All privately run places which tend to be nicer and more homely are prohibitive price wise. It isn't an undertaking which is going to last 2-3 years, I mean it can be a 20-30 year carry on. So it's Hobson's choice, you're back to public institutions.
Question: What would you consider the best solution?
Answer: That she pre-deceases us!

Comment. On our scale of disability Krystyna was a severely disabled child. She could perform with

help some of the activities of every day life such
as washing, dressing and eating and was not difficult to manage except perhaps when she was out or in
the night. However she still needed a lot of care
and attention. Even though she attended school and
stayed in the school hostel during the week, it was
a full-time job for Mrs. Hatch running the house and
caring for Krystyna. As in most households she
expected and received minimal help from her husband.
    Krystyna imposed severe restrictions on Mrs.
Hatch's activity and family life in general. Her
husband's health had suffered and her son Simon had
to forgo many of the pleasures enjoyed by his peers.
Caring for Krystyna imposed direct and indirect
costs on the family that were difficult to quantify
but were undoubtedly substantial. Like most mothers
Mrs. Hatch could see no end ot the caring and could
see no way in which Krystyna could survive without
her.

Informal Support in the Community
    Mr. and Mrs. Hatch had little contact with
relatives. They were both only children and both
sets of parents were dead. They had lost contact
with other relatives and did not expect or get help
from relatives. Instead Mrs. Hatch had developed a
circle of supportive friends. She described herself
as a friendly person and said 'I do get on well with
many people'.
    Mrs. Hatch found that Krystyna could cause a
problem in the development of friendship and like
many mothers had adopted a strategy to deal with the
problem.

> If we make friends with someone and then find
> out that they have a handicapped child, we
> don't ditch them which we've had happen to us
> very often. We sort of make friends with
> people and then when children have come into
> the conversation and we've said straight out
> that we have a handicapped child, we don't see
> these people any more.
> Question: Why?
> Answer: Because they don't know how to talk
> to you after that, as though because you have a
> handicapped child you're different. You find
> out who your true friends are.

Many individuals did come through the filtering
process and Mrs. Hatch had developed a circle of

211

friends that provided practical help.

> Question: What practical help have you
> received from friends?
> Answer: Friends have her for the day when
> they know that mother's getting absolutely
> desperate. They sense when everything's got
> too much. When the ceiling's fallen in in one
> of the bedrooms, friends just arrived like
> magic and spirited her away. They cover us for
> weddings. They provide a general back up and
> in the holidays. Friends are always prepared
> to have us out for lunch. Friends take her out
> for the day to relieve the tedium of just
> Krystyna and I together all the time. The
> children are in it too. They meet in the
> holiday times. They meet their peers and have
> somebody they know, someone to play with, some-
> one to visit as any other child would visit
> their school friends.

Friends also provided emotional and moral
support. Mrs. Hatch used her friends, especially if
they had similar problems, as a source of information and advice.

> Question: What other help do friends give?
> Answer: Discussions, the realisation that
> they have been through similar situations. A
> voice on the other end of the phone. It is
> helpful if it's a new concept or some new idea
> that's coming up. It's a good idea to share
> ideas, talk it over, thrash it out. At the
> same time there are the people who want to
> spend time going back and saying when my
> Johnny ...   Well going back never did anybody
> any good really. One has to look to the
> future, think of new ideas. I think that's
> true not just of mentally handicapped people.

An obvious source of friends for Mrs. Hatch was
the mothers of other mentally handicapped children.
Mrs. Hatch had established a close relationship with
one mother but generally her circle of friends was
not limited to the parents of handicapped children.

> Question: Have you become good friends with
> anyone who has a mentally handicapped child?
> Answer: Yes, there is one woman, she has a
> little girl. She was born normal but she got
> meningitis and became brain damaged. I found

that she used to seek me out and talk to me and
I used to try and talk to her. It sort of
brought us together. I think she needed somebody to talk to; somebody who would not only
show sympathy but also understanding and who
would be able to share experiences. We have
shared many problems over the years. She's
problems which I haven't got and I've problems
which she hasn't got. When problems come up
we can talk in complete trust and confidence.
We discuss our deepest fears and worries for
the future. I think our friendship gave her
reassurance. I would say the benefit was
mutual because through our friendship I came to
realise just how much I had learned over the
years about handicapped children. I have become friends with other people who have
mentally handicapped children but I don't count
any other parents of mentally handicapped
children among my close circle of friends.

Mrs. Hatch's source of help and practical
support were not limited to her friends but also
included her neighbours.

Question: Do you and your neighbours do things
for each other?
Answer: Yes. Sit up with the other one's
children while the ambulance whips off somebody in the middle of the night. One side I
have a very elderly lady. I collect prescriptions, shop and sweep the path when it's
snowing. The other side is a young family.
You know, just general, if she's desperate
she'll turn to me, if I'm desperate I'll turn
to her.

Generally Mrs. Hatch found people were both
sympathetic to her, to Krystyna and to the mentally
handicapped.

Question: What do you think is the general
public's attitude towards children who are
mentally handicapped?
Answer: Very much improved over the last
few years. There's still a tremendous amount
of ignorance. So many of my friends have
said that knowing Krystyna and knowing Paul
when he was alive has opened their eyes and has
made them aware of the problem. All my friends
support us to the hilt in ventures for the

school. They'll all support us by coming and
visiting the school. By visiting the school
they see more and more varied handicapped
children and all the time they're becoming more
and more aware. There still must be great
quantities of the public who have no idea of
the plight of families with people who are
mentally handicapped. It is ignorance but all
the time people are becoming aware. The mentally handicapped are becoming more acceptable,
they're not shut away in the little spare room
any longer.

Comment. In many ways the Hatchs' were a classic
nuclear family. Work and employment had brought and
kept the Hatchs' in Hull. They had no close relatives and made little use of kinship as a source of
support and help. Instead Mrs. Hatch had developed
a network of mutually supporting friendships.

The role of formal services
As two of her three children had been born
severely handicapped Mrs. Hatch had long and extensive experience of professionals. Her initial
encounters, especially with the medical profession,
had been negative but Mrs. Hatch had adopted a similar strategy to the one she used to gain informal
support. She established close relationships with
specific professionals whom she trusted and she
classified them as friends and used them as her main
source of help and advice.

I have created a back up crew of friends. I
have a social worker who works in the paediatric
department of the Infirmary. She's always
available on call as a friend but obviously her
advice and guidance is valuable. I have a
nursing sister who is also a friend.

She used her special relationship with these
'friends' to bypass professionals whom she saw less
informed or less co-operative. For example she
described her use of her paediatrician in the
following way:

On at least three occasions with our family
doctor we've had to go over his head and ring
the paediatrician, another family friend, who
has immediately reacted because he knows us and

our circumstances. On each of these occasions
which ever child it was had been admitted to
hospital within an hour of us contacting the
paediatrician. But we could not get the family
doctor to listen, visit or anything.

Generally Mrs. Hatch was very critical of
professionals who were not her friends, especially
her family doctor.

Question: What do you think is the family
doctor's responsibility towards the family
concerning handicapped children?
Answer: I think he should look upon the
family as a unit, as any other family. I think
that he should have the sense to know that even
if the mother is in a great state and in a
flurry and a fluster that basically she's in
that state because of a reason and not just
dismiss it out of hand. Also, to be adult
enough to appreciate that his patients are
adult enough, and by that I'm speaking of myself or my husband, and listen to what we have
to say and act on it. So my opinion of that
family doctor is nothing. In the case of Paul
and the last illness before he died, he told
me that I was exaggerating, being melodramatic.
The child was then admitted to hospital and
never came home from hospital. Paul's bowels
had packed up which I told the doctor. He said
I was melodramatic. Paul died and after he
died the doctor never called, rang up, or said
were we alright. I come from a family where
uncles were G.P.s and I believe in the old
family care where if there's a bereavement in
the family, the doctor calls round to say are
the rest of you alright or just to say a word.
We never saw sight, sign nor hair of our family
doctor.
Question: What do you think your family doctor's
attitude is to mental handicap?
Answer: He doesn't want to know. He doesn't
want to be bothered. It takes up too much of
his time. He can't just reach for his
prescription pad and write out Valium or
Librium which is his stock in trade.
Question: How best do you think your family
doctor can help you care for Krystyna?
Answer: Just listen to us when we call for
help. Help us to face the next problem. Be
aware of what the next problem is probably

going to be and be there ready and waiting. I
mean obviously with Krystyna the next problem
is menstruation. Well already we've crossed
this bridge with the paediatrician who is now
sitting and waiting and we are sitting and
waiting so that when it happens we're ready with
a plan of action.

Mrs. Hatch was critical of other professionals.
She identified the high turnover of health visitors
and social workers as a special problem.

Question: Would you like someone - a health
visitor or a social worker - you could see
regularly?
Answer: I find that with health visitors and
social workers they change so frequently and
you've got to go back to square one everytime a
different one arrives. Instead of you gaining
any ground, they're benefitting from your
experience. The one who called (a social
worker) about three months ago was in her
probation year and she was using me to learn as
much as anything else.

Mrs. Hatch was one of the few mothers who found
fault with the school teachers.

Question: What about Krystyna's teachers, do
you find them helpful?
Answer: Krystyna's particular teacher at the
moment over-compensates. I think she fusses.
I know Krystyna can't write or draw and she
knows Krystyna can't draw but she still insists
on sending home these pseudo-child like things
which she has drawn to make them look as if
they have come from Krystyna. But we're not
kidding anybody so it's all a great big game
or something. She gets very wound up with the
children. In fact she's too conscientious in
a way and very overbearing with them at times,
and no sense of humour.

Mrs. Hatch's use of informal social relations
as a source of support and help extended to the
local voluntary organisations. Mrs. Hatch was the
secretary of the local branch of MENCAP and Mr.
Hatch the chairman of Krystyna's school PTA. In her
discussion of the MENCAP Mrs. Hatch stressed the
intellectual and educational benefits she gained
from her membership.

Question: What advantages do you gain from
membership?
Answer: Interesting discussion and talks
when there have been guest speakers. We get
doctors, psychologists, health visitors and all
sorts of social workers coming to talk. They
have been very good. There was one man, a
psychologist, who came to talk about sexual
behaviour in mentally handicapped adolescents.
I found it very interesting indeed. Because of
Krystyna's age it is my next most worrying
problem. It extends our minds, educates us,
helps us, definitely I'm all for it. The
society is a forum for a change of thoughts and
ideas with parents of other handicapped people.
One obviously passes over snippets of information and hears what things are in the pipe-
line.

Mrs. Hatch also saw MENCAP as a useful source of
help, especially for family holidays.

The Society organises holidays and outings for
the children. This is a good thing and I have
always involved Krystyna. I like the Society's
holiday accommodation. The family can have a
good holiday with Krystyna and I don't feel too
bad at the way she behaves because everybody
sort of behaves the same way. There's also the
newsletter and Parents Voice which we get
regularly. They make interesting reading. I
think it is important that the Society can
provide a forum like that. It's like a thread,
you feel attached, you're not alone.

MENCAP provided Mrs. Hatch with an outlet for
her social energies and allowed her to establish an
identity as a competent caring person who contributed to the well-being of others.

Question: How do you get involved in the
Society's activities?
Answer: Well, I'm the current secretary. We
raise funds to help the children. We've bought
prams, slides, paints and things. Things that
will help the children. We have a separate
account now which we're hoping eventually to
get a hydrotherapy pool for the school which
will benefit all the children. If the Society's
got any raffles and things like that, I try
and do the tickets. If it wants anything for

tombolas or for the garden fetes or anything like that I try and send something. It's great fun. When you help to raise funds and you see where they're going and what they're doing it is great. You're helping everybody.

Comment. As an articulate and well-educated middle class women Mrs. Hatch demanded and in some cases was given an equal status with the professionals. She described these professionals as her friends and used these friends to obtain the services and resources she needed from various agencies. She had no difficulty in obtaining the various allowances she was entitled to. She was generally critical of other professionals with whom she could not establish a long-term informal relationship.

In contrast to most of the mothers in our study, Mrs. Hatch was actively involved in the organisation of the local branch of MENCAP. This involvement was very important for Mrs. Hatch. It provided her with a source of intellectual stimulation, mutual support and with an opportunity to help others.

Discussion

The Hatches could be described as an archetypal middle class nuclear family. Mr. Hatch had followed his job and the family had moved away from a network of kinsfolk. Mrs. Hatch replaced the traditional network of kin with a network of friends that she recruited from the neighbourhood, from voluntary organisations such as MENCAP and from the professionals inside statutory agencies. These friends provided Mrs. Hatch with the extra aid and support she needed and the ability to maintain her identity as a normal competent adult and mother through mutual exchange and helping others.

MRS. JONES

Background

Mrs. Jones had 7 children, 4 were mentally handicapped. Lisa, the eldest, was 18 years old. She was mentally handicapped and spent part of her time in residential care and part at home. She attended an Adult Training Centre. Edward was 16 years old. He lived at home and attended an ordinary school. His twin brother, Robert, was

severely mentally handicapped, and had lived in a
mental handicap hospital since the age of 5. Mrs.
Jones had agreed to his admission as a doctor told
her that if he was not admitted he would retard
Edward's growth and development. Derek was 14
years old, lived at home and attended an ordinary
school. Maura, the subject of our interview, was
the fifth child. She was 13 years old, lived at
home and attended an ESN(S) school. Tania was 11
years old, lived at home and attended an ordinary
school. Bill, the youngest, was 10, he lived in a
school hostel and attended an ESN(M) school.

The Joneses lived in a four bedroomed council
house on an estate on the outskirts of Hull. The
estate was bleak and fairly rundown. Some flats and
houses had been vandalised. The house lacked basic
amenities. There was no inside toilet. There was
no central heating. The Joneses used coal for
heating. The gas and electricity had been cut off
for non-payment of bills and at the time of the
interview they had only been partially reconnected.
The Joneses used the small dining room as their
living room as they could not afford to heat the
larger living room. They had applied for rehousing
and had been on a waiting list for 7 years. Mrs.
Jones said they were not a priority 'in spite of our
situation because we are not a medical case'.

Discovering the Handicap

When Mrs. Jones became pregnant with Maura she
was already familiar with mental handicap having
two prior mentally handicapped children. She had
been told after the birth of her first child, Lisa,
that there was a 50% chance that another child
would be mentally handicapped but she was convinced
that she would have a normal child, 'I just didn't
think it could happen. I just wouldn't let it sink
in that anybody could have three'.

The pregnancy was relatively normal. A fort-
night before Maura was born she had an accident and
was admitted to a nursing home. The birth was unproblematic and nothing seemed to be the matter.
However Maura did not develop normally. When Maura
was two, Mrs. Jones became aware that she was not
developing properly. Maura was still crawling and
she was not talking 'as two year olds should'. She
obtained an appointment with a hospital consultant.

Question: What were you told?
Answer: I was just told, with having other

mentally handicapped children, to expect the
same about Maura, and I would just have to
make the most of it. I was just told in a
blunt way, I wasn't told in any special way.
With Maura not being my first handicapped child
I knew the effect it would have on the family,
but it broke my heart.
Question: Did you discuss with a doctor the
risk of having another child?
Answer: My doctor gave me no advice until
Maura was born. When I got to Maura, my own
doctor gave me the advice. He said 'Look Mrs.
Jones, it's not fair to you and it's not fair
to anybody else that you should have another
child born like this, because now we know it's
going to happen all the time'. When Maura was
born I wasn't able to take the pill and my
doctor asked if I'd have the operation. I
said no. I thought I'd gone through enough. I
had a word with my husband who volunteered to
have the operation. But by the time he had the
operation I was already expecting Bill.

Most mothers in our study had little or no
experience of mental handicap when their handicapped
child was born. They had to make use of a confusing
situation by relying heavily on the advice and
information of professionals. Mrs. Jones was
exceptional. When Maura was born she had already
had experience of two mentally handicapped children
and therefore had her own stock of experience to
draw on. She neither expected nor received any
help:

I would have liked to have known a lot about
how to deal with their behaviour, some more
information, booklets on how to care for a
mentally handicapped child. I now know there
are societies that can help you but nobody told
me about these. I didn't get any help from
anybody but I wasn't really bothered.

Comment. Like most mothers in our study Mrs. Jones
received very little help and assistance from
professionals. With four mentally handicapped children she had learnt to cope without their advice.
There appeared to be a lack of communication between
Mrs. Jones and the professionals. She appeared to
pay little attention to the advice and information
she was given. For example she was warned after

the birth of her first handicapped child that there
was a high risk that subsequent children would be
handicapped. She had three more handicapped children.

Care in the Family

In terms of disability Maura Jones was similar
to Krystyna Hatch. Like Krystyna she had developed
some capacity to care for herself.

> Dressing. She needs a lot of help, she's able
> to dress herself but is unable to tie her shoe
> laces.
> Bathing. She needs help, because left to her-
> self she takes a long time to wash or bath,
> even then she lacks the manual dexterity for a
> thorough wash or bath.
> Eating. She needs no extra help, can eat at
> table with the rest of the family.
> Toiletting. She uses the toilet alone, but is
> not toilet trained and she wets herself at
> night.
> Walking. She walks alone but is unsteady on
> her feet. She's prone to falling down and
> injuring herself if not supervised.

Like Krystyna, Maura needed a lot of help but there
were some areas in which she was more independent
than Krystyna. Krystyna had to be fed, and soiled
herself at night. Krystyna scored 11 on our disability scale and was classified as severely disabled
and Maura scored 7 and was classified as moderately
disabled.

Mrs. Jones had six children apart from Maura
to look after and she had to learn to 'take things
in my stride'. Nevertheless Maura did present
special problems and there were aspects of Maura's
care that were difficult, especially getting Maura
dressed, changing her at night and supervising her.

Mrs. Jones found dressing Maura difficult when
she was in a hurry.

> Question: What difficulty does this (dressing)
> create?
> Answer: She's very tense and it's difficult
> trying to dress her. When you try to put her
> jumpers on she tenses up and you're having to
> pull her all the time. It causes a lot of
> temper sometimes because there're mornings
> when she won't dress for school. Her brother

had to actually hold her while I zip her and
button her into everything.

Maura's incontinence created a problem at
night and was a social embarrassment.

Question: What difficulty does this (Maura's
incontinence) create?
Answer: Well I've got three girls in one
bedroom and if Marua wets at night, I've got to
put on the light and wake the other two. I
have to run the bath and bath her, if not it's
first thing in the morning. If I find when I
go in in the morning that She's wet the bed
that means that I have to bath her before she
goes to school. You wouldn't do that with a
normal 13 year old but I couldn't rely on Maura
to do that. It wasn't so difficult when she
was younger. But I find it more difficult now
because if she wakes up and she's got anything
on she'll take it all off and then if she wets
it is very difficult because everything gets
wet. I get the disposable nappies, but I wish
they would allow more rubbers. They allow four
pairs a year, and of course a girl of 13, she
needs more because they keep tearing, and then
of course she soaks the bed right through.
It's difficult because she suffers with consti-
pation. If you take her out she uses the
phrase that she wants to go but she doesn't.
Another problem is when you take Maura to
someone's home, especially if they don't know
Maura. You tend to be on tenterhooks all the
time. You say 'come on let's have you
toileted', and yet you know that if you're not
careful you'll make life a misery by doing it.
It's awfully embarrassing if someone's pants
are full of awful smells and all the rest of it.
It causes a lot of washing and a lot of heart-
aches at times.

Maura could walk but with difficulty and this
restricted Mrs. Jones and Maura.

Question: What problems do Maura's walking
create?
Answer: It creates many problems. She can't
walk distances, so one difficulty is when Maura
goes anywhere it's got to be transport all the
time ... She's limited to where she can go or
where I'd like to take her, because it's a bit

frustrating for me at this time of year taking
her into town with so many visitors, and her
getting pushed about. Her brother is very
helpful, he takes her into town on a Saturday
afternoon other wise she wouldn't get anywhere
at the weekends ... She's very clumsy as well
so she bumps into people, not intentionally,
and if she bumped into an old person she could
hurt them.

Even though Maura was usually well behaved she
still needed a lot of supervision because of her
general lack of awareness and epileptic fits.

She couldn't go out to play, whether any child
would want to play with her I don't know. If
she did go out in the back yard you'd have to
watch her in case she had a dizzy spell. She's
split her lip, she's broken her nose, she's
done damage to her chin and she's split her
head open, just with having her dizzy spells.
You've always got to keep your eyes on her
because she's a child that likes to do what she
wants to do. If she sees something at the other
side of the road she'll dash across to get it.
You've always really got to have a hold of her.
She did take an old man's pipe out of his
mouth once. She saw this pipe in his mouth and
thought I'll have that, and just took it. The
gentleman was very nice, but I couldn't be
perturbed about it because they could see she
was handicapped.

Maura did have the odd bad day and then Mrs.
Jones had problems.

Question: What about Maura's behaviour?
Answer: She is stubborn. She gets in some
really bad moods at times, and you cannot cope
with her. Some days she can be really bad.
When we have company this is the time Maura
starts showing off in her own way, and it can
be really annoying at times. It's what you
think they think about your child, then you get
nasty with yourself. That's when you feel you
have got to tap her.

Unlike Mr. Hatch, Mr. Jones was unemployed and
therefore available to help but like Mr. Hatch
he did very little in the way of caring for Maura or
looking after the house. Mrs. Jones said her

husband was only really willing to help in an
emergency.

> He doesn't seem very interested but when it
> comes to the time he knows I'm not able to cope,
> then he'll step in and help out. If he knows
> I'm able to do it myself, I get no help what
> so ever. But if he knows I'm really incapable
> of being able to help myself that's when I'll
> say he's good.

Like Mrs. Hatch, Mrs. Jones accepted the
division of responsibility within the household as
right and proper. She was pleased that her husband
could take over in an emergency but also saw his
incompetence as establishing her status as a competent mother.

> The first time I had to go into hospital they
> came round from the social services to see if
> they should put the kids in a home and my
> husband said 'Not while I'm here'. It was a
> strange experience for him. I was away for
> two weeks. I realise now he couldn't cope with
> the family and me being away from home for long.
> He was lost without me.

Normally when Mrs. Jones had to be away she
made arrangements for Maura to be cared for.

> The last time I was away was when I had
> thrombosis and I went in for ten days. I made
> arrangements for Maura to be taken to Westlands.
> I'd rather her be in Westlands than be at home.
> Her dad isn't cruel to her, he's good. But he
> tends to go out to put a bet on and will say to
> Paul 'Keep an eye on her while I nip to the
> shop', and to me that's wrong. That's why I
> think she'll be safe and properly looked after
> if she was away.

Caring for Maura was difficult and put a strain
on Mrs. Jones and the family but with six other
children - three normal and three handicapped
children - it was difficult to identify the distinctive problems of caring for Maura and the specific
impact Maura had on the family. Indeed Mrs. Jones
sometimes mixed the children and their problems up
as in the following discussion of the impact of
Maura on her health.

Question: Have there been any effect on your
health because of caring for Maura at home?
Answer: Well, yes. My health has suffered
because of lifting her and straining my spine.
Then the lumps under my arms which I suffer
through stress and strain, plus nerves. I
worried more when she was at the training
centre (Lisa). She came home with bruises. I
was worried all the time what they were doing
to her. I knew she was being hit at the centre
and I knew she wasn't happy there. She showed
it in the tantrums she used to have when she
came home at night. This worried me. It
didn't help my nerves. I find that I can't mix
in with people it's very hard. I feel
different from them. They've got normal children. When I go out I fear that they're going
to say their children are running about and
I'm hoping they're not going to ask me. I get
too tensed up and I'm too frightened to go out.
People don't understand why you're getting so
nervous and why you don't like mixing in with
them. I can't actually talk about the children
without it affecting my nerves.

Mrs. Jones found coping with life difficult and
had sought advice and help from her family doctor.

Question: Do you have to see a doctor about
your nerves?
Answer: Yes, I've gone periodically to the
doctor. He gives me pills which don't do any
good. I think to myself, now, if the doctor
rather than give me drugs, could send me some-
where and help me in another way. I've taken
drugs for seventeen years, but the drugs are
doing me no good. If he could send me some-
where for help, or to somebody who could help
me to help myself then I think I would be a lot
better off than taking drugs, sat here taking
drugs all my life.

Mrs. Jones' workload was generally heavy and on some
days she can barely cope.

Question: Which aspects of daily care would
you want more help with?
Answer: Washing, washing, washing! On the
bad days when I've got stacks of washing. When
the children are wetting the bed, when I get in
bad humours. My brain is saying can I do it,

am I going to make it. I often have them days.
That's when I wish I had more help.

Like most mothers Mrs. Jones found Maura an
additional expense and one which, with her limited
financial resources, she could ill-afford. As in
Mrs. Hatch's case she identified lost opportunities.

Question: Do you think Maura restricts you in
getting a job more than a normal child?
Answer: Yes, definitely. Many a time I've
thought I would like a change of atmosphere.
But you know that everything is going to be
neglected. The children are going to get neglected, and then you're going to come home at
the weekend, to piles of washing, piles of
everything, because everything would go to pot.
I know it would if I went to work, even though
I would sometimes like the change from the four
walls. No way could I even dream of going to
work.

Mrs. Jones clearly felt that she should be
compensated for the financial costs of caring for
Maura.

Question: Do you think there's a need for
financial help for families caring for children
who are mentally handicapped?
Answer: Yes, I think they should really
compensate us a little bit more, because we
have to give up our lives. It's not the
government's fault that we have these children.
They may turn round and say 'it's your fault,
you had them'. This is a thing that can
happen to anybody, but this is the attitude
people give you. They think you went and had
these children, it's not our fault. We get the
attendance allowance but I don't think that is
sufficient. If the child is in a home or a
hospital it will cost more than £18.60. Yes,
we do need more than what we get. It would pay
for the extras you couldn't afford because of
the restrictions on the family life.

Mrs. Jones devoted all her time to caring for
her family and running the house. The whole household was geared to the needs of its handicapped
members. The Joneses got by with a restricted
routine involving few activities outside the house

We have a large family and we find that we need
to live to a pattern, we can cope a lot better
now with a pattern. You've got to stick to a
pattern and that's the best way I can put it.
You must stick to a pattern with these children. Break the pattern and you've got problems.
So this is one reason why we don't go out.

Holidays were impossible.

Question: What about holidays?
Answer: A lot of the holiday places don't
take the mentally handicapped. One year we
wanted a caravan and we tried all over and
when we said that there were three mentally
handicapped also in the family, they didn't
want to know. We never bothered again.

Mrs. Jones was preoccupied with the present and
the problems of coping. She had not devoted a great
deal of thought to the future. She was concerned
about Maura leaving school and going to the Adult
Training Centre because Lisa, her eldest daughter,
had found the change difficult.

Question: Do you think any difficulties may
arise in the future in connection with Maura's
education?
Answer: The main problem is when she gets to
the age of sixteen. I wouldn't like her to be
shoved straight into the Adult Training Centre.
They take them out of school and shove them
straight away with adults. It just didn't work
with Lisa. Lisa was placed with adults. It
broke my heart, because even though she was
sixteen, to me she was a child. In the Centre
they were all jealous of her because there were
a lot of older people with different handicaps.
They used to knock her about. She was in
hospital twice and in the end I took her out of
the centre altogether. Your problems start
then because you know you can't cope with them
at home all the time.

Her fears about the future were vague and non-
specific. Her children would have to accept what
they got.

Question: What do you think will happen in the
future if you or both parents are too old to
look after her?

Answer: It's frightening to think about.
You wonder are they going to be put in a home,
a mental home? I would like the handicapped
to be all together, not separated. I would
like somebody, like myself, who knew a lot
about them to be able to look after them. As
things are now, if I found I was sick and it
was very hard to cope, then I wouldn't mind her
being fostered into another family. But as I
can cope I can look after her myself.

Comment. For Mrs. Jones, Maura was just one problem amongst the many she had to cope with. Maura
was her most disabled child and her incontinence and
problems with walking created additional problems,
but these were small additions. It was the overall
size of the task that created the restrictions and
led to the limited life style of the Joneses.

Informal Support in the Community
    Mrs. Jones did have relatives living close by
but they provided little support. All of them had
their own problems. Her parents were dead and her
husband's parents were elderly.

His parents are getting on now and they would
find it a strain to have her (Maura) for a few
days because they don't really know her. I
would be far more worried about her with them
than I'd be if she was at the school hostel.

Her own brothers and sisters were preoccupied with
their own families and didn't have any time or
resources to help her.

I have brothers and sisters living away from
home but I couldn't turn to them because they
all have their own problems with bringing up
their own children. None of my sisters want
to know... My sisters all live in Hull but
we don't see each other, never have done since
my two boys were born.

Unlike Mrs. Hatch, Mrs. Jones had few friends
and had not developed a network of support in the
community. She was relatively isolated.

Question: Have you become good friends with
anyone who has a mentally handicapped child?

Answer: Audrey ... if Audrey's got any
problems she'll come round and ask for advice,
we're not close friends. I haven't got any
friends.

Mrs. Jones found her neighbours hostile and
was unable to develop a supportive relationship with
them.

Question: Do you like living in this area?
Answer: No I don't. People here do not
accept the mentally handicapped. They're
really rotten to them. They just don't accept
them. They've been beaten up. They take the
mickey out of them. Not just the young ones,
I'm on about adults as well. Not only the
children suffer, I get it as well. People
around here have upset me talking about the
children being as they are. They've said 'put
them up against the wall and shoot them, get
them in the garden and chain them up, they're
not fit to be on the streets'. It's not as
though I let them out on the street.

Mrs. Jones had been trying to change houses for
seven years and it was one of her main preoccupa-
tions.

Question: Why do you want to leave this area?
Answer: Whilst I've been in this area I've
been sick with worry because we've had a lot of
vandalism. I don't know whether you heard of
the family whose house was set on fire because
neighbours disapproved of their handicapped
children. Well, they did it a different way
with us. They put our windows through. They
more or less tried to drive us out - if you
don't go on your own, right we'll drive you
out. That's the way they've done it. I get on
to the police but they're not interested
because my bairns are mentally handicapped.
They should bring something out to protect the
mentally handicapped!
Question: What effect has this experience had
on you?
Answer: Most of the society (MENCAP) people
who I've spoken to have said the public around
them are marvellous and they accept the
mentally handicapped. I don't know because
I've never been anywhere else. It can really
hurt, especially when they call the kids

idiots. It hurts me deep inside to think I
have these idiots, and God must have given
them for some reason. It hurts the parents
more than it hurts the bairns.

On the other hand Mrs. Jones was quite willing
to use neighbours in a crisis.

Question: Who would you turn to at short
notice for assistance?
Answer: It would depend on what it was. If
a problem cropped up on a fairly long term
basis I'd probably approach the school. I
would approach them rather than friends,
neighbours or relatives... On the other hand,
if the emergency would last for a couple of
hours or so then I would leave her with neighbours.
Question: When was the last time you had to
turn to someone for assistance?
Answer: It was when Lisa, my eldest daughter, needed to go to hospital. She was
kicked at the centre. I was in bed. I had a
breakdown and the doctor had been to see me.
My husband's mother had had a stroke and he was
away. My neighbour, Margaret, came across to
see what the problem was. I explained and
Margaret said 'Don't worry about it', and she
went to hospital with Lisa.

Comment. Mrs. Jones lived in a rather hostile and
unfriendly world. Despite her extensive and
difficult problem she found it difficult to make
friends and had not developed a supportive network
of relatives and friends. She was very much on her
own.

The Role of Formal Services
     With her large family Mrs. Jones had extensive
experience of welfare services and the professionals.
However she lacked the skills and ability of Mrs.
Hatch and did not know how to establish fruitful
working relations with these professionals.
Generally she found the professionals unhelpful and
unsympathetic.
     She described her relationship with her family
doctor in the following way:

Question: How helpful has been the support

you've received from your family doctor?
Answer: When they are mentally handicapped
you're a little bit more concerned about these
children than you are with the normal ones,
because they seem to get an illness more than
the normal ones. When you say to your doctor
'My child is mentally handicapped, can I have
a doctor'? You have to wait your turn. I
wouldn't say I've had a lot of help from my
doctor.
Question: What do you think is the family
doctor's responsibility towards the family
concerning the handicapped child?
Answer: I would expect him to come out when
she was ill. But I'd say 'Do you mind coming
out to see Maura'? 'You bring her to the
surgery'! I'd say 'Well she's handicapped',
and he'd say 'What difference does it make, you
can bring her to the surgery'! He doesn't
realise that it costs you money all the time to
make it to the surgery. I have a lot of problems with my doctor. When they were very young,
and took poorly all hours of the night, the
doctor would say 'Who do you think you are
ringing me at this time of night'? I think
they should be a bit more sympathetic to the
mentally handicapped and their parents.
Question: How best do you think your family
doctor can help you care for Maura?
Answer: I would like to be able to go to
him and ask him for advice as she grows older,
about sexual problems and things like this I
would like to know.

Mrs. Jones saw her family doctor as a useful
resource but one that she obtained at rather a high
cost. In contrast she had little use for either her
health visitor or for her social worker. She did
not want to accept their advice and found they were
unable to obtain benefits for her.

Question: How helpful has been the support
you've received from health visitors?
Answer: No, I never really bothered with
health visitors. I didn't have a lot of
patience with them. Half of them didn't have
kids of their own, and they tried to tell me
how to bring mine up and it just didn't work.
Question: How helpful has been the support
you've received from your social worker?
Answer: None. They haven't got the

patience. My social worker is one of those who
tells me how well her kids are coming on at
school, brags about how she goes swimming at
dinnertime. That's not helping me, is it? Who
wants to know what's happening in her family.
When it comes to my problems, she doesn't want
to know about them. I ask her where I can get
this from and where I can get that from. Like
when I got the money stopped for the bairns for
stopping at the hostel. I wanted to fight the
decision because other mothers fought and had
their attendance allowance restored. She said,
'I know nothing at all about the attendance
allowance so I can't help you in any way at
all'. We've been trying to get out of this
house for the past seven years and get a bigger
house so that we could have Robert home for a
holiday. I asked if she'd write me a letter
which helps when you're dealing with the housing corporation. She said 'You'll have to wait
until I come back because I've got this other
girl to see to. She's got to go to court in
Newcastle, and I must see her first'! This was
a normal child. I reported her. I rang the
social services and said I want a social worker
who understands the needs of the mentally
handicapped. She's not a caring person. She
came round and said 'I know you don't like me,
there's not many that do, but if you ever need
me anytime give me a ring'. I said 'never'.
She said to me 'Well you do need a medal for
what you've done'. I said 'I don't want a
medal, I want a little bit of help and advice'.
Every mother who has a mentally handicapped
child needs a medal, I wouldn't say just me.

Mrs. Jones was not hostile to all professionals.
She found the school and school teachers very helpful.

Question: What about her teachers, do you find
them helpful?
Answer: They have been helpful. Maura used
to go to the day centre. She used to come home
and go to sleep, she'd no interest in anything.
Then she started the school. She's pleased
with herself now. She goes on holidays which
we pay for. They teach her to do things, like
cookery. They're teaching her to write her
name.

Mrs. Jones was aware of the special financial benefits available to her and had applied for both the attendance and mobility allowance. She had obtained the lower rate of attendance allowance but was unsuccessful with the mobility allowance.

> I get the attendance allowance, but this doesn't help really with the times she has to go out. I have been told that she has a slight spastic condition possibly brought on by a stroke during the fits. She can walk and doesn't qualify for the mobility allowance. I applied in the first instance and was turned down. Then when this test case came on of a child who did get the mobility allowance, I went back to the tribunal and had a medical. I went before a public tribunal, but they turned my application down because she's not sufficiently immobile to qualify.

Comment. Mrs. Jones found it difficult to establish working relations with professionals. Although she was able to obtain basic resources such as attendance allowance, she did not have the necessary skills to get the long term support she needed and therefore had to rely very much on her own resources.

Discussion

Mrs. Jones was an atypical mother and the Joneses were an atypical family. She had the largest family, the most mentally handicapped children and possibly the heaviest workload of all the mothers we talked to. There were signs that she could not cope. One of her children was a long term resident in a mental handicap hospital. The house was dirty and run down. She was unable to pay the bills. The family could not live in parts of the house. The family had antagonised their neighbours and the professionals that were trying to help them. However despite the mess and chaos Mrs. Jones soldiered on and when we talked to her the family were surviving, albeit on a day to day basis.

CONCLUSION

We hope that in these two case studies we have shown the dangers of generalization. Mrs. Hatch and Mrs. Jones both cared for a mentally handicapped

daughter and Krystyna Hatch and Maura Jones had
similar handicaps and similar needs. Both mothers
had to provide the bulk of care and both families
were subject to considerable restrictions on their
activities. These restrictions were similar to
those experienced by families with pre-school children but unlike these families, the restrictions were
likely to persist for the forseeable future. Both
mothers had developed strategies for coping and had
developed a routine to enable them to cope with the
heavy burden of caring for their handicapped children.
    However the differences between the mothers and
families was far greater than the similarities. Mrs.
Hatch was an articulate middle class woman with the
extensive social skills that she could use to
mobilise a range of informal and formal support.
Her experience of the world and mental handicap was
very different to Mrs. Jones. She lived in a
sympathetic and supportive environment that she
could use, even educate. Mrs. Jones was less
articulate, had little education and few social
skills. She did not have the ability or skill to
mobilise support. She was isolated and lived in an
unsympathetic and hostile environment and barely
got by.

Chapter 10

CONCLUSION - WHAT DIRECTION COMMUNITY CARE?

INTRODUCTION

Our study of mothers with severely handicapped
school children was descriptive and exploratory.
We did not start with a particular theory to test,
rather we wanted to find out, by talking to
mothers, about their daily experiences of caring for
their mentally handicapped school children and we
used theory to help us organise the talk and their
accounts.

We talked to a relatively small group of
mothers who lived in North Humberside about a
relatively limited set of topics. We did not conduct a large scale postal questionnaire of a
national sample of mothers. Our material is therefore limited and we hope that there will be many
more studies that are both wider in scope and more
analytic in design.

In our study and in this book we accepted
mothers' accounts of their situation and their
assessment of their relationship with others at face
value. If we had talked to others we would undoubtedly have got different accounts. However it is
mothers who provide the bulk of the care and therefore we believe their version should take precedence.
Professionals have little difficulty in making their
views known but services should be designed around
the needs and perceptions of mothers not those of
professionals.

In this concluding chapter we shall draw out
the implication of our study for the development
of networks of support in this country. In the
first section we highlight the findings of our
study and emphasise the light these findings throw
on the shortcomings of current policies and services
for mentally handicapped children and the mothers

who care for them. In the second and third sections
of the chapter we shall discuss possible innovations
that will both improve the quality of care of children living at home and provide support and assistance to mothers. In the second section we shall
discuss ways of enhancing the informal support of
families through the development of self-help groups
amongst parents of mentally handicapped children.
In the third section we shall discuss methods of
improving the support parents receive from formal
agencies.

MOTHERS IN NORTH HUMBERSIDE

In this section we shall discuss the findings
of our study. We shall discuss the role of mother
as the main carer; the problems of everyday care;
and the role of formal agencies.

Mothers of Mentally Handicapped Children
Both professionals and researchers often assume
that families and mothers of mentally handicapped
children must somehow be damaged by the experience.
In our study mothers stressed their own normality
and competence and the similarity of their family
to other families. Voysey also talked to parents of
handicapped children and found a similar desire to
stress normality and normal family life. This was a
reflection of reality for these parents 'because it
is as normal parents that others, both informal and
formal agencies treat them'.[1] Our mothers had
their problems and were under stress but so do other
mothers who have young children. The mothers in our
study were, to use Winnicott's phrase, 'ordinary
good enough mothers'[2] with ordinary families and
leading ordinary lives.
The difference lay mainly in these mothers'
lack of preparation for caring for a mentally handicapped child. For most mothers the usual
preparatory socialization of relatives, friends,
Dr. Spock, etc. is enough but mothers with mentally
handicapped children are faced with distinctive
problems. They do not know what to expect and they
do not know how to deal with problems that can be
associated with mental handicap such as epilepsy.
The mothers in our study did not need psychiatric
help to enable them to 'adjust', 'accept' or
'resolve their guilt feelings'. They wanted to be
'treated as adults', to be told what to expect and

to be given practical advice and help that would
enable them to care for their child and develop his
or her potential to the full.

The care of mothers is the basis of community
care for mentally handicapped children and there is
no substitute to the care and involvement mothers
provide. As the Court Committee pointed out 'We
have found no better way to raise a child than to
reinforce the ability of his parent(s) to do so'.[3]
But the involvement of a mother with her child is
both a strength and a weakness. Caring for a
handicapped child is demanding and can be lonely
work. The mothers in our study had different
capacities and abilities to care for their children
and to mobilise the necessary support.

All the mothers in our study, whatever their
child's needs and their problems in fulfilling
these needs, wanted to care for their child at home
and wanted to provide and maintain a normal home
environment for their child. In the words of one
mother 'home is the right place for all my children
to live'.

The mothers talked about their children as
people who were handicapped. Their children were
not 'spina bifida', 'spastic', 'Down's', or 'a
mongol' but children and members of their family,
albeit members with special needs. Officially all
the children in our study were classified as severely mentally handicapped but this broad classification concealed far more than it revealed. The
range of abilities amongst severely mentally
handicapped children was far greater than amongst
other children of the same age. Each child was
unique, had a unique range of abilities and disabilities and was a unique person within the context
of a particular household and family. Individual
families had children with very different needs and
had different resources they could draw on to
satisfy these needs. The strategy adopted by
individual families varied according to the child-
rens' needs, the family resources and their
perception of the situation.

Daily Care
    Mothers' desire to provide and maintain a
normal family life usually involved considerable
sacrifices. The extra work involved was usually
considerable and the mothers generally took on the
majority of it, especially the extra housework and
child care. Mothers did get help from their

husbands, relatives and friends but this help was usually restricted to child-minding activities or moral support.

There were costs. All mothers experienced relative deprivation. There were activities or opportunities that they would have undertaken or had if their child had been normal. The family as a whole experienced deprivation. Some mothers became preoccupied with their handicapped child and other members of the family were deprived of the attention they would otherwise have received. In the words of one mother 'I wanted to do everything I could to help her. I didn't want help from anyone, or anybody else to take her away from me and it got so bad, I was leaving my other 3 children and their father out'.

Although the mothers presented their family as a normal family and most said the birth of their handicapped child had brought the family together, most also acknowledged the strain created within the family. Some mothers said their husband did not understand the extra work created and were unsympathetic to their needs. In one case a mother of a severely mentally handicapped boy who was overactive and difficult to manage said her husband insisted on her keeping the house spotless and expected that a cooked meal would be ready for him when he returned from work.

Most mothers could deal with the day to day problems but the future was to many a source of anxiety and worry. Unlike mothers with other young children who could expect their child to become more independent and therefore could expect a steady reduction in the care and supervision of their child, the mothers in our study expected little improvement and most looked ahead to a life of caring and the associated restrictions.

The Role of Formal Services

The Seebohm Committee on Local Authority and Allied Personal Social Services advocated a 'community based and family-oriented service' that would 'enable the greatest possible number of individuals to act reciprocally, giving and receiving services for the well-being of the whole community'.[4] We could find little evidence of a sensitive coordinated system of support for the mothers we talked to.

We found that mothers had a remarkably low opinion of the majority of professionals they came

into contact with. There was little evidence of
continuity of support and little evidence that
generalist or generic practitioner had much knowledge of, or interest in the needs of mentally
handicapped individuals and their families. The
exception were the school teachers at the special
school. The majority of mothers found them both
helpful and useful but even here there were costs.
The provision for education for mentally handicapped
children was segregated from the provision of other
children and some mothers felt their children were
deprived of educational experiences and found problems with transport.

There are a large number of agencies that are
willing and able to help the mentally handicapped
and their families. To many mothers this network of
services was confusing and few mothers had a comprehensive knowledge of the different agencies, their
workers and the services they provided.

Many mothers were unaware of the facilities
they could use. For example, 70% did not know about
aids, applicances and home adaptations and 88% did
not know about the laundry service or home help
service. Similar problems existed with financial
assistance. The introduction of financial schemes
that help families with handicapped children is
undoubtedly a welcome innovation but many mothers
did not have the right information. 60% of the
mothers we talked to did not know about the Family
Fund and 26% did not know about the attendance
allowance. In the case of another welcomed innovation, short-term care, a rather different problem
emerged. Mothers were aware of the availability of
the service but there were considerable worries
about the equitability of distribution of the available service. Many mothers felt the best periods
were being unfairly allocated.

Support services for the mentally handicapped
are now divided between a number of different
agencies. There is no single agency or practitioner
that can provide comprehensive information about
the range of available services or guide mothers
through the network of services. Most mothers we
talked to found out about the services from other
mothers. Some co-ordinating and integrative
mechanism is needed so that mothers of mentally
handicapped children do not fall through the welfare
net.

Discussion

Community care is a fine piece of government rhetoric. The positive attitudes to the mentally handicapped and their families implicit in it should be welcomed when contrasted to the hostility implicit in the 1913 Mental Deficiency Act and the colony system associated with it. Furthermore as an official commitment to dismantling the segregated system of institutional care it should also be welcomed. However our study indicates the danger of the policy. The policy has different meanings and currently the main emphasis is on the development of a network of small residential facilities in the community. Specialist services and facilities for the mentally handicapped are being dismantled but they are not being replaced by active support for mothers caring for their severely handicapped children. These mothers are providing community care with a minimum of informal and formal support.

In the remainder of this chapter we explore two alternative and complementary ways of providing more support. The first involves developing informal support through self-help and the second involves building on statutory services but developing a network of contact points or individuals within these services.

ENHANCING THE CARING CAPACITY OF THE COMMUNITY

Until the 1960s the shortcomings of welfare provisions for various client groups was seen as evidence that more welfare and welfare agencies were needed of a more sophisticated variety. There was a consensus that the development of the welfare state was a good thing and this development would continue. This optimism has in the late 70s been replaced by a more pessimistic attitude.

The criticisms of the welfare state have been popularised by Ivan Illich. Illich has argued that the welfare state creates the very problems it purports to solve[5] and professionals, rather than helping people, take away people's capacity to care for themselves.[6] Although there is little general support for the radical position adopted by Illich, many commentators on the welfare state would agree that welfare agencies are large bureaucracies that tend to be slow, impersonal and insensitive to the needs of individual clients. Professional intervention is not only expensive but can produce a state of dependence in the client who seeks help.

240

Professionals often have limited accountability either to the agencies that employ them or to the clients who use their services yet they frequently exert considerable influence and control over the lives and welfare of their clients.[7]

The reduction in the caring capacity of the community is not a result of or created by development of welfare agencies and professionals. Rather both are a product of the changing structure of society associated with industrialization and urbanization. These changes have reduced mechanisms for mutual support in the community such as kin groups and there is little evidence to show that neighbourhood in British towns or villages can provide an effective mechanism for mutual support.[8] In our study the burden of care fell on the family and especially the mother and there was little evidence of systematic community support.[9]

The problem can be defined in two different ways. How can the mentally handicapped and their families get the information or support they need without having to rely on or become dependent on formal agencies and professionals and how can the caring capacity of the community be enhanced to provide informal support and help for the mentally handicapped on the basis of mutual reciprocity?

One solution suggested to these problems is the development of self-help groups amongst families of the mentally handicapped. The parents of mentally handicapped children have, through their experiences of caring for their child and through finding and using various methods of support, become experts. Indeed as many mothers in our study stressed some professionals looked to them for advice and guidance. Furthermore the parents of mentally handicapped children have a mutual interest and share certain experiences. If the parents of mentally handicapped children choose to stress their common experiences and identity they can form a mutually supporting group or a self-help group.[10]

The self-help, mutual aid or co-operative approach to social deprivation has a long history but in the last decade it has been increasingly adopted by groups who experience stigma, social deprivation and/or health problems. For example individuals with drinking problems have formed Alcoholics Anonymous, individuals with gambling problems have formed Gamblers Anonymous, and homosexuals have formed The Campaign for Homosexual Equality.[11]

Self-help groups have been created for a

variety of reasons and a variety of purposes.
Robinson and Henry have identified some of the
reasons for the development of self-help groups in
health as: disillusionment with established
services, hostility to established professions, a
change in the conception of the role and efficacy of
state, a search for an alternative to traditional
social support and an ideological rejection of
contemporary values such as individualism.[12]
       Whatever the reasons for the establishment of a
self-help group all successful groups share certain
characteristics. Successful groups establish an
identity and life of their own. Members feel that
their contributions are valued, that they obtain
benefits from belonging and that group is mutually
beneficial. The common problem or identity that
draws people together is seen as more important than
the differences between members. The group is self-
running and self-governing. Indeed, as Robinson and
Henry suggest, membership of a successful self-help
group may become a 'way of life'.[13]
       The relationships which self-help groups
establish with formal services and agencies is both
interesting and complex. Some self-help groups are
explicitly established in opposition to and as a
rejection of formal agencies and their professionals.
For example, Johnson, whose son had muscular
dystrophy and, who was a founder member of a local
group, said 'When I started the Hugh Johnson Club
the parents were adamant that no social worker
should be asked to help'.[14] However many groups
also rely on professionals. In many cases the
specific problem that brings the group together is
defined by professionals. Groups have worked out
their relationships with professionals in different
ways. The most successful groups, such as
Alcoholics Anonymous, have been able to reverse the
traditional relationship of subordination that
clients have in the professional-client relationship. Alcoholics Anonymous maintains a distance
from formal services but it is seen as a useful
asset by service providers. Practitioners, who have
no ready solution to offer problem drinkers, can
refer them to a local group of Alcoholics Anonymous.
Policy makers, in thinking about the development of
services for problem drinkers, can draw on the
expertise of Alcoholics Anonymous.
       Most progressive practitioners describe the
relationship between the parents of mentally handicapped children and professionals as a partnership.
If the relationship is a partnership then it is one

based on terms by the professionals. They define
the problems and provide the solutions.[15] The
development of self-help groups could be the basis
for a real partnership. Self-help groups can act as
an alternative to the bureaucratised insensitivity
of welfare agencies.[16] Local self-help groups can
act as a resource centre and source of mutual
benefit. The services of professionals would be one
of the resources and professionals would have an
important role to play in referring potential
members to the group.

There are relatively few self-help groups
amongst the parents of mentally handicapped children.
One group, Contact a Family, was set up in 1974 and
has tried to develop a network of neighbourhood
self-help groups in London. Contact a Family
defines its objectives in the following way:

> To give families with a handicapped child
> living at home contact with other families who
> are in the same situation and area as them-
> selves;
> To bring together these families so that they
> can exchange information and share experiences,
> give each other mutual support, understanding
> and practical help;
> To enable these families to meet as near as
> possible to their home;
> To have frequent contact and somewhere central
> to meet and share activities;
> To give parents, through being part of a local
> group the opportunity to press for better
> services and say collectively what their group
> needs are;
> To encourage families to organise services that
> they need locally, e.g. holiday play-schemes,
> baby-sitting and transport schemes;
> To enable families with handicapped children
> to benefit as a whole, not just the handicapped
> child but also the parents and brothers and
> sisters;
> To give these handicapped children and their
> families the opportunity to take a more active
> part in their local community.[17]

It is easier to identify the advantages of
self-help groups than it is to identify the
processes by which a successful self-help group is
formed and how self-help groups can be fostered
amongst the parents of the mentally handicapped.
Robinson and Henry have examined the accounts that

existing groups have made of their origins.

> Three main aims tend to be emphasised in
> groups' accounts of their origins: failure of
> existing services, recognition of the value of
> mutual help and the role of the media. The
> stress given to any one of the themes varied
> greatly from account to account but, as in
> commentators' accounts, the failure of existing
> services to provide satisfaction for people
> with problems was given most weight.[18]

Establishing a self-help group is very much a
social process. It depends on a group of individuals recognising a common problem and a common
grievance or identity and meeting to develop a
programme to deal with this problem. The obvious
starting point and basis for a network of self-help
groups amongst the families of mentally handicapped
people are existing voluntary agencies such as
MENCAP. Some mothers in our study already treated
the local branch of MENCAP as if it were a self-
help group. However this development was relatively
informal and implicit. The local branches had
limited autonomy and limited membership. Less than
half the mothers in our sample belonged to MENCAP.
To develop fully as self-help group branches would
have to develop their own programme of independent
activity. An obvious starting point would be a
review of local services and parents' experiences of
them. This would pool experience and knowledge and
help to heighten group consciousness.

Comment. Traditional community support no longer
exists in industrial society and support from professionals is often inadequate and can actually be
counterproductive and create a sense of dependency
amongst clients. Self-help groups offer an
alternative. Individuals can pool their experiences
and resources and the group can act as a supportive
community. Self-help groups have tended to develop
spontaneously as a reaction to specific dissatis-
faction. Little work has been done on the system-
development of a network of groups. However there
are amongst the parents of the mentally handicapped
organisations that could form the basis of this
type of systematic development.

DEVELOPING COMMUNITY SERVICES

90% of severely mentally handicapped children
live with their families at home.[19] An effective
policy of community care should fulfil several
requirements. It should primarily be concerned with
the needs of the families caring for their children.
It should seek to anticipate and meet the unique and
changing needs of individual families. It should
provide a comprehensive, coordinated and easily
accessible locally based service. In our study we
could find little evidence of such a service and in
this section we discuss the basic constituents of
such a service.

The Underlying Philosophy
        In his study of institutions, Wolfensberger[20]
has shown that all policies for mentally handicapped
people embody and reflect deeply held social values
and beliefs about the nature of mental handicap.
This is true whether these policies are government
statements such as White Papers, the operating
manuals of local welfare agencies or the day to day
actions of service providers. In Chapter 1 we
showed how attitudes to the mentally handicapped and
their families have shifted in the last hundred
years and how the principles of custodial care
implicit in the 1913 Mental Deficiency Act were
based on a negative view of the mentally handicapped
and their families.
        The situation has undoubtedly improved and
official policy is now based on a more sympathetic
view of the mentally handicapped and their
families. Publication of documents such as the
DHSS White Paper Better Services for the Mentally
Handicapped[21] indicate a growing awareness of and
interest in the rights of mentally handicapped
people. At an international level the Declaration
of the Rights of Mentally Handicapped Persons[22]
shows an equivalent awareness. The Jay Committee
gave these rights form by proposing three principles
as the basis of policy for mentally handicapped
peoples:

        Mentally handicapped people have a right to
        enjoy normal patterns of life within the
        community; Mentally handicapped people have a
        right to be individuals; and
        Mentally handicapped people will require
        additional help from the communities in which

245

they live and from the professional services if
they are to develop to their maximum potential
as individuals.[23]

However the committee pointed out that these
principles have to be interpreted and given concrete
form and a range of operational issues are involved
including: where should mentally handicapped people
live; what sort of living environment should they
have and how should services be organised? In this
section we shall make some suggestions for improvements in the organisation of services.

Basic Services
        MENCAP has produced a check list of questions
to enable parents, voluntary groups and professionals to evaluate services provided locally and
identify shortcomings. The check list identifies
the services which MENCAP believes are essential, if
mentally handicapped children and their families are
to enjoy a normal pattern of life in the community.
We reproduce the items in MENCAP list as we feel it
gives the range of services and facilities that
should constitute an effective service.

1.   Regular full support from relevant specialist
      services, for example, paediatrician, speech
      therapist, psychologist, psychiatrist, physio-
      therapist;
2.   Regular support from specialist social worker
      and/or health visitor. This should include
      visits at home at intervals of not more than
      two months;
3.   Visits by professionals, which should be
      documented in reports to the appropriate
      authority and these reports should be available
      to parents;
4.   Parents should have the opportunity of counsel-
      ling and advice, short-term relief, clinics,
      opportunity classes, etc;
5.   Full information regarding statutory benefits
      and services of all kinds should be readily
      available and should be conveyed to parents by
      specialist social workers and/or community
      mental handicap nurses;
6.   Priority placement on local authority housing
      lists should be available to families with a
      severely mentally handicapped child;
7.   Parents' 'workshops' to assist parents with the
      care of their child and to provide information

about support services for the families should
be provided by the local agencies;
8.   A full laundry service;
9.   Special equipment, drawsheets, nappies, suit-
     able wheelchairs, washing machines;
10. Adaptations to the homes in the form of ramps
     to doorways, hoists, etc., should be available
     if required;
11. Home help and other kinds of support for
     families should be available;
12. Local short-term care should be available on
     request for a variety of periods including
     overnight, for weekends, Mondays to Fridays, or
     in emergencies;
13. Options for short-term care should include
     foster homes and childrens homes;
14. A 'day care' programme should be available
     throughout all school holidays;
15. Any child irrespective of how difficult, if
     managed by the parents, should have access to
     short-term facilities; and
16. Local authority social and leisure activities
     should be available or that financial support
     is given to voluntary agencies to arrange these
     activities.[24]

The general availability of specific services
does not guarantee that individual families will
get access to the specific service they require.
Families vary in their awareness and in their
ability to exploit resources. The services have to
be organised around the needs of specific families
and specific children.

Individual Programme Plans
     The starting point for a comprehensive service
should be the needs of individual children and
their families. Individual programme plans are a
useful way of creating improved service co-ordina-
tion. A plan is developed by all those involved in
caring for the child and represents agreed objectives and activities. The different participants in
the caring process are brought together periodically
to assess the needs of the child and his or her
family, identify particular service needs or service
objectives and review progress. Carle sees
individual programme plans as a natural development
of the view that each person is unique and should
receive the assistance appropriate to his or her
particular need in his or her specific environment.[25]

Review meetings should be the main forum in which individual plans or 'life plans' are agreed.[26] These meetings should involve both parents and professionals and should be based on shared decision-making. Review meetings can pool information from different participants. Detailed and up-to-date assessment must be available. Each child should be regularly assessed in his or her own environment, not the artificial environment of an assessment centre. Like the meeting itself, the assessments should include the whole range of individuals involved, especially the child's guardians or parents. The programme would include a statement of long and short term goals, steps required to reach the goals, resources required and responsibilities of different participants and mechanisms for monitoring and reviewing progress.

The concept of an individual programme has been officially endorsed[27] and there are a number of experimental schemes using it[28] but it has not become an accepted part of the routine services in the same way as case conferences for non accident injuries cases. One of the clearest discussions of the idea of the individual programme plan can be found in the strategy for the development of mental handicap services in Wales proposed by a Welsh working party. The Welsh working party recommended services should be based on:

> A system of individual plans (which) will help ensure that a team of relevant professionals is assembled around each client at regular intervals to agree objectives, to contract to provide services and to review progress.[29]

The working party specified that these plans should be associated with regular review meetings:

> All professionals concerned with an individual meet at regular (6 monthly) intervals together with the client and family to plan the short and long-term aims for that person.[30]

An individual programme plan can create up to date information about the mentally handicapped child and his or her needs. However the plan needs to be put into action and the necessary resources and services mobilised. Above all the activities of different agencies and their workers need to be co-ordinated. Our study has drawn attention to the shortcoming of formal services and the problem of

coordination. For example many mothers in our study
lacked basic information about the availability of
welfare services and mothers who had obtained the
information had usually got it in a haphazard way.
The ignorance of mothers of these services was often
related to ignorance amongst service providers of
the services provided by different agencies.
Lloyd-Bostock has pointed out that lack of communication between professionals involved with a family
is one reason why parents receive uncoordinated
services and conflicting advice.[31] The individual
programme plans needs to be supported by a mechanism
of service coordination such as the 'named person'
system.

Named Person

Both the Court Committee[32] and the Warnock
Committee[33] identified the fragmented and uncoordinated nature of welfare provision as a major
shortcoming in services for handicapped children.
The Warnock Committee believed that these shortcomings could be overcome through a key worker or
named person system. The different agencies in
contact with a family and a child would agree that
one person would act as the main contact for that
family or child. The Warnock Committee recommend
that 'one person should be designated as Named
Person to provide a point of contact for the parents
of every child who has been discovered to have a
disability or who is showing signs of special needs
or problems'.[34]

In the view of the Warnock Committee the named
person should be the person most frequently in contact with the child and his or her family. In the
early period of childhood, the health visitor has
responsibilities for visiting all children. Therefore the Warnock Committee recommended that at this
stage the health visitor should act as the named
person.[35] Studies have shown[36] that parents react
more positively to health visitors than social
workers. However when the child reaches school age
the health visitor becomes less important and
families with mentally handicapped children develop
relations with Special Schools. The Warnock
Committee recommended that the head teacher of the
special school should act as the Named Person for
the school years.[37] In the transition from school
to adult life it is more difficult to identify a
dominant service or service provider. The Warnock
Committee recommended that 'the specialist careers

officer should act as Named Person for young people
with special needs and their parents or should ensure that another professional takes on the function
of providing a single point of contact for them
during the transition from school to adult life'.[38]
     The Welsh working party on services for the
mentally handicapped also identified the named person as the lynch pin of the new pattern of services
they were proposing. The Working Party recommended
that in each area a key worker should be identified
as a point of contact for families. They described
the role of this worker in the following way:

> A named professional should be assigned as the
> main point of contact with each mentally
> handicapped person and family. The key worker
> may come from one of a range of disciplines,
> but is most likely to be the social worker,
> psychologist, members of the nursing team or
> ATC staff. A particular professional input is
> not the important matter. What is crucial is
> that the client and family have ready access to
> the expertise of the Community Mental Handicap
> Team and its contacts. This access will be
> most effectively provided if a key worker is
> identified as the main contact.[39]

     A successful named person could form the lynch
pin of an effective community service for the
mentally handicapped. As Mittler has pointed out
parents would 'know that a specific person is always
available to give advice, to guide them through the
maze of services and to ensure that they receive all
the help that they need'.[40]

Comment. Community care and the associated positive
attitudes to the role of the family are to be welcomed. However the actual position of support to
the families leaves a lot to be desired. Part of
the problem related to the low priority accorded to
the mentally handicapped within agencies and part to
the fragmented response of different agencies. The
development of individual plans and the use of
named persons would both create more awareness within agencies of the problems and needs of mentally
handicapped children and their families and would
also improve the service received by families.

FEMINISM AND COMMUNITY CARE [41]

In the Preface we stressed that we saw this
study as a pilot study that would generate insights
that other studies could develop. We have been
criticized for this approach by some reviewers who
felt that we should have had a clearer theoretical
focus to our study [42]. As we made clear in our
Preface this study is not atheoretical rather we
have decided to make the theory implicit rather
than explicit. However as this has caused misunderstandings we shall in this section draw out one of
the implicit theoretical themes in our study,
feminism, and discuss the role of sociologists in
developing services for mentally handicapped
people.

As we showed in Chapter 2 sociological ideas
and research have undoubtedly played an important
part in undermining the assumptions behind the
administrative and legal framework established by
the 1913 Mental Deficiency Act. However, agreement
on an alternative framework has proved more
elusive. Sociologists and researchers have done a
good demolition job but they have been less helpful
with alternatives.

In so far as an alternative has emerged it is
community care. However, there is no precise and
agreed meaning of community care. For example a
group of officials in the D.H.S.S. recently
reviewed policies for the development of community
care because there was 'some uncertainty about the
general policy objectives underlying the concept of
community care' [43]. The authors of the report
acknowledged that the term '"community care" seems
to mean very different things depending on the
context in which it is used' [44]. Part of the
confusion arises because the three main schools of
sociological ideas which have informed critiques of
previous policies have also contributed alternative
definitions of community care.

The critique of policies which developed out
of labelling theory and associated ideas was based
on the view that, as far as possible, individuals
should not be labelled mentally handicapped. If
they were, then they should not be excluded from
services provided for the rest of the population but
should be given access to these services. The
additional services, that they received, should
enable them to return as far as possible and as
quickly as possible to the normal patterns of life
enjoyed by the rest of society. It is a view of

community care as desegregation and as integration
of mentally handicapped people into the community.

The critique which developed out of community
studies was based on the view that formal agencies
should not supplement or replace the family or the
community but, as far as possible, they should
support communities and families in caring for
dependent people. It is a view of community care
as care by the community and the family.

The critique of contemporary policies which
developed out of criticisms of large scale
instititutions was based on the view that large
scale institutions were intrinsically bad and
damaging to their inmates. By fostering the
dependency of their inmates, institutions created
the very problems they were supposed to be solving.
The solution was to shut institutions and where
necessary to replace them with small home-like
residential units in the community. It is a view
of community care as care in the community.

We shall argue in this section that feminist
ideas offer not only a general critique of community
care but also a critique of these three alternative
definitions of community care.

Feminism is a more recent phenomenon than the
three main schools of ideas discussed in
Chapter 2 of this book. It has come to occupy
a central place not only on sociological ideas but
also in other social science and humanities
disciplines. Like most sociology, feminist
sociology is concerned with the formation of and
relation between social groups, however unlike most
other sociologists, feminist sociologists argue
that one type of social grouping is evident in and
fundamentally important in all societies, that is
social groupings based on the gender of group
members. Feminist sociologists argue that not only
are these groupings important in all societies but
they have been neglected in sociological research
as most sociologists have been men.

Amongst feminist sociologists there is a
difference in emphasis on the relationship between
gender-based groupings and other forms of social
groupings. At one end of the spectrum of opinion,
radical feminists argue that gender based groupings,
roles and relationships are the dominant form of
social organisation and refer to dominance by males
or patriarchy as the main oppressive force in
contemporary societies. At the other end of the
spectrum marxist feminists argue that gender
relationships and conflict are only part of the

wider class struggle between the owners of the means of production and workers. In between these two extreme positions are socialist feminists who ackowledge the importance of social groupings based on both gender and social class. They argue that class struggles and gender struggles are equally important and the allocation of resources and division of labour in society is based on the way that these two forms of social conflict inter-act. Sociologists working within this framework and using this perspective have contributed most to discussions about the role of women as carers in capitalist society. One example of this feminist perspective was a renewed interest in the family, especially in gender roles and division of activities in the family which we discussed in Chapter 6.

Recent writers who have explicitly or implicitly adopted a feminist perspective have found that the division of domestic labour is unequal and that women provide most of the care for children, the sick and elderly. [45] The ideology of family life and the division of labour in the family produces and reproduces this differential time allocation, in which women are allocated the tasks of providing for health, nursing the sick, teaching about health, mediating with health and social services and generally coping with crisis. [46] The unequal division of labour is reproduced not only in the family but also in the wider workforce predominantly in part-time and lower paid jobs. Their work outside the house is generally considered as secondary to their responsibilities at home. The provision of child care and support for dependent relatives means that the development of a career for women is very difficult.

Feminists argue that the state maintains and reinforces the unequal relationship between men and women. The role of the state can be most clearly seen in the ways in which social security benefits are provided. [47] The critics of these policies argue that these policies are based on the false assumption that women as wives are dependent on their husbands. The assumption that married women are dependent on their husbands can be seen in the conditions attached to the payments of non-contrib-utory invalidity pensions and invalid care allowances. In the case of invalidity care allowances these conditions and the associated sex inequalities are being challenged with some success in the European Court.

Our study of Community Care was influenced both theoretically and methodologically by feminist studies. In particular we followed Oakley's methodology in examining the allocation of caring activities within the household, for example we examined men's participation in terms of child-minding, child care and household activities. Our findings confirmed the findings of other researchers using a similar approach. The mothers we talked to were caring for children who required far more care and supervision than other children of the same age. Moreover these mothers could not look forward towards a decline in their responsibilities and workload. Caring for the child tended to dominate the mother's and the family's life and in spite of the increased workload there was little evidence of a more equitable distribution of responsibilities between family members.

In all the areas we investigated fathers rarely took on major responsibility. There was a difference between the activities with which fathers sometimes helped and those with which they never helped. Most fathers sometimes helped with house-hold activities, play activities and supervision but few helped with activities that involved close and intimate contact with the child. Fathers had the power to legitimately avoid, if they so wished, those tasks they found less interesting and rewarding. For example many of the children in the study generated large amounts of extra washing yet 94% of the fathers in the study never provided any help with the washing or ironing.

Mothers in the study took the brunt of the physical care of their mentally handicapped child. Conventionally supervision and leisure activities are not identified as female activities in the same way as physical care of children and housework and women tended to receive more assistance with these activities. However the community care of mentally handicapped children in our study was really care by women who received little additional support and assistance. It was, for most of the women in our study, a life of hard work and social restriction.

Viewed from a feminist perspective community care is not care by, through or in the community but by individual women living at home. Dixon et al describe community care in the following way:

> Governments talk of taking caring back to the community; they never say that "community"

means "women" - that women are to be unpaid
carers for people whom society prefers to
forget about. [48]

In each of the separate meanings of community
care women are expected to act as the main carers.
In the view of community care as integration and
the associated concept of normalisation, the
dominant model of normality is the family in which
the husband is the bread winner and the wife the
home maker. Other divisions of responsibility or
patterns of living are not seen as normal. In the
view of community care as care by the community, it
is the family or rather women at home that are
expected to provide the bulk of the care. Not only
are they seen as a relatively cheap resource but
their lost career and work opportunities are easily
disregarded. In the definition of community care
as care in small units in the community again it is
women who are expected to provide the bulk of the
cheap labour.

Each of these definitions can be subjected to
detailed criticism from the feminist perspective.
Community care, as a critique of institutional care,
has been developed mainly as a family model of
care. [49] There is an implicit assumption that all
forms of institutional care are bad and life in a
nuclear family is both desirable and normal in
contemporary society. The view of community care as
the integration of mentally handicapped people into
the community is closely associated with the
normalisation ideology. In this ideology the
dominant model of normality is also that of the
nuclear family in which the husband plays the
active economic role and the wife is the carer for
the dependent children in the household. Both
models of community care can be subjected to the
same criticism. Nuclear families are not
statistically 'normal'. Although 6 out of 10 people
currently live in parents and children households,
as Chester points out, the strict stereotypes of the
nuclear family, "breadwinning husband plus housewife-
applies to only 15 per cent of households". [50] It
is not clear that nuclear families are necessarily
desirable when viewed from a women's point of view.

In reality women often have to earn a living
outside the home and therefore they end up with a
double role or burden as main carer and as wage
earner. Caring for dependent people is often seen
as 'second-rate' work that is accorded low status
and low rewards. Feminist sociologists would argue

that only when caring for mentally handicapped people is acknowledged as 'real work' and adequately supported materially and emotionally will community care be a real alternative to institutional care.

The third meaning of community care is care by the community. Feminist sociologists argue that care by the community usually means care by women living in isolation and receiving minimal support by the community. [51] The Equal Opportunities Commission, in their submission to the Social Service Committee of the House of Commons on 'Community Care' stated that community care policies which seek to extend the provison of informal care have a greater impact upon women than men. Their research provided evidence that:

> the pattern of health and social service provision tends to reinforce women's caring role, by assuming that it is appropriate for women to carry a heavier burden of care than might be expected of a man in comparable circumstances. There was evidence of more informal and service support for male carers than for their female counterparts. [52]

Women's caring work for the family has been aptly named 'a labour of love' [53] and for many women 'loving' means 'labour'.

Arguments that women's natural role is in the family do not identify or allow for the hard work entailed. Feminist sociologists have argued that community care only appears to be cheaper than institutional care because it involves a transfer of costs from the state to women. Women, who have to provide the bulk of 'community care' experience two forms of cost which are easily overlooked, the loss of earnings which includes both actual losses and missed opportunities, and the emotional costs in terms of psychological well-being. Brown and Harris [54] have shown in their study of depression that women,who care for dependent relatives, experience higher levels of morbidity than women who do not have that burden. It is possible that the long term costs of providing therapeutic and health care to these women may turn out to be greater than the short term savings.

The Social Services Committee Report on Community Care [55] showed that some of the short-comings identified in this study and by other researchers are beginning to influence discussions

amongst policy-makers. Although there is
relatively little evidence of academic critics, and
in particular feminist critics having a direct
influence on the Committee report, it is clear that
the Committee was influenced by the general
atmosphere of concern about Community Care. In its
report, the Social Services Committee supported the
concept of community care but was critical of the
ways in which it was being implemented. They
stated that:

> We wholeheartedly support a policy of
> community care for mentally disabled people.
> It cannot be done overnight. It cannot and
> must not be done on the cheap... The stage
> has now been reached when the rhetoric of
> community care has to be matched by action,
> and where the public are understandably
> anxious about the consequences. There is
> a general and growing groundswell of opinion
> which is questioning the way in which
> so-called community care policies are
> operating in practice. [56]

The Committee felt a need to define community
care because as it pointed out 'the phrase "community care" means little in itself' and that 'it has
become a slogan, with all the weakness that that
implies'. [57] Indeed the Committee suggested it
might be best to abandon the phrase community
care and replace it with a phrase like individual
care. They decided to retain the phrase and
suggested that the following principles should
underlie the practice of community care:

> Appropriate care should be provided for
> individuals in such a way as to enable them
> to lead as normal an existence as possible
> given their particular disabilities and to
> minimise disruption of life within their
> community. [58]

The Social Services Committee recognised that
there were different general principles underlying
the various definitions of the term and identified
four such principles:

> i   a preference for home life over
>   'institutional care';
> ii the pursuit of the ideal of
>   normalisation and integration and

avoidance so far as possible of
separate provision, segregation and
restriction (i.e. the least
restrictive alternative);
iii a preference for small over large;
iv a preference for local services over
distant ones;

These four principles are related to the three
main streams of sociological ideas we identified in
our discussion in Chapter 2. The preference for
home life relates to the criticism of institutions,
the pursuit of integration relates to the insights
provided by labelling theory and the preference for
small localised services relates to a concern with
care by the community.

In each of these areas, the Social Services
Committee endorsed the principles and objectives
but seriously criticised the practices of community
care. The Committee endorsed the closure of large
institutions and the development of alternative
facilities in the community but felt that this
process had been badly planned and managed. In
particular the Committee felt that more attention
had been devoted to the running down of institutions
than to the development of alternatives with the
consequence that:

The pace of removal of hospital facilities
for mental illness has far outrun the
provision of services in the community to
replace them. It is only now that many
people are waking up to the legacy of a
policy of hospital rundown which began over
20 years ago. Many of the horror stories
of mentally ill people living on the streets
or miserably in board and lodging are the
results of an earlier era. Whatever the
weaknesses of present policies and practice,
everybody must be aware of the need for
appropriate community services to be in
place before the process of hospital rundown
races ahead yet further: what evidence from
Sheffield referred to as 'building the
infrastructure of community services'.
Putting pressure on authorities to close or
run down hospitals without similar incentives
or resources to develop alternative services
is putting the cart before the horse. [60]

Although criticising the large institutions,

Committee did recognise that they performed an important function as asylums. They argued that this function was essential for the care and protection of many severely disabled people:

> Earlier community care policies were embarked on in the apparent belief that it was the institutions which created many of the disabilities of those within them, and that modern medical or psychological techniques would lead to a massive reduction in the need for long-term care. There are now only vestiges of such a blithely over-optimistic attitude. While the disabilities of long-stay patients may well be heightened by institutional care, the simple facts are that there is little prospect of major change for the better for many disabled people. Significant progress can be made through appropriate social programmes, to a degree which would surprise our forefathers. Severely disabled people can be helped. But many people need long-term care, wherever and by whomever it is provided, because of their intrinsic disabilities, and not because of the effects on them of institutions. There is also a growing recognition that 'institutions' - meaning primarily hospitals - may have fulfilled at least one function which has to be replicated should they be replaced: that of 'asylum', by which is meant the provision of shelter and refuge. 25 years after the 1959 Act, informed opinion is slowly returning to the idea that there will always be a substantial number of mentally disabled people who are entitled to some sort of protection and support, which may involve their partial withdrawal from the rest of the community. In rediscovering this 'asylum' function, the lessons of the hospital inquiries of the last 15 years, from Ely and Whittingham to Normansfield, must not be forgotten. These inquiries provided an indictment of the possible effects on patients and staff of living in vast institutions, isolated from outside observation and often insulated from professional supervision. The conditions prevailing in the back wards of some mental illness and mental handicap hospitals are one part of the reality which must never be forgotten. The concept of

259

asylum has nothing inherently to do with
large or isolated institutions. Asylum
can be provided in a physical or psychological sense in the middle of a normal
residential community: traditionally indeed,
in the midst of a busy church. We must
face the fact that some people need asylum.[61]

The Committee clearly felt that integration
of mentally disabled people into the community was
important but again felt that in practice little
had been done to facilitate this integration.
The Committee felt that it was important to recognise the public's anxieties about mentally disabled
people:

Without arrogance, people's anxieties,
whether legitimate or exaggerated, must
be understood and assuaged. Some mentally
handicapped and mentally ill people are
severely behaviourally disturbed,
embarrassing, unpredictable and therefore
socially unattractive. The problem is that
public opinion, if not properly formed,
tends to stigmatise all mentally handicapped
and mentally ill people in this way. [62]

The Committee felt that the Government should
engage in more systematic campaigns to educate the
public and thereby foster the integration of
mentally handicapped people into the community.
The third major meaning of community care is
care that is shared by the community and a
recurrent theme in the Committee's report is that
the burden of care is in fact concentrated. As
the Committee pointed out:

The vast majority of mentally ill and
mentally handicapped people are not and
may never be in hospital. The almost
obsessive concentration in public policy
on the mechanisms for 'getting people out
of hospital' has sometimes obscured the
basic fact that most mentally ill or
handicapped people already live in the
community, whether with their families,
in lodgings, group homes, hostels or private
accommodation. Different figures are
quoted: a common claim in respect of mental
illness is that 10 per cent of care is
provided by hospitals while 90 per cent of

the 'patients' are in the community. In
mental handicap, the proportions are
broadly similar a figure of around 80 per
cent being sometimes mentioned. As a
councillor and parent of a mentally
handicapped child put it to us in
Lancashire -

'Community care goes on anyway.' [63]

The Committee acknowledged the central role of
families and in particular the role of mothers in
providing care in the community for mentally
disabled people:

Many witnesses have told the Committee of
the sometimes intolerable burden of care
that is placed on the families of mentally
ill and mentally handicapped people who are
living at home. Constant demands may exact
a heavy toll on families, and particularly on
parents. According to the Social Policy Unit
at the University of York -

'The "community care" of young mentally and
multiply impaired young adults involves
arduous and unremitting physical work and
watchfulness, similar to the care and
supervision needed by a young child but
extending over a lifetime and becoming
increasingly onerous as both parents and the
young person grow older. Despite this growing
burden, there is no evidence of any involvement by the wider community - friends,
neighbours, volunteers or even extended family
members - in providing any of the care which
is needed from day-to-day. Instead, the
burden of care falls largely on the young
person's mother and results in marked
financial, physical and emotional costs.'

As the Equal Opportunities Commission (EOC)
told us -

'community care policies which seek to extend
the provision of informal care have a greater
impact upon women than men'. [64]

The Committee felt that the needs of these
carers had been badly neglected and recommended
that the needs of these families should become a

central focus in plans to develop community care:

> Community care depends heavily at the end of
> the day on relatives caring for their own
> family members. There is a danger that the
> establishment of new and expensively staffed
> services will produce a continuation of the
> present relative neglect of families caring
> in the community, to their personal and
> financial cost. We recommend that all
> community care plans provide a statement of
> their impact on families caring for mentally
> disabled relatives and specify the actions to
> be taken in consequence. [65]

The development of sociological ideas in the
1960's had an important impact both directly through
research and indirectly through generating a climate
of opinion about services for mentally handicapped
people. Their impact was greater in demonstrating
the inadequacies of traditional policies than in
generating alternatives. However there was a
general agreement that mentally handicapped people
should have community care and the different school
of ideas influenced different concept of community
care.

Feminism has had a radical impact not only on
sociology but also on a range of other academic
disciplines. Feminist sociologists view community
care as care by women. They argue that the main
burden of caring for dependent people has always
fallen on women and in so far as community care
does involve any substantial changes it will reduce
the rewards and support received by women and
increase their burden of care.

Although there is little evidence of a direct
impact of feminist ideas on official policy, the
general climate of opinion has become more critical
of community care. This is clear in the Social
Services Committee report on community care.
Although the committee endorsed the principles of
community care, it was critical of its practice.
In particular the Committee acknowledged that
families provide the bulk of care for dependent
people in the community and they have received few
benefits from the policy. The Committee argued that
the needs of carers must be seriously addressed.

This section has been a section about the
impact of sociological ideas on social policy for
mentally handicapped people. Ideas are elusive.
They can be difficult to define and their

histories and influences are difficult to identify.
Researchers using sociological ideas have
successfully undermined existing or emerging policy
for mentally handicapped people but we have also
shown that they have been less successful in
developing alternatives. In the past 30 years the
consensus over policies have been replaced by
confusion and competiton.

Generally this confusion and competition is
regarded as bad. Service providers often hanker
after a golden era in which there was a simple grand
design for services and this grand design was
embodied in a government statement and was implemented by a government agency. It is possible to
argue that the 1913 Mental Deficiency Act embodied
such a grand design and services developed for
nearly 50 years along the lines laid out by this
grand design. The only problem was that it was the
wrong grand design.

Community care has not provided an alternative
grand design. Perhaps there is no real need for or
advantage in a grand centrally inspired design.
Services for mentally handicapped people will
develop most effectively if central government
gives a firm commitment to providing funding and
encourages local agencies to sensitively experiment
with services. If these experiments are
effectively assessed, especially in terms of the
ways in which they meet the needs of mentally
handicapped people and their families and if the
results of the studies are effectively disseminated
then more effective patterns of services should
develop.[66]

NOTES

1.   M. Voysey, A Constant Burden: The
     Reconstitution of Family Life, Routledge and
     Kegan Paul, 1975, p.27.
2.   D.W. Winnicott, An Ordinary Devoted Mother
     and her Baby: Nine Broadcast Talks, Privately
     Printed, p.47, 1949.
3.   Fit for the Future: Report of the Committee on
     Child Health Service (Chairman: Professor
     S.D.M. Court), Cmnd. 6684-I, H.M.S.O.,
     1976, p.2.
4.   Report of the Committee on Local Authority and
     Allied Personal Social Services (Chairman:
     Sir F. Seebohm), Cmnd. 3705, H.M.S.O., 1968,
     para.2.
5.   I. Illich, et al., Disabling Professions,

Boyars, 1977.

6. I. Illich, <u>Medical Nemesis</u>, Calder and
    Boyars, 1975.
7. See, for example, P. Wilding, <u>Professional
    Power and Social Welfare</u>, Routledge and Kegan
    Paul, 1982; E. Friedson, <u>Profession of
    Medicine: A Study of the Sociology of Applied
    Knowledge</u>, Harper and Row, 1970.
8. J. Finch and D. Groves, 'Community care and
    the family: a case for equal opportunities',
    <u>Journal of Social Policy</u>, 9, 4, 487-511, 1980.
9. Ibid., and D.H.S.S. <u>A Happier Old Age: A
    Discussion Document on Elderly People in Our
    Society</u>, H.M.S.O., 1978.
10. M. Loney, 'The politics of self-help and
    community care' in A. Brechin, P. Liddiard
    and J. Swain (eds.), <u>Handicap in a Social
    World</u>, Hodder and Stoughton, 1981, p. 302.
11. For the wide range of problems and activities
    dealt with by particular self-help and mutual aid
    groups as well as recent literature on the
    self-help approach see D. Robinson and
    W. Henry, <u>Self-help and Health: Mutual Aid for
    Modern Problems</u>, Robertson, 1977; D. Robinson
    and Y. Robinson, <u>From Self-help to Health</u>,
    <u>A Guide to Self-Help Groups</u>, Concord Books,
    1979; J. Chisholm and O. Gillie (eds.),
    <u>The 'Sunday Times' Self-Help Directory</u>,Times
    Newspapers, 1975; <u>Self-Help and the Patient:
    A Directory of Organisations concerned with
    Particular Diseases and Handicaps</u>, The
    Patients' Association, 7th Edition, 1980:
    J.D. Williamson and K. Danaher, <u>Self-Care in
    Health</u>, Croom Helm, 1978; <u>The Journal of
    Applied</u> Behavioural Science, Self-Help Groups,
    Special Issue, 12, 3, 1976; A.H. Katz and
    E.I. Benden (eds.), <u>The Strength in Us:
    Self-Help Groups in the Modern World</u>, View-
    points, New York, 1976; and G. Caplan and
    M. Killilea (eds.) <u>Support Systems and Mutual
    Help: Multidisciplinary Exploration</u>, Grune and
    Stratton, New York, 1976.
12. Robinson and Henry, <u>Self-Help and Health</u>,
    p. 11.
13. Ibid., p. 116.
14. M. Johnson, 'Personally speaking, muscular
    dystrophy', <u>Community Care</u>, p. 12, 20/11/1980.
15. See, for example, Association of Professions
    for Mentally Handicapped, <u>Collaboration
    between parents and professions</u>, Mental
    Handicap Papers, No. 9, Kings Fund Centre, 1976.

16. R. Hadley and S. Hatch, 'Why our social service volunteers deserve more official backing', The Times, 23 November 1977.
17. Voluntary Organisations: An NCVO Directory 1980/81, Bedford Square Press, 1981. See also A. Jones, 'Voluntary teaching: Kith and Kids', New Psychiatry, 1, 5, 14/11/1975 and M. Collins and D. Collins, Kith and Kids: Self-Help for Families of the Handicapped, Souvenir Press, 1976.
18. Robinson and Henry, Self-Help and Health, p. 12.
19. D.H.S.S., Mental Handicap: Progress, Problems and Priorities, D.H.S.S., 1980, p. 5.
20. W. Wolfensberger, The Origins and Nature of Institutions, Human Policy Press, Syracuse University, Syracuse, 1974.
21. D.H.S.S., Better Services for the Mentally Handicapped. Cmnd. 4683, H.M.S.O., 1971, paras. 3 and 88.
22. United Nations General Assembly, Declaration on the Rights of Mentally Retarded Persons, Resolution, 2856, 26th session, 1972, para. 88.
23. Report of the Committee of Enquiry into Mental Handicap Nursing and Care, Vol. I, (Chairman, Peggy Jay), Cmnd. 7468-I, H.M.S.O., 1979, paras 88-90.
24. MENCAP, Residential Care of the Mentally Handicapped, MENCAP, no date.
25. N. Carle, 'Key concepts: individual programme plans', CMH Newsletter, 26 Autumn 1981, 3-4.
26. Report of the Committee of Enquiry into Mental Handicap Nursing and Care, para. 93.
27. See, for example, Welsh Office, All Wales Strategy for the Development of Services for Mentally Handicapped People, Welsh Office, 1983; North Western Regional Health Authority, Services for People who are Mentally Handicapped: A Model District Service, Manchester, April 1982; and Sheffield AHA(T) and Sheffield Metropolitan District, Strategic Planning of Services for the Mentally Handicapped, December 1981.
28. For example, Welsh Office, NIMROD: Report of a Joint Working Party on the Provision of a Community based Mental Handicap Service in South Glamorgan, The Welsh Office, vols. 1 and 2, July 1978; R. Blunden, Individual Plans for Mentally Handicapped People: A Draft Procedural Guide, Mental Handicap in Wales Applied Research Unit, Cardiff, 1980.

S. Revil and R. Blunden, Goal Planning with Mentally Handicapped People in the Community: Report on the Evaluation of the Use of Goal Planning Techniques by Health Visitors, Mental Handicap in Wales Applied Research Unit, Cardiff 1980.
29. Welsh Office, All Wales Strategy, p. 28.
30. Ibid., p. 24.
31. S. Lloyd-Bostock, 'Parents' experiences of official help and guidance in caring for a mentally handicapped child', Child: Care, Health and Development, 2, 325-38, 1976.
32. Fit for the Future (Court Report).
33. Special Educational Needs, Report of the Committee of Enquiry into the Education of Handicapped Children and Young People, (Chairman Mrs. H.M. Warnock) Cmnd. 7212, H.M.S.O., 1978.
34. Ibid., para.5.13.
35. Ibid., para. 5.14.
36. Ibid., para. 5.14 and R. Daniel, 'The Health Visitor' in V. Shennan, (ed.), Right from the Start, MENCAP, 1981; and Association of Professions for the Mentally Handicapped, Mental Handicap - The First Twelve Months, APMH Project Paper, 1981.
37. Special Educational Needs, para. 9.29.
38. Ibid., para. 10.94.
39. Welsh Office, All Wales Strategy, pp. 24 and 28.
40. P. Mittler, People not Patients: Problems and Policies in Mental Handicap, Methuen, 1979, p. 64; L. Ward, People First, King's Fund Project Paper No. 37, 1983 pp. 15-16. See also the handbook edited by G.B. Simon (ed.), Local Services for Mentally Handicapped People, British Institute of Mental Handicap, Kidderminster, 1981.
42. We would like to thank B.N. Ong and G. Manthorpe for their help with initial drafts of this section and the Controller of Her Majesty's Stationery Office for permission to use extracts from the Second Report of the Social Services Committee, Session 1984-85, Community Care, with Special Reference to Adult Mentally Handicapped and Mentally Ill People, (Chairman; Renee Short), HC, 13-I, H.M.S.O., 1985/
42. M. Bayley, Review, Journal of Social Policy, Vol 14, pp. 583-4, 1985.
43. D.H.S.S. Report of a Study on Community Care,

D.H.S.S., 1981, para 11.
44. Ibid. para 2.1.
45. A. Oakley, The Sociology of Housework,
    M. Robertson, 1974; M. Nissel and
    L. Bonnerjea, Family care of the handicapped
    elderly: who pays? Policy Studies Institute,
    1982; D. Wilkin, Caring for the Mentally
    Handicapped Child, Croom Helm, 1979.
    G. Carey, 'Community Care - Care by Whom?
    Mentally Handicapped Children Living at Home',
    Public Health, Vol. 96, pp. 269-78, 1982.
46. H. Graham, Women, Health and the Family,
    Wheatsheaf Books, 1984.
47. H. Land, 'Who cares for the family?' Journal
    of Social Policy, Vol. 7, pp. 357-84, 1978.
48. G. Dixon, C. Johnson, S. Leigh and N. Turnbull,
    'Feminist Perspectives and Practice' in
    G. Craig, N. Derricourt and M. Loney (eds.)
    Community Work and the State, Routledge and
    Kegan Paul, p. 64.
49. G. Dally 'Ideologies of Care: A Feminist
    Contribution to the Debate', Critical Social
    Policy, Vol. 3, no. 2, 1983.
50. R. Chester, 'The Rise of the Neo-Conventional
    Family', New Society, pp. 185-8, 9th May 1985,
    p. 185.
51. Equal Opportunities Commission, Caring for the
    Elderly and Handicapped: Community Care
    Policies and Women's Lives, Equal Opportunities
    Commission, 1982 and A. Walker, Community
    Care: The Family, the State and Social Policy,
    B. Blackwell and M. Robertson, 1983.
52. Equal Opportunities Commission, Submission by
    the EOC to the Social Services Committee of
    the House of Commons on 'Community Care',
    Equal Opportunities Commission, 1984.
53. J. Finch and D. Groves, A Labour of Love:
    Women, Work and Caring, Routledge and Kegan
    Paul, 1983.
54. G. Brown and T. Harris, The Social Origins of
    Depression, Tavistock, 1978.
55. Second Report of the Social Services Committee.
56. Ibid. para. 233.
57. Ibid. para. 8.
58. Ibid. para 11
59. Ibid. para 10
60. Ibid. para 30
61. Ibid. paras. 25-26.
62. Ibid. para 130
63. Ibid. para. 24
64. Ibid. para. 167

65. Ibid. para. 168
66. An excellent example of the type of research
    we envisage is Glendinning's study of the
    resource worker project in which a specialist
    worker provided a 'single door' to services
    and provided families caring for a severely
    disabled child with information, advice,
    practical help and support.
    C. Glendinning, A Single Door: Social Work with
    the Families of Disabled Children, Allen and
    Unwin, 1986.

SUBJECT INDEX

Adaptation 134, 193, 239
    247, home adaptations
    93, 177; equipment
    193
Avon 94
Asylum 259-660

Bathing 131
Bedtime and sleeping 126
Benefits 246, 253-4;
    attendance allowance
    179, 190-1, 194, 198n,
    226, 232, 233, 239;
    Financial assistance
    170, 185, 190-5, 207,
    239; Financial
    resources 226
Better Services for the
    Mentally Handicapped
    26, 27, 33n,
    39, 40, 41, 51, 61,
    65n, 66n, 176, 245,
    265
Binet 5, see I.Q.
    Testing
Board of Control 12, 14,
    15, 16, 17, 18, 19,
    21, 32n, see Wood
    Committee
Board of Education 5, 14
Brooklands 37, 38

Careers Officer 249
Central Council for the

Education and
    Training of Social
    Workers (C.C.E.T.S.W.)
    197n
Central Health Services
    Council 180, 196n
Centre 230; Junior
    Training Centre 180;
    Adult Training
    Centre 185, 209, 210,
    218, 227, 250
Child-minding 140, 179-
    180; baby-sitting
    138, 151, 158-9, 163,
    186, baby-sitters
    94, 149
Chronically Sick and
    Disabled Act 175
Colony 10, 14, 17, 18,
    20, see Institutions
Commissioners in
    Lunacy 9, 10, 30n,
    31n
Committee of Enquiry,
    Mental Handicap
    Nursing and Care,
    see Jay Committee
Committee on Local
    Authority and Allied
    Personal Social
    Services, see
    Seebohm Committee
Communication 80, 81
Community Care 24, 34-

INDEX OF MOTHERS AND FAMILIES

AUTHOR INDEX